Anonymous

Translation of the Syriac Peshito Version of the Psalms of David

Anonymous

Translation of the Syriac Peshito Version of the Psalms of David

ISBN/EAN: 9783337302979

Printed in Europe, USA, Canada, Australia, Japan

Cover: Foto ©Lupo / pixelio.de

More available books at **www.hansebooks.com**

A TRANSLATION

OF THE

SYRIAC PESHITO VERSION

OF THE

PSALMS OF DAVID;

WITH

NOTES CRITICAL AND EXPLANATORY,

BY THE

Rev. ANDREW OLIVER, M. A.

אין אמר ואין דברים
בלי נשמע קולם :

BOSTON:
E. P. DUTTON AND COMPANY.
LONDON: TRÜBNER AND COMPANY.
MDCCCLXI.

Entered according to Act of Congress in the year 1861, by
ANDREW OLIVER,
in the Clerk's Office of the District Court for the District of Vermont.

RIVERSIDE, CAMBRIDGE:
STEREOTYPED AND PRINTED BY H. O. HOUGHTON.

TO

THE MEMORY OF MY BROTHER,

THE LATE PETER OLIVER,

THIS VOLUME IS INSCRIBED, IN TESTIMONY OF

RESPECT AND LOVE.

PREFACE.

THE publication of the present work, from its unusual character, may seem to demand a few words of explanation and apology. The idea of translating the Syriac Psalter, and adding such notes as my limited information and the slender resources at my command might enable me to append, was suggested while casually inspecting a copy which had been placed in my hands, and observing its general fidelity to the original, and at the same time certain curious discrepancies which seemed to me to be full of interest to the critical student of the Sacred text.

The Syriac version of the Old Testament is of great antiquity, though the precise date to which it may be referred has never been satisfactorily determined. The Syrian writers themselves are extravagant in their assertions upon this point, — some going so far as to say that portions of it were made by the command of Solomon, for the use of Hiram king of Tyre, and other portions by the command of Abgarus, king of Edessa in the time of our Lord. It is referred by others to the hand of Asa, a priest of the Samaritans, of St. Thaddæus the Apostle, and of St. Mark the Evangelist. It is claimed that it must be as old as the Apostolic era, because St. Paul, in quoting from the Psalms, (Ephes. iv. 8,) differs both from the Hebrew and the Septuagint, and agrees with the Syriac in an important peculiarity; to this, however, it has been replied, that the Syriac version of this passage may have been subsequently formed according to St. Paul's quotation. The latest date assigned is the second or third century after Christ. The general opinion, however, seems to be in favor of an earlier date; and, in the absence of any evidence to the contrary, the concurrent testimony of the Syrians themselves, for whose use it was designed, and none of whom refer it to a later period than the close of the first, or the beginning of the second, century, would seem to be entitled to great respect. Of modern critics, Bishop Walton, Carpzov, Leusden, Bishop Lowth, and Dr. Kennicott, refer it to the first century; Michaelis to the close of the first, or to the earlier part of the second, century, at which time the Syrian Church was in its most flourishing condition. Dathe inclines to the latter opinion, and regards the Syriac version as a certain standard by which to judge of the state of the Hebrew text in the second century. It is held in the utmost esteem by Aramæan Christians of every sect, is quoted by St. Ephraem Syrus in the fourth century, as generally known, and is commended by him and other Syriac writers for its fidelity to the original. Two facts may be considered as settled beyond any dispute by internal evidence: the translation was made before the vowel points were added to the Hebrew text; and, as respects the Psalms, the translator was a convert to Christianity. In proof of this I should not adduce the titles to the Psalms, which may have been subsequently added by another hand; but it will be observed that in Psalm cx. the original is made to contain a reference to the eternal generation of the Son of God.

Another source of interest which this version possesses above all others is the fact that the Syriac language is so closely related to the Hebrew as to illustrate its meaning in obscure and difficult passages. There is little doubt that the pure Hebrew as a spoken tongue had passed out of use before the period of our Lord, and had been succeeded by the various dialects which are known as the Chaldee, Syriac, and Aramæan. The vernacular of the Jews is called Hebrew, indeed, in the New Testament, because it was the native language of the people, though in the lapse of time it had undergone many modifications, and especially in consequence of the captivity, and the more widely extended intercourse of the people with the surrounding nations. In the opinion of Bishop Walton, there were three dialects of the Chaldee or Syriac tongue. First, the Babylonian, the purest of all, in which Daniel and Ezra wrote. Secondly, the dialect of Jerusalem, used by the Jews after their return from the captivity. Of this there were probably subordinate dialects, as that, for example, which St. Peter used, and which betrayed his Galilean origin. Thirdly, the dialect of Antioch, or the Maronitic. This is the dialect of the Syriac version. These three languages, however, or rather dialects of the same language, are closely allied to each other, and have a common basis in the Hebrew. What is therefore called Hebrew by the writers of the New Testament doubtless closely resembled it in its grammatical structure, and in many of its verbal forms, but was probably substantially the same that we call Syriac. Our Lord's exclamation on the cross, in the opening words of Psalm xxii., is a mixture of Hebrew and Syriac. In other instances in which the original words of the vernacular are preserved by the Evangelists and Apostles, they are found to be Syriac rather than Hebrew, at least in a majority of cases, and never, that I am aware, except perhaps in one or two instances, do they correspond to the pure Hebrew forms of the Old Testament. The words *Talitha cumi*, for example, (Mark v. 41,) are a pure Syriac form. The same may be said of the compound word *Maran-atha* (1 Cor. xvi. 22). *Aceldama* (Acts i. 19) is Syro-Chaldaic. *Golgotha*, found in three of the Evangelists, though derived from a root common to this whole family of languages, does not correspond exactly to any word which they contain, but thus much may be said, that it resembles the Syriac as nearly as it does the Hebrew equivalent. There is some difference of opinion as to the derivation of *Mammona*, which occurs several times, but Schleusner says it is Syriac in its origin, and according to Tertullian it was the name of the Syrian or Phenician Plutus. *Abba*, a word also of not infrequent occurrence, is a Syriac or Chaldee, and not a Hebrew, form. *Boanerges* (Mark iii. 17) would seem to be a corruption of *Boanereges; reges*, in Syriac, signifying *thunder*, though in Hebrew it has not this meaning. *Corban* (Mark vii. 11) is Hebrew, but *Corbanan*, (Matthew xxvii. 6,) translated *the treasury*, is Syriac. Of proper names, *Thomas* would seem to be a Syriac form, and *Martha* and *Tabitha* are such undoubtedly; and it is a curious and significant fact, that in the composition of certain proper names, the word *Bar*, *the son of*, is universally substituted for *Ben*, which would have been the earlier or Hebrew use, as *Bar-Jona*, *Bartholomew*, *Barnabas*, *Bartimæus*, *Barabbas*.

Whether or not, however, the Syriac, as we have it, was the vernacular of our Lord and His Apostles, it is at least most certain that it has a close affinity to the Hebrew, and this circumstance alone gives it a peculiar interest to the Biblical student, and establishes the critical value of the old Syriac versions. The relation of the Hebrew to this family of languages would probably find a pretty exact parallel in the history of the Latin, formerly the spoken tongue of the Roman people, but which has degenerated into the various dialects of the Italian peninsula.

With regard to the editions of the Syriac Psalter, the first was published at Paris by Erpenius, in 1625, from two manuscripts brought from the East. Dathe edited this text in 1768, adding vowel-points and notes. In the same year (1625), Gabriel Sionita published at Paris an edition with vowel-points. This is the text of the Paris Polyglott, published in 1645, and also of Walton's Polyglott, published in 1657, carefully collated however with four independent manuscripts. The edition which I have used in the following translation was published in London a few years since for the use of the Syrian Christians. It seems to be identical with the text of Walton, differing as that does from the text of Erpenius. While engaged in the translation, the Rt. Rev. Dr. Southgate of New York, sent me a copy of the Syriac Psalter, presented to him in the East by Mar Yacoob, and which was published under circumstances so interesting, that I shall make no apology for inserting here an extract from his letter, he having kindly given me permission to do so.

"The history of the book is full of interest. Mar Yacoob was sent by his Patriarch to Russia, on an ecclesiastical mission. On his return, the Emperor of Russia made him a handsome present in money. With that money he determined to do some good to his people. He came to Constantinople, hired a very small house, went to a type founder, and, in company with him, with great labor and difficulty, succeeded in casting a font of type from models made by himself. Then he hunted about the city, and at length succeeded in finding an old press, which belonged to the Jesuit Mission, and had been cast aside as useless. He purchased it, and carried it with the type to his house. Then he entered a printer's office, and, for a small fee, was allowed to watch the operations there for a few days. He then bought paper, went home, set up his type with his own hands, with his own hands worked the press, and, finally, with sore travail and patience, struck off an edition of a thousand Psalters; — the first printing ever done in the Syrian nation. He afterwards went to a bookbinder's, paid him for a few weeks' apprenticeship in his shop, then purchased his leather and other materials, with the necessary tools, went home, shut himself up for a month or two, and bound his books. Of these books yours is one of the copies; made entirely by the hands of the Syrian Bishop of Jerusalem; and the first book printed in the Syrian Church; of which Church, Mar Yacoob has since become, as he well deserves to be, the Patriarch. Few human works have so interesting a history."

Upon a careful examination of the text of this volume, I have discovered that it substantially agrees with the text from which I have made my translation, though it occasionally differs from that, as that differs from the text of Erpenius. It is without vowel-points, and the same titles are added which are found in the polyglott of Walton. With regard to the differences between the several texts, to which I have alluded, so far at least as I have had an opportunity of comparing them, I ought here to observe, that they are minute and trifling in their character, and seldom affect the meaning of the passages where they occur. They are precisely such differences as we should expect to find between copies of the same work preserved for ages in a manuscript form, and multiplied by manual transcription. To have noted them, therefore, in the margin, would have increased the bulk of the work, without contributing materially to its value. I may add, as regards those Psalms which differ most widely from the Hebrew, that in the opinion of Dathe they became gradually corrupted through a more frequent use and repetition in the offices of the Church.

The following rules have guided me in my translation: I have adhered as closely as possible to the version of King James, carefully preserving the old English diction so sacred and venerable from its long association with the Word of God. Proper names I have translated according to their common English orthography. Passages conveying no intelligible meaning I have contented myself with literally translating, in preference to suggesting any meaning of my own which could not be extracted from the original without doing violence to the text. I have retained the titles of the Psalms. It is not proved, but neither is it disproved, that these titles were the work of the Syriac translator, and whatever may be said of their authoritative value, and however unintelligible some of them may appear to be, they will be allowed to be interesting as an ancient commentary upon this portion of the Word of God. I have also retained the division of the Psalms into Books, and the subdivision into Grades, and what appears to be a rubrical direction or musical notation, connected with a ritualistic use of the Psalms with which I am not familiar. In a few instances, and but a few, I have not translated the copula when occurring at the commencement of a clause or passage, and not essential to its meaning, and when it could not have been preserved in the translation without an awkward redundancy. I may mention here that I have noted all the instances, or nearly all, in which the Syriac, where differing from the Hebrew, agrees with the Greek version of the Seventy.

I do not flatter myself that the book is free from serious errors and defects; but for such, if any be found, I shall only plead in apology the novelty of the enterprise, and the want of those literary facilities which are seldom found in the libraries of parish clergymen. I shall be abundantly satisfied, if what I have done serves to awaken an interest in a department of sacred literature which I cannot but think has been too much neglected.

I desire here to record my grateful acknowledgment to the Rt. Rev. Dr. Southgate, and the Rev. Drs. Crusé and Turner of New York, and the Rev. Dr. Jenks, of Boston, for encouragement and assistance in my undertaking.

RECTORY, BELLOWS FALLS, VERMONT,
July 15th, 1861.

THE BOOK OF THE PSALMS

OF

DAVID,

KING AND PROPHET.

PSALM I.

A summary of the instruction concerning the various Christian graces, which is contained in the canon of the nine Beatitudes in Matthew.

1. BLESSED is the man that walketh not in the way of the unjust, and standeth not in the counsel of sinners, and sitteth not in the seat of the mockers;
2. But his delight *is* in the law of the Lord, and in his law will he meditate day and night.
3. He shall be like a tree planted by a stream of waters, that bringeth forth his fruit in his season; his leaves also do not fall; and all that he doeth he bringeth to perfection.
4. Not so the wicked; but *they are* like the chaff which the wind driveth away.
5. Therefore the wicked shall not stand in the judgment, nor sinners in the congregation of the righteous.
6. For the Lord knoweth the way of the righteous; but the way of the wicked shall perish.

PSALM II.

Concerning the call of the Gentiles; and Prophetic allusion to the Passion of the Messiah.

1. Wherefore do the heathen rage, and the people imagine a vain thing?
2. The kings of the earth stand up, and the rulers thereof, and take counsel together against the Lord and against his Anointed, *saying*,
3. Let us break their bands asunder, and loose their yoke from us.
4. He that sitteth in the heavens shall laugh, and the Lord shall have them in derision.
5. Then shall he speak against them in his wrath, and vex them in his sore displeasure.
6. I have set my King upon my holy hill of Zion, that he may proclaim my covenant.
7. The Lord said unto me, thou *art* my Son, and this day have I begotten thee.
8. Ask of me, and I will give thee the heathen for thine inheritance, and the bounds of the earth *for* thy possession.
9. Thou shalt rule them with a rod of iron, and break them in pieces like a potter's vessel.

Ps. II. Ver. 6. *That he may proclaim my covenant,* ܘܢܰܟܪܶܙ ܟܠ ܩܝܳܡܝ. A.V.* *I will declare the decree,* אֲסַפְּרָה אֶל־חֹק. The translator probably took the verb in the Hiphil conjugation, and read אַסְפִּרָה אֶל־חֻקִּי, *I will cause him to declare my decree.*

Ver. 9. *Thou shalt rule them,* ܬܶܪܥܶܐ ܐܶܢܘܢ. A. V. *Thou shalt*

* Authorised Version.

10. Be wise, now, O ye kings, and be instructed, ye judges of the earth.

11. Serve the Lord with fear, and lay hold of him with trembling.

12. Kiss the Son, lest he be angry, and ye perish from his way;

13. For his wrath is quickly kindled: Blessed are all they that put their trust in him.

PSALM III.

Written by David concerning good things to come.

1. Lord, how are mine oppressors increased! Many there are that rise up against me.

2. Many *there be* which say unto my soul, There is no deliverance for thee in thy God.

3. But thou, O Lord, *art* my protector, and my glory, and the lifter up of my head.

4. I cried unto the Lord with my voice, and he heard me out of his holy hill.

5. I lay me down and sleep, and awake, for the Lord sustaineth me.

6. I will not be afraid of ten thousand of the people that have surrounded me, and set *themselves* against me.

7. Arise, O Lord my God, and deliver me; for thou hast smitten all mine enemies upon their cheeks, and thou hast broken the teeth of the wicked.

break them, תֵּרְעֵם. LXX., Ποιμανεῖς αὐτούς. In both translations the verb was derived from רָעָה instead of רָעַע.

Ver. 11. *And lay hold of him,* ܘܐܚܘܕܘܗܝ.

8. Salvation is of the Lord, and thy blessing is upon thy people forever.

PSALM IV.

A Psalm of David.—Concerning those things that he suffered.

1. When I cried unto thee, thou heardest me, O my God, and the preserver of my righteousness; in mine afflictions thou hast enlarged me; have mercy upon me, and hear my prayer.
2. O ye sons of men, how long will ye hide mine honour, and love vanity, and seek after falsehood; forever?
3. Know ye that the Lord hath separated the chosen one to himself in a wonderful manner; the Lord will hear when I call upon him.
4. Be ye angry, and sin not; commune with your own hearts, and meditate upon your beds.
5. Offer the sacrifices of righteousness, and put your trust in the Lord.
6. *There be* many that say, Who will show us *anything* good? Let him lift up the light of his countenance upon us.
7. O Lord, thou hast put thy joy in my heart, since

Ps. IV. Ver. 1. *Thou heardest me,* ܫܡܥܬܢܝ. A. V. *Hear me,* עֲנֵנִי. The translator seems to have read עֲנִיתָנִי. The LXX. in one version have εἰσήκουσας.

Ver. 7. *And oil.* This is not in the Hebrew. The LXX. have καὶ ἐλαίου. *In peace together.* These words in the Hebrew are construed with the succeeding clause.

the time that their corn, and wine, and oil, increased in peace together.

8. I will both lay me down and sleep; for thou, O Lord, shalt make me to dwell alone in tranquillity.

PSALM V.

A Psalm of David. — A prayer in the name of the Church, when he went early into the House of the Lord.

1. Hear my words, O Lord, and consider my meditation;
2. And listen to the voice of my cry, my King, and my God.
3. For it is to thee *that* I pray: O Lord, in the morning thou shalt hear my voice, and in the morning will I prepare myself, and appear before thee.
4. For thou art God, and hast no pleasure in wickedness: the evil man shall not dwell with thee;
5. Nor shall the proud stand in thy sight: Thou hatest all them that deal falsely;
6. And thou shalt destroy all them that speak lies: the blood-shedding and deceitful man, shall the Lord abhor.
7. But I will enter thy house in the abundance of thy mercy, and I will worship in thy holy temple.
8. Lead me in thy fear, O Lord, and in thy righteousness; because of mine enemies, make thy way direct before me.

Ps. v. Ver. 3. *Will I prepare myself,* اَتْهَيَّأُ. A. v. *Will I direct my prayer unto thee,* אֶעֱרָךְ־לְךָ.

9. For there is no truth in their mouth, but iniquity is within them; their throats are like open sepulchres, and their tongues are perverse.

10. Condemn them, O Lord, and let them fall through their own counsels; cast them out in the greatness of their iniquity, for they have provoked thee to anger.

11. And let all them that hope in thee be glad in thee; they shall praise thee forever, and thou shalt dwell among them; let all them that love thy Name be strengthened in thee.

12. For thou shalt bless the righteous; O Lord, thou shalt cover me like an acceptable shield.

PSALM VI.

A Psalm of David. — Doctrine and instruction; also concerning mercy.

1. O Lord, rebuke me not in thine anger, neither correct me in thy displeasure.

2. Have mercy upon me, O Lord, for I am weak: heal me, O Lord, for my bones are shaken.

3. My soul also is sore troubled; but thou, O Lord, how long?

4. Return, O Lord, and deliver my soul, and save me for thy mercy's sake.

5. For in death there is no remembrance of thee; and who will give thee thanks in the pit?

Ver. 11. *And thou shalt dwell among them,* ܘܬܸܫܪܹܐ ܒܗܘܿܢ. A. V. *Because thou defendest them,* וְתָסֵךְ עָלֵימוֹ. LXX., Καὶ κατασκηνώσεις ἐν αὐτοῖς.

6. I am weary with my groaning, and every night wash I my bed, and moisten my couch with my tears.

7. Mine eye is grieved through indignation, and troubled because of all mine enemies.

8. Depart from me, all ye workers of falsehood, for the Lord hath heard the voice of my weeping.

9. The Lord hath heard my supplication; the Lord hath received my prayers.

10. Let all mine enemies be ashamed and broken; let them turn and perish suddenly.

PSALM VII.

A Psalm of David. — The conversion of the Gentiles to the Faith, and a confession of the Trinity.

1. O Lord my God, in thee have I put my trust; save me, and deliver me from all my persecutors.

2. Lest they tear my soul like a lion, and there be no one to save or deliver.

3. O Lord my God, if I have done this; and if there be iniquity in my hands;

4. And if I have requited him who hath done me

Ps. VII. Ver. 2. *And there be no one to save or deliver,* ܘܠܝܬ ܕܡܦܨܐ. A. V. *Rending it in pieces while there is none to deliver,* פֹּרֵק וְאֵין מַצִּיל. The Heb. פרק means both *to deliver* and *to tear in pieces.* The translator took it in the former sense, and constructed the sentence accordingly. So the LXX., μὴ ὄντος λυτρουμένου μηδὲ σώζοντος.

Ver. 4. *And if I have requited him who hath done me evil,* ܐܢ ܦܪܥܬ ܠܡܢ ܕܐܒܐܫ ܠܝ. A. V. *If I have*

evil, and if I have oppressed mine enemies without cause;

5. Let the enemy pursue my soul and take it; and let him tread my life down to the ground, and lay my glory in the dust.

6. Arise, O Lord, in thy wrath, and exalt thyself above the necks of mine enemies: awake for me in the judgment which thou hast appointed.

7. And the congregation of the nations shall surround thee, and for their sakes shalt thou return on high.

8. The Lord shall judge the heathen: judge me, O Lord, according to my righteousness, and according to mine innocency.

9. Let evil be consummated upon the wicked, but guide thou the righteous, O righteous God, that searcheth the heart and the reins.

10. My helper also, *and* the God that delivereth them that are upright in heart.

11. The Lord *is* a judge of truth: he is not angry every day, but he returns.

rewarded evil unto him that was at peace with me, אִם־גָּמַלְתִּי שׁוֹלְמִי רָע. The Hebrew, however, will bear the other construction. LXX., εἰ ἀνταπέδωκα τοῖς ἀνταποδιδοῦσί μοι κακά.

Ver. 6. *And exalt thyself above the necks of mine enemies,* ܘܐܬܬܪܝܡ ܡܢ ܓܠܐ ܕܚܣܡܝ̈ܟ. A. V. *Lift up thyself because of the rage of mine enemies,* הִנָּשֵׂא בְּעַבְרוֹת צוֹרְרָי. For בְּעַבְרוֹת, the translator probably read בְּעָרְפוֹת.

Ver. 11. *He is not angry every day, but he returns,* וְלֹא רָגֵז ܕܠܐ ܪܓܙ ܘܐܠܐ ܗܦܟ. A. V. *And God is angry with the wicked every day. If he turn not,* וְאֵל זֹעֵם בְּכָל־יוֹם: אִם־לֹא יָשׁוּב. The translator for וְאֵל read וְאַל. The LXX. give a sim-

12. He hath whet his sword and bent his bow, *and* made *it* ready ;

13. He hath prepared, and will prepare for himself the instruments of wrath ; he hath made his arrows for the persecutors.

14. For the unrighteous man is in travail, and hath conceived falsehood, and brought forth oppression.

15. He hath graven and digged a pit, and he hath fallen into the pit which he hath made.

16. His iniquity shall return upon his own head, and his wickedness shall fall upon his own pate.

17. I will give thanks unto the Lord, according to my righteousness, and I will sing praise unto the Name of the Lord most high.

PSALM VIII.

A Psalm of David. — A prophecy that sucklings, children and youth should sing with Hosannas to the Lord.

1. O Lord, our Lord, how excellent is thy Name in all the earth! Thou that hast set thy glory above the Heavens.

2. Out of the mouth of children and youth hast thou ordained thy praise, because of thine enemies, that the avenging enemy might be brought to nought.

---

ilar meaning to the first clause, μὴ ὀργὴν ἐπάγων καθ᾽ ἑκάστην ἡμέραν.

Ver. 14. *For the unrighteous man is in travail.* Heb., *Behold, he travaileth with iniquity.*

Ps. VIII. Ver. 2. *Thy praise,* ܝܟܘܒܚܐ Heb., עֹז, *strength.* LXX., *αἶνον.*

3. For they have seen thy Heavens, the work of thy fingers, the moon and the stars which thou hast ordained.

4. What is man that thou art mindful of him? and the son of man, that thou visitest him?

5. Thou hast made him a little lower than the angels; thou hast clothed him with glory and honour.

6. Thou madest him to have dominion over the work of thy hands; and thou hast put all things under his feet.

7. Sheep and all cattle; also the beasts of the fields.

8. The fowls of the air, and the fishes of the sea, that walk through the paths of the seas.

9. O Lord, our Lord, how excellent is thy Name in all the earth!

PSALM IX.

A Psalm of David.—The Session of the Messiah, and *his* reception of the kingdom, and frustration of the enemy.

1. I will give thanks unto the Lord with my whole heart, and I will tell of all thy wondrous works.

2. I will rejoice and be glad in thee, and will sing unto thy Name, O thou most Highest.

3. When mine enemies turn backward, they shall stumble and perish at thy presence.

4. For thou hast maintained my right and my cause, and thou sittest on the Throne, a righteous judge.

Ps. VIII. Ver. 3. *For they have seen,* ܚܙܘ ܓܝܪ. A. V. *When I consider,* כִּי־אֶרְאֶה. The Hebrew gives a better sense.

5. Thou hast rebuked the heathen, and destroyed the wicked, and hast put out their names forever and ever.

6. Mine enemies have perished by the sword forever; thou hast overthrown cities and caused their memorial to perish.

7. But the Lord abideth forever; his throne is established for judgment:

8. That he may judge the world in truth, and the heathen in righteousness.

9. The Lord is a refuge for the poor, and their helper in times of affliction.

10. And all that know thy Name shall put their trust in thee; for thou, O Lord, never failest them that seek thee.

11. O sing unto the Lord which dwelleth in Zion, and proclaim his works among the heathen:

12. For he remembereth to avenge their blood, and forgetteth not the cry of the poor.

13. Have mercy upon me, O Lord, and consider my subjection to them that hate me, thou that liftest me up from the gates of death;

14. That I may tell of all thy wondrous works: in

Ps. IX. Ver. 6. *Mine enemies have perished by the sword forever*, ܚܒ݂ܟ݂ܝ݂ܒܟ݂ܐ ܚܡ݂ܘ ܚܣ̈ܦ݂ܐ ܠܥܠܡ. A. V. *O thou enemy, destructions are come to a perpetual end,* הָאוֹיֵב תַּמּוּ חֳרָבוֹת לָנֶצַח. The translator probably read חֲרָבוֹת, *swords*, the word with the other pointing meaning *destructions*, as if the sentence were אוֹיְבַי תַּמּוּ בֶּחֳרָבוֹת לָנֶצַח. The LXX. understood the word in the same way, though they cast the sentence into a different form, τοῦ ἐχθροῦ ἐξέλιπον αἱ ῥομφαῖαι εἰς τέλος.

Ver. 14. *In the gates of the daughter of Zion.* In the original this forms part of the first hemistich of the verse.

the gates of the daughter of Zion I will rejoice in thy salvation.

15. The heathen have sunk into the pit which they have made; and in the net which they have hid is their foot taken.

16. The Lord maketh known the judgment that he doeth, and the wicked is taken in the work of his own hands.

17. The wicked shall be turned into hell, and all the people that forget God.

18. For the poor is not alway forgotten; and the hope of the poor thou shalt not suffer to perish forever.

19. Arise, O Lord, and let not man prevail, and let the heathen be judged in thy sight.

20. Appoint unto them a law-giver, that the heathen may know that they are men.

PSALM X.

A Psalm of David. — Concerning the exultation of Satan over Adam and his race; and how the Messiah defeated his boasting.

1. Why standest thou afar off, O Lord, and turnest away thy face in times of affliction.

Ver. 20. *Appoint unto them a law-giver,* ܐܩܝܡ ܠܗܘܢ ܣܐܡ ܢܡܘܣܐ. A. v. *Put them in fear, O Lord,* שִׁיתָה יְהֹוָה. For מוֹרָה לָהֶם, *fear,* the translator read מוֹרֶה, from the root יָרָה, meaning *law-giver*. The LXX. similarly; κατάστησον κύριε νομοθέτην ἐπ' αὐτούς.

2. Through the pride of the wicked, the poor is consumed: let them be taken in the counsel which they have devised.

3. For the wicked glorieth in his own lusts; the unrighteous man is called blessed, but the Lord is angry.

4. The wicked in his pride doth not enquire *after God*, neither is God in all his thoughts.

5. His ways are always profane; thy judgment is far above out of his sight, and he despiseth all his enemies.

6. He saith in his heart, I shall not cease to meditate evil throughout all generations.

7. His mouth is full of cursing; deceit and fraud are under his tongue, iniquity and oppression.

8. He sitteth in ambush in *his* dwelling, and secretly slayeth the righteous.

Ps. x. Ver. 2. *Through the pride of the wicked, the poor is consumed*, ܚܦܘܚܕܗܘܢ ܘܢܐܒܕ ܢܩܡ ܡܣܟܢܐ. A. V. *The wicked in his pride doth persecute the poor*, בְּגַאֲוַת רָשָׁע יִדְלַק עָנִי. The Hebrew, however, will bear the other construction, which the LXX. also adopted, ἐν τῷ ὑπερηφανεύεσθαι τὸν ἀσεβῆ ἐμπυρίζεται ὁ πτωχός.

Ver. 3. *The unrighteous man is called blessed, but the Lord is angry*, ܟܦܪ ܡܒܪܟ ܘܥܘܠܐ ܪܓܙ. A. V. *And blesseth the covetous, whom the Lord abhorreth*, וּבֹצֵעַ בֵּרֵךְ נִאֵץ יְהֹוָה. For בֵּרֵךְ the translator seems to have בֹּרַךְ in the passive; so the LXX. καὶ ὁ ἀδικῶν ἐνευλογεῖται.

Ver. 6. *I shall not cease to meditate evil throughout all generations*. According to the common version, *I shall not be moved; for I shall never be in adversity*.

In verses eight and nine there are verbal variations, though the sense of the original is preserved.

9. His eyes watch the poor; he layeth snares to catch the poor in the drawing of his net.

10. He shall be humbled and fall, and in his bones *there shall be* weakness and pain.

11. He saith in his heart, God hath forgotten; he hath turned away his face, and will never behold.

12. Arise, O Lord my God, lift up thy hand, and forget not the poor.

13. Wherefore doth the sinner provoke God to anger, saying in his heart that he will never take vengeance?

14. Thou seest that there is iniquity and wrath, and thou providest that he be delivered into thy hands; the poor committeth himself unto thee, and thou art the helper of the fatherless.

15. Break thou the arm of the sinner; let the sin of the wicked seek him, and let him not be found.

16. The Lord is King forever and ever; the heathen have perished out of his land.

Ver. 10. *He shall be humbled and fall, and in his bones there shall be weakness and pain,* ܗܘ ܢܬܡܟܟ ܘܢܦܠ. ܘܒܓܪܡܘܗܝ ܟܐܒܐ ܘܚܫܐ. A. V. *He croucheth, and humbleth himself, that the poor may fall by his strong ones,* וְדִכָּה יָשֹׁחַ וְנָפַל בַּעֲצוּמָיו חֵלְכָּאִים. This difference is easy of explanation, if we suppose the translator for the last two words to have read בַּעֲצָמָיו חַיִל וּכְאֵבִים.

Ver. 14. *Thou providest that he be delivered into thy hand,* ܘܡܙܡܢ ܐܢܬ ܕܢܫܬܠܡ ܒܐܝܕܝܟ. According to the common version of the whole passage: *thou hast seen it; for thou beholdest mischief and spite to requite it with thine hand.* The translator connected the second verb תַּבִּיט with the words לָתֵת בְּיָדְךָ, otherwise slightly varying the construction.

17. Thou hearest, O Lord, the desire of the poor, and thine ear inclineth into the preparation of their heart; to judge the fatherless and the poor, that *the wicked* may no more destroy men from the earth.

PSALM XI.

A Psalm of David. — When the people grieved, because he and his sons were driven into captivity; and *signifying* now to us victory over the adversary.

1. In the Lord put I my trust; how say ye to my soul, flee, and dwell upon the mountains like a bird?
2. For, lo, sinners have bent their bow; they have made ready their arrows upon the string, that they may privily shoot at the upright in heart.
3. For they have overthrown that which thou hast established; but what doeth the righteous?
4. The Lord *is* in his holy temple; the Lord's seat *is* in heaven; his eyes behold, and his eyelids try, the children of men.
5. The Lord trieth the righteous; *but* the wicked, and them that love wickedness, his soul hateth.

Ver. 17. *Thine ear inclineth unto the preparation of their heart.* A. V. *Thou wilt prepare their heart, thou wilt cause thine ear to hear.*

That the wicked may no more destroy men from the earth. A. V. *That the man of the earth may no more oppress.*

Ps. XI. Ver. 3. *For they have overthrown that which thou hast established,* ܗܢܳܐ ܘܰܐܗܦܶܟ݂ܘ ܡܶܬ݂ܩܢܰܬ݂. A. V. *If the foundations be destroyed,* כִּי הַשָּׁתוֹת יֵהָרֵסוּן. For הַשָּׁתוֹת the translator seems to have read הֲשִׁתִּיתָ. The LXX. give the same meaning to the passage: ὅτι ἃ κατηρτίσω καθεῖλον.

6. Snares have come down upon the ungodly like rain; fire and brimstone, and the wind of the plague, *shall be* the portion of their cup.

7. For the Lord is righteous, and loveth righteousness, and his countenance doth behold the thing that is just.

PSALM XII.

A Psalm of David. — The contention of the wicked, and a prophecy of the coming of the Messiah.

1. Save, Lord; for the godly man faileth, and truth is perished from the earth.
2. Men talk of vanity, and speak every one to his neighbour with divided lips and a double heart.
3. The Lord shall destroy all divided lips, and tongues that speak proud things;
4. Which say, we will magnify our tongue; the lips are ours; who is Lord over us?
5. Because of the spoil of the poor, and the sighing

Ps. xii. Ver. 4. *We will magnify our tongue,* جفّي نَعزْت. A. V. *With our tongue will we prevail,* לִלְשֹׁנֵנוּ נַגְבִּיר. LXX, τὴν γλῶσσαν ἡμῶν μεγαλυνοῦμεν.

Ver. 5. *And will execute deliverance openly,* ةادحج ܚܢܘܠܐ ܒܣܘܦܢܐ. A. V. *I will set him in safety from him that puffeth at him,* אָשִׁית בְּיֵשַׁע יָפִיחַ לוֹ. If we suppose the translator to have read אוֹפִיעַ, *I will manifest myself openly,* instead of יָפִיחַ לוֹ, we can easily account for the form into which he has cast the sentence.

of the humble, now will I arise, saith the Lord, and will execute deliverance openly.

6. The word of the Lord is a pure word; *as* chosen silver which is tried in the earth, and purified seven times.

7. And thou, O Lord, shalt keep them: save me and deliver me from this generation forever.

8. For the wicked walk on every side, as *with* the arrogant pride of the children of Edom.

PSALM XIII.

The power of the adversary, and the expectation of the Lord, and of the help that cometh from him.

1. How long wilt thou forget me, O Lord? forever? How long wilt thou turn thy face from me?

2. How long wilt thou put grief in my soul, and

Ver. 8. An obscure and difficult passage, in which the Syriac differs most widely from the Hebrew. The Hebrew is סָבִיב רְשָׁעִים יִתְהַלָּכוּן כְּרֻם זֻלּוּת לִבְנֵי אָדָם; translated, *the wicked walk on every side when the vilest men are exalted.* The Syriac is ܕܪܫܝܥܐ ܒܚܕܪܐ ܡܗܠܟܝܢ. ܐܝܟ ܪܘܡܐ ܐܟܝܠܐ ܕܒܢܝ ܐܕܘܡ, literally, *the wicked walk on every side, like the vile altitude of the children of Edom.* I have suggested one translation in the text; another may be, *the wicked walk on every side, as upon the high places of Edom devoted to the vilest purposes of idolatrous worship.*

Ps. XIII. Ver. 2. *Wilt thou put grief,* ܬܣܝܡ ܟܐܒܐ. A. V. *Shall I take counsel,* אָשִׁית עֵצוֹת. The translator may have read תָּשִׁית עֶצֶב.

sorrow in my heart every day? How long shall mine enemy be exalted over me?

3. Consider and hear me, O Lord my God, and lighten mine eyes, that I sleep not in death.

4. And let not mine adversary say, I have prevailed against him; *neither* let mine oppressors rejoice over me when I am moved.

5. But I have put my trust in thy mercy; my heart shall rejoice in thy salvation;

6. And I will praise the Lord who hath delivered me.

PSALM XIV.

A Psalm of David. — The expectation of the Messiah.

1. The wicked man saith in his heart, There is no God. They are corrupt and become abominable in their doings, and there is none that doeth good.

2. The Lord looked down from heaven upon the children of men, to see if there were any that would understand and seek after God.

3. They are all gone out of the way together, and are become reprobate, and there is none that doeth good; no, not one.

4. And they have no knowledge, all the workers of iniquity, eating up my people, as if they would eat bread; neither have they called upon the Lord.

5. There were they in great fear, because God is in the generation of the righteous.

6. They have shamed the counsel of the poor, because God is his confidence.

7. Who will give salvation unto Israel out of Zion? When the Lord bringeth back the captivity of his people, Jacob shall rejoice, and Israel shall be glad.

(LAUD, AND THE BEGINNING OF THE GRADE.)

PSALM XV.

A Psalm of David. — Perfect repentance towards God.

1. Lord, who shall dwell in thy tabernacle, and who shall rest upon thy holy hill?
2. He that walketh without blemish, and doeth righteousness, and speaketh the truth in his heart;
3. He that useth no deceit with his tongue, and doeth no evil to his friend, and receiveth no reward against his neighbour;
4. In whose eyes the angry man is despised, and who honoureth them that fear the Lord; that sweareth to his friend, and deceiveth *him* not;
5. That giveth not his money upon usury, and taketh no reward against the innocent. Whoso doeth these things is just, and shall never be moved.

Ps. xv. Ver. 3. *That useth no deceit,* ܡܢ ܢܟܠܐ. A. V. *That backbiteth not,* לֹא־רָגַל. LXX, ὃς οὐκ ἐδόλωσεν. *Reward,* ܡܘܣܦܐ. Heb., חֶרְפָּה *reproach.*

Ver. 4. *The angry man,* ܚܛܝܐ. Heb., נִמְאָס *a vile person.* *To his friend,* ܠܫܒܒܗ. Heb., לְהָרַע *to his own hurt.* The translator read לְהָרֵעַ, and so the LXX, τῷ πλησίον αὐτοῦ.

Ver. 5. *Is just,* ܟܐܢ הוּ.

PSALM XVI.

A Psalm of David. — The election of the Church, and the resurrection of the Messiah.

1. Preserve me, O Lord, for in thee have I put my trust.
2. I have said unto the Lord, thou art my Lord, and my goodness is from thee.
3. *The goodness,* also, of the saints and excellent ones that are in the earth, in whom is all my desire.
4. Their last sorrows shall be quickly multiplied, and I will not pour out their libations of blood, neither will I make mention of their names with my lips.
5. The Lord is the portion of mine inheritance, and of my cup; thou returnest to me mine inheritance.

Ps. xvi. Ver. 2. *And my goodness is from thee,* ܘܛܒܬܝ ܡܢܟ. A. v. *My goodness extendeth not to thee,* טוֹבָתִי בַּל־עָלֶיךָ.

Ver. 3. *The goodness also of the saints,* ܐܦ ܛܒܬܐ ܕܩܕܝ̈ܫܐ. A. v. *But to the saints,* לִקְדוֹשִׁים.

Ver. 4. *Their last sorrows shall be quickly multiplied,* ܢܣܓܘܢ ܟܐܒܝܗܘܢ ܐܚܪܝܐ ܒܥܓܠ. The Hebrew is very obscure from ellipsis. It is rendered in the common version, *their sorrows shall be multiplied that hasten after another God,* יִרְבּוּ עַצְּבוֹתָם אַחֵר מָהָרוּ. The words that create the difficulty are אַחֵר מָהָרוּ, which the Syriac translator rendered by the words ܐܚܪܝܐ ܒܥܓܠ, meaning *last* and *quickly.*

Ver. 5. *Thou returnest to me mine inheritance,* ܡܗܦܟ ܐܢܬ ܠܝ ܝܪܬܘܬܝ

6. The lines have fallen unto me in goodly places; yea, mine inheritance is pleasant to me.

7. I will bless the Lord who hath given me counsel; my reins also chasten me in the night season.

8. I have set the Lord always before me, and he is on my right hand, so that I shall not be moved.

9. Wherefore my heart was glad, and my glory rejoiced; my flesh also shall rest in tranquillity.

10. Because thou hast not left my soul in hell, neither hast thou suffered thy Holy One to see corruption.

11. Thou shalt show me thy way of life, and I shall be satisfied with the joy of thy countenance, and with the pleasantness of the victory of thy right hand.

ܐܢܬ ܗܘ. A. V. *Thou maintainest my lot,* אַתָּה תּוֹמִיךְ גּוֹרָלִי. LXX, σὺ εἶ ὁ ἀποκαθιστῶν τὴν κληρονομίαν μου ἐμοί.

Ver. 9. *In tranquillity,* ܒܣܒܪܐ. A. V. *In hope,* לָבֶטַח.

Ver. 11. *I shall be satisfied with the joy of thy countenance, and with the pleasantness of the victory of thy right hand,* ܐܣܒܥ ܚܕܘܬܐ ܘܒܢܨܚܢܐ. ܥܡ ܟܣܝܣܬܐ ܘܐܚܕܐ ܕܝܡܝܢܟ.

A. V. *In thy presence is fulness of joy; at thy right hand there are pleasures forevermore,* שֹׂבַע שְׂמָחוֹת אֶת־פָּנֶיךָ נְעִמוֹת בִּימִינְךָ נֶצַח. The latter is the word translated, *forevermore.* The same root in Syriac expresses the idea of victory, and we may conjecture that the translator read, אֶשְׂבַּע שְׂמָחוֹת פָּנֶיךָ וּנְעִמוֹת נֶצַח יְמִינֶךָ.

PSALM XVII.

Written by David. — A prayer.

1. Hear, O Holy Lord, and consider my supplication, and listen to my prayer, which *proceedeth* not from deceitful lips.
2. Let my judgment go forth from thy presence, and let thine eyes behold the thing that is just.
3. Thou hast searched my heart, and hast visited me in the night; thou hast proved me, and hast not found any wickedness in me.
4. And the deeds of men have not passed through my mouth in the word of the lips, but thou hast kept me from evil ways.
5. And thou hast supported my goings in thy paths, that my footsteps should not slip.

Ps. XVII. Ver. 1. *Hear, O Holy Lord,* ܡܫܡܥ ܡܪܝܐ ܩܕܝܫܐ. A. V. *Hear the right, O Lord,* שִׁמְעָה יְהוָֹה צֶדֶק. For צֶדֶק, the translator read צַדִּיק.

Ver. 3, 4. *And hast not found any wickedness in me. And the deeds of men have not passed through my mouth in the word of the lips,* ܘܠܐ ܐܫܟܚ ܒܝ ܥܘܠܐ: ܘܠܐ ܥܒܕܐ ܕܒܢܝ ܐܢܫܐ ܕܚܛܝܢ ܘܐܚܝܕܝܢ ܒܡܡܠܠܐ ܕܣܦܘܬܐ. A. V. *And shall find nothing: I am purposed that my mouth shall not transgress. Concerning the works of men, by the words of thy lips,* etc. בַּל־תִּמְצָא זַמֹּתִי בַּל־יַעֲבָר־פִּי : לִפְעֻלּוֹת אָדָם בִּדְבַר שְׂפָתֶיךָ. For זַמֹּתִי *I am purposed,* the translator seems to have read זִמָּתִי *mine offence,* and to have otherwise varied the construction, perhaps as follows : בַּל־תִּמְצָא זִמָּתִי בַּל־יַעֲבְרוּ פִּי פְעֻלּוֹת אָדָם בִּדְבַר שְׂפָתַיִם. The latter part of verse 4 also varies from the Hebrew.

6. I have called upon thee, for thou hast heard me; incline thine ear unto me, O God, and hear my words.

7. And make thy Holy One a wonder, and a deliverer to them that put their trust in thee from them that rise up against thy right hand.

8. Keep me as the pupil of the eye, and hide me in the shadow of thy wings;

9. From these wicked that oppress me; *from* the enemies of my soul that set themselves against me.

10. Shut their mouth which speaketh proud things:

11. They did praise me, and now they surround me; and they have fixed their eyes *upon me* that they may cast me to the earth;

12. Like a lion that is greedy of his prey, and like a lion's whelp that lurketh in a secret place.

Ver. 7. *And make thy Holy One a wonder, and a deliverer,* ܘܦܪܘܩܐ ܠܐܝܠܝܢ ܕܣܒܪܝܢ. A. v. *Show thy marvellous loving kindness, O thou that savest,* הַפְלֵה חֲסָדֶיךָ מוֹשִׁיעַ. The difference here can be partly explained by supposing the reading to have been חֲסִידְךָ *thy saint,* for חֲסָדֶיךָ *thy loving kindness.*

Ver. 10. *Shut their mouth which speaketh proud things,* ܣܟܘܪ ܦܘܡܗܘܢ ܘܟܠ ܡܟܬܒܢܝܬܐ. A. v. *They are inclosed in their own fat; with their mouth they speak proudly,* חֶלְבָּמוֹ סָגְרוּ פִּימוֹ דִּבְּרוּ בְגֵאוּת. For סָגְרוּ *they are inclosed,* the translator evidently read סְגֹר *shut or close up;* omitting the word חֶלְבָּמוֹ *their own fat.*

Ver. 11. *They did praise me, and now they surround me,* ܡܫܒܚܝܢ ܗܘܘ ܟܕ ܦܪܣܘ. A. v. *They have now compassed us in our steps,* אַשֻּׁרֵנוּ עַתָּה סְבָבוּנִי. For אַשֻּׁרֵנוּ *our steps,* the reading was אִשְּׁרוּנִי *they did bless me.*

13. Arise, O Lord, before them, and cast them down, and deliver my soul from the wicked, and from the sword.

14. And from the dead that die from thy hands, O Lord, and from the dead of the pit, thou shalt divide them in life. Fill their belly also with thy treasures. Let the children be satisfied, and let them leave the residue to their children.

15. But I shall behold thy face in righteousness, and I shall be satisfied when thy truth is awakened.

Ver. 13. *And from the sword.* Common version, *which is thy sword.*

Ver. 14. *And from the dead who die from thy hands, O Lord, and from the dead of the pit, thou shalt divide them in life.* It is easier to account for this version than to suggest any tolerable meaning to the words. The Hebrew is מְמְתִים־יָדְךָ יְהוָֹה מְמְתִים מֵחֶלֶד חֶלְקָם בַּחַיִּים. Translated, *from men which are thy hand, O Lord, from men of the world which have their portion in this life.* For מְתִים *men,* מֵתִים was read, meaning *the dead.* For מֵחֶלֶד *of the world,* the Syriac has ܒܓܘܒܐ *of the pit.* The root חלד in that language signifying *to dig,* and hence *a pit.* For חֶלְקָם *their portion;* the translator read תְּחַלְּקֵם *thou shalt divide them.*

Ver. 15. *When thy truth is awakened,* ܒܩܘܫܬܟ ܐܬܬܥܝܪܬ. A. V. *When I awake, with thy likeness,* בְּהָקִיץ תְּמוּנָתֶךָ. For תְּמוּנָתֶךָ *thy likeness,* the reading was אֲמוּנָתֶךָ *thy truth.* A different meaning, in other respects, was given to the words.

PSALM XVIII.

A Psalm of David. — A thanksgiving. — Also concerning the ascension of the Messiah.

1. I will love thee, O Lord, my strength;
2. My hope also, my refuge, and my deliverer; the strong God in whom I trust; the horn also of my salvation, and my glorious refuge.
3. I will cry unto the Lord, and *so* shall I be saved from mine enemies.
4. For the pains of death compassed me, and the floods of ungodly men troubled me.
5. The cords of hell came about me, and the snares of death prevented me.
6. In mine affliction, I called unto the Lord and cried unto my God, and he heard my voice from his temple, and my cry before him entered into his ears.
7. The earth shook and trembled, and the foundations of the hills were moved and rent asunder, because he was wroth with them.
8. There went up a smoke in his anger, and fire flamed from his countenance, and coals were kindled by it.
9. He bowed the heavens and came down, and *it was* dark under his feet.
10. He rode upon the cherubim and did fly; he did fly upon the wings of the wind.
11. He made darkness his secret place, and his pavilion was round about him, dark waters with the clouds of the skies.

12. Through the splendour of his tabernacle, he made his clouds hailstones and coals of fire.

13. And the Lord thundered in heaven, and the Most High uttered his voice, hailstones and coals of fire.

14. He sent forth his arrows, and scattered them, and he multiplied his lightnings, and troubled them.

15. And the fountains of waters were seen, and the foundations of the world were revealed at thy rebuke, O Lord, and at the blasting of the breath of thy displeasure.

16. He sent from on high and delivered me, and took me out of the great waters.

17. He saved me from my powerful enemies, and from them that hated me, who were too strong for me.

18. They prevented me in the day of my trouble, but the Lord was my helper;

19. And brought me forth into a large place, and delivered me, because he delighted in me.

20. And the Lord requited me according to my

Ps. xviii. Ver. 12. *Through the splendour of his tabernacle, he made his clouds hailstones and coals of fire.* As given in the English version: *at the brightness that was before him, his thick clouds passed, hailstones and coals of fire. Through the splendour of his tabernacle,* ܗܒ ܐܣܢܘ ܘܥܢܢܘܗܝ. A. V. *At the brightness that was before him,* מִנֹּגַהּ נֶגְדּוֹ. The other variation arose probably from reading עָבַד *he made,* for עָבְרוּ *they passed.*

Ver. 14. *He multiplied his lightnings,* ܘܒܪܩܘܗܝ ܐܣܓܝ. A. V. *He shot out lightnings,* בְּרָקִים רָב. The root רָבַב has both meanings. LXX., ἀστραπὰς ἐπλήθυνε.

righteousness, and according to the purity of my hands hath he recompensed me.

21. For I have kept the ways of the Lord, and have not rebelled against my God.

22. For all his judgments *were* before me, and his laws I did not put away from me.

23. And I was without blemish with him, and guarded myself from transgressions.

24. And the Lord requited me according to my righteousness, and according to the purity of my hands in his eyesight.

25. With the holy thou shalt be holy, and with the perfect thou shalt be perfect.

26. With the elect thou shalt be elect, and with the froward thou shalt be perverse.

27. Thou shalt deliver the poor people, and the lofty eyes shalt thou humble.

28. Thou shalt light my candle; the Lord my God shall make my darkness to be light.

29. For through thee shall I run against a troop, and with *the help of* my God shall I leap over the wall.

30. The Lord's way is without blemish; the word of the Lord is tried, and he is the helper of all that put their trust in him.

31. For there is no God but the Lord, and there is no one so strong as our God.

32. *It is* God that hath girded me with strength, and made my way without blemish.

Ver. 26. *With the elect thou shalt be elect,* ܟܡ ܓܒܝܐ ܬܬܓܒܐ. A. V. *With the pure thou wilt show thyself pure,* עִם־נָבָר תִּתְבָּרָר. LXX., μετὰ ἐκλεκτοῦ ἐκλεκτὸς ἔσῃ.

33. He hath made my feet like *the feet* of an hart, and hath set me up on high.

34. He hath taught my hands to war, and hath strengthened mine arms like a bow of steel.

35. Thou hast given me the shield of salvation; thy right hand shall support me, and thy correction shall nourish me.

36. Thou hast enlarged my steps under me, that my feet should not be moved.

37. I will pursue mine enemies and overtake them; and I will not return till I have destroyed them.

38. I will smite them, and they shall not be able to stand, but shall fall under my feet.

39. Thou shalt gird me with strength in the battle, and shalt throw down beneath me all them that rise up against me.

40. Thou shalt break mine enemies before me, and I will put to silence them that hate me.

41. They shall cry, and there shall be no one to help them; they shall pray unto the Lord, and he shall not hear them.

Ver. 34. *And hath strengthened mine arms like a bow of steel,* ܘܐܘܫܛ ܘܣܢܦ ܐܝܟ ܩܫܬܐ ܕܢܚܫܐ. A. V. *So that a bow of steel is broken by mine arms,* וְנִחֲתָה קֶשֶׁת־נְחוּשָׁה זְרוֹעֹתָי. LXX., καὶ ἔθου τόξον χαλκοῦν τοὺς βραχίονάς μου. Both translators, for נִחֲתָה, *is broken,* seem to have read נִחַתָּ, *thou hast made.*

Ver. 35. *And thy correction shall nourish me,* ܘܡܪܕܘܬܟ ܬܪܒܝܢܝ. A. V. *And thy gentleness hath made me great,* וְעַנְוָתְךָ תַרְבֵּנִי. The translator read עֲפוּתְךָ תְרַבְּנִי. Similarly the LXX., καὶ ἡ παιδεία σου αὐτή με διδάξει.

42. I will beat them as small as the dust before the wind, and I will trample them as the mire of the streets.

43. Thou shalt deliver me from the strivings of the people, and shalt make me the head of the heathen: a people that I have not known shall serve me;

44. And *with* the hearing of the ear they shall hear me; the strange children shall subject themselves to me.

45. The strange children shall be consumed, and shall be lamed from their paths.

46. The Lord liveth, and blessed is he that strengtheneth me: the Lord my Saviour is exalted.

47. *It is* God that avengeth me, and subdueth the heathen under me, and delivereth me from mine enemies.

48. Set me up also above them that rise up against me, and thou shalt save me from wicked men.

Ver. 42. *I will trample them,* ܘܐܕܘܫ ܐܢܘܢ. A. V. *I did cast them out,* אֲרִיקֵם. The translator read אֲדִיקֵם, which is found in the parallel passage, II. Sam. xxii. 43.

Ver. 45. *Shall be lamed from their paths,* ܘܢܬܚܓܪܘܢ ܡܢ ܫܒܝܠܝܗܘܢ. A. V. *And be afraid out of their close places,* יַחְרְגוּ מִמִּסְגְּרוֹתֵיהֶם. The Hebrew text in this place is doubtful, the parallel passage in II. Sam. xxii. 46, having יַחְגְּרוּ, instead of יַחְרְגוּ. The translator adopted the former reading, giving it the meaning of the Syriac verb ܚܓܪ, *to be lame;* reading also מִמְּסִלּוֹתֵיהֶם, *from their paths.* LXX., καὶ ἐχώλαναν ἀπὸ τῶν τρίβων αὐτῶν.

Ver. 47. *And delivereth me from mine enemies.* In the Hebrew this is the commencement of ver. 48.

49. For this cause will I give thanks to thee, O my Lord, among the Gentiles, and sing praises unto thy Name.

50. Great deliverance giveth he to his King, and sheweth mercy to his Anointed, to David, and to his seed forever.

PSALM XIX.

A Psalm of David. — Deliverance of the people from Egypt. — *Unfolding* to us theological truth.

1. The heavens declare the glory of God, and the firmament sheweth his handy-work.

2. Day unto day uttereth speech, and night unto night sheweth knowledge.

3. There is no speech nor language where their voice is not heard.

4. Their annunciation hath gone forth into all the earth, and their words into the ends of the world. In them hath he placed his tabernacle above the sun;

5. And he is like a bridegroom that goeth forth from his chamber; he rejoiceth like a strong man to run his course:

Ps. XIX. Ver. 4. *Their annunciation,* ܣܘܢܚܗܘܢ. A. V. *Their line,* קַוָּם. The Syriac here would favour the conjecture that the Hebrew should be קוֹלָם. The LXX. have ὁ φθόγγος αὐτῶν.

His tabernacle. Heb., *a tabernacle. Above the sun,* ܡܢ ܫܡܫܐ. A. V. *For the sun,* לַשֶּׁמֶשׁ. The LXX. have still another variation, ἐν τῷ ἡλίῳ, *in the sun.*

6. And his going forth *is* from the ends of heaven, and his setting *is* in the ends of heaven, and there is nothing hid from the heat thereof.

7. The law of the Lord *is* without blemish, and converteth the soul; the testimony of the Lord *is* true, and giveth wisdom to the little ones.

8. The commandments of the Lord *are* right, and rejoice the heart; the precept of the Lord *is* elect, and enlighteneth the eyes.

9. The fear of the Lord *is* clean, and endureth forever; the judgments of the Lord *are* true and righteous altogether.

10. And more to be desired *are they* than gold and precious stones; sweeter also than honey and the honeycomb.

11. Moreover thy servant shall carefully observe them; and if he keep them, he shall be greatly rewarded.

12. Who understandeth *his* transgressions? Cleanse thou me from secret *faults*.

Ver. 6. *His setting*, ܡܲܫܟܒܗ; literally, *his bed* or *couch*.

Ver. 7. *The little ones*, ܠܫܒܪܐ. A. V. *The simple*, פֶּתִי. LXX., νήπια.

Ver. 10. *Precious stones*, ܟܐܦܐ ܛܒܬܐ. A. V. *Much fine gold*, פַּז רָב. LXX., λίθον τίμιον πολύν.

Ver. 11. *Thy servant shall carefully observe them*, ܥܒܕܟ ܢܬܙܗܪ ܒܗܘܢ. A. V. *By them is thy servant warned*, עַבְדְּךָ נִזְהָר בָּהֶם. The verb used here is the same, but it has the signification which I have given it in the Syriac conjugation Ethpeel. The version of the LXX. is, ὁ δοῦλός σου φυλάσσει αὐτά.

13. Keep thy servant also from iniquity, that the wicked may not get the dominion over me, and I may be purified from sins.

14. Let the words of my mouth, and the meditation of my heart, be acceptable in thy sight, O Lord, my helper and my redeemer.

PSALM XX.

A Psalm of David — when he prayed to be delivered from the battle of the Ammonites; and *teaching* us now that it is prayer that helpeth us.

1. The Lord hear thee in the day of affliction, and the name of the God of Jacob defend thee;
2. Send thee help from his sanctuary, and protect thee out of Zion.
3. The Lord remember all thine offerings, and anoint thy burnt sacrifices.
4. The Lord grant thee according to thine own heart, and fulfil all thy counsel.
5. And we will rejoice in thy salvation, and in the

Ver. 13. *That the wicked may not get the dominion over me.* A. V. *Let them not have dominion over me: then shall I be upright.*

Ps. xx. Ver. 3. *Anoint,* يُدْهِن. The word in the Hebrew is the same, meaning *to make fat*, and, secondarily, *to accept as fat.*

Ver. 4. *All thy counsel*; literally, رأي, or, *according to all thy counsel.*

Ver. 5. *Shall we be exalted,* نَتَعَاظَم. A. V. *We will set up our banners,* נְדַגֹּל. The translator probably read נִגְדַּל, and also the LXX., who have μεγαλυνθησόμεθα.

name of our God shall we be exalted; the Lord accomplish all thy desire.

6. Now is it known that God hath delivered his Anointed, and heard him from his holy heaven with the strength and deliverance of his right hand.

7. Some *put their trust* in chariots, and some in horses; but we will be strong in the Name of the Lord our God.

8. They are bowed down and fallen, but we are risen and prepared.

9. The Lord shall deliver us, and our King shall hear us in the day that we call upon him.

PSALM XXI.

A Psalm of David.— Supplication for those things that are profitable to a righteous man.

1. The King shall rejoice in thy strength, O Lord, and exceeding glad shall he be of thy salvation.

2. Thou hast given him the desire of his heart, and hast not denied him the preparation of his lips.

3. For thou hast prevented him *with* an excellent blessing, and hast placed upon his head a glorious crown.

Ver. 6. *Is it known.* Heb., *know I. With the strength and deliverance.* Heb., *with the saving strength.*

Ver. 7. *We will be strong,* ܢܬܓܒܪ. A. V. *We will remember,* נַזְכִּיר. Perhaps the translator read נַגְבִּיר. LXX., μεγαλυνθησόμεθα.

Ps. XXI. Ver. 2. *The preparation of his lips,* ܘܡܬܩܦܗ ܕܣܦܘܬܗ; a Syriasm for prayer.

Ver. 3. *A glorious crown.* Heb., *a crown of pure gold.*

4. He asked life of thee, and thou gavest him length of days forever and ever.

5. His glory shall be great in thy salvation; glory and majesty hast thou laid upon him.

6. For thou hast made him a blessing forever and ever, and hast made him glad with the joy of thy countenance.

7. Because the King putteth his trust in the Lord, and in the mercy of the Most High he shall not be moved.

8. Thy hand shall find out all thine adversaries, and thy right hand shall find out them that hate thee.

9. Thou shalt make them like a furnace of fire in the time of wrath; the Lord shall burn them in his anger, and the fire shall consume them;

10. And thou shalt destroy their fruit from the earth, and their seed from among the children of men.

11. Because they intended evil against thee, and imagined a device, and were not able to perform *it*.

12. Thou shalt place a mark upon them, and carry into effect thy preparation against the face of them.

13. Be thou exalted, Lord, in thine own strength; so will we sing and praise thy power.

Ver. 12. *Thou shalt place a mark upon them, and carry into effect thy preparation against the face of them,* ܐܶܬܿܠ ܟܰܣ ܗܘܢ: ܘܢܰܙܘܢ ܒܝܢ ܩܠܠ ܟܿ ܟܠ ܩܿܘܒܿܝܗܘܢ. The Syriac expresses the general sense of the original without adhering very closely to the words; though the Hebrew is somewhat obscure from ellipsis.

PSALM XXII.

A Psalm of David — when his persecutors mocked him. — Concerning also the sufferings of the Messiah, and the calling of the Gentiles.

1. My God, my God, why hast thou forsaken me, and removed my salvation far from me through the words of mine offences?

2. O God, I cry unto thee in the daytime, and thou hearest not; and in the night season, and thou dost not regard me.

3. Thou *art* holy, and dwellest in Israel, thy praise.

4. My fathers trusted in thee; they trusted in thee, and thou didst save them.

5. They cried unto thee, and were delivered; they put their trust in thee, and were not ashamed.

Ps. xxii. Ver. 1. *Hast thou forsaken me,* ܡܫܒܩܬܢܝ. This is the *Sabachthani* of the gospels. The Hebrew word is different.

And removed my salvation far from me through the words of mine offences, ܘܐܫܬܡܐ ܡܢܝ ܦܘܪܩܢܝ ܒܡܠܠ ܣܟܠܘܬܝ. A. V. *Why art thou so far from helping me, and from the words of my roaring?* רָחוֹק מִישׁוּעָתִי דִּבְרֵי שַׁאֲגָתִי. The principal variation here is in the word ܣܟܠܘܬܝ *mine offences,* corresponding to the Hebrew, שַׁאֲגָתִי, *my roaring.* Both our translator and the LXX., who have τῶν παραπτωμάτων μου, seem to have read שְׁגִיאֹתַי, *my errors,* from root שָׁגָה.

Ver. 2. *Thou dost not regard me,* ܠܐ ܡܣܟܐ ܠܝ. The verb ܡܣܟܐ means *to expect, to delay.* It has been conjectured, however, that its primary meaning is *to consider attentively,* and thence *to expect or delay.* This would justify the translation which I have adopted. The Hebrew is, וְלֹא־דוּמִיָּה לִי, translated, *and am not silent.*

6. I am a worm and no man: the scorn of men, and outcast of the people.

7. All they that see me mock me; they shoot out their lips and shake their heads, *saying*,

8. He trusted in the Lord *that* he would deliver him, and let him deliver him, if he delighteth in him.

9. For thou wert my confidence from the womb, and my hope from my mother's breasts.

10. I was cast upon thee from the womb, and thou *art* my God from my mother's belly.

11. Be not thou far from me, for affliction is near, and there is no one to help *me*.

12. Many oxen have surrounded me, and the bulls of Bashan have compassed me about.

13. They gaped upon me *with* their mouth, like a lion that roareth and rendeth.

14. I am poured out like water, and all my bones are out of joint; my heart is like wax, and my bowels are melted within me.

15. My strength is dried up like a potter's vessel, and my tongue cleaveth to the roof of my mouth, and thou hast cast me into the dust of death.

16. For dogs have compassed me about, and the congregation of evil men have surrounded me; they pierced my hands and my feet;

Ver. 14. *And my bowels are melted within me,* ܘܐܬܦܫܰܪ̈. A. V. *It is melted in the midst of my bowels,* נָמֵס בְּתוֹךְ מֵעָי. The translator seems to have read נָמַסוּ בְּתוֹכִי מֵעָי.

Ver. 15. *To the roof of my mouth,* ܠܚܶܟܳܐ ܬܚܬ; literally, *to the heavens of my palate.* Heb., *my jaws.*

Ver. 16. *They pierced,* ܒܰܙܥܘ. This would favour the conjecture that the Heb. כָּאֲרִי should be כָּרוּ or כָּאֲרוּ.

17. And all my bones cry out; they look and stare upon me.

18. They parted my garments among them, and cast lots upon my vesture.

19. But be not thou far from me, O Lord.

Section.

My God, my God, look *upon me* to help me;

20. And deliver my soul from the sword, and my unity from the power of the dogs.

21. Save me from the lion's mouth, and my humility from the horn that is exalted.

22. That I may declare thy Name to my brethren, and praise thee in the midst of the congregation.

23. Ye that fear the Lord, praise him, and honour him all ye seed of Jacob, and fear him all ye seed of Israel.

24. For he hath not despised nor rejected the cry of the poor, nor turned away his face from him; but when he cried unto him he heard him.

Ver. 17. *And all my bones cry out*, ܘܢܒܓܕܘܢ ܟܠܗܘܢ ܓܪ̈ܡܝ. A. V. *I may tell all my bones*, אֲסַפֵּר כָּל־עַצְמוֹתָי. For אֲסַפֵּר, perhaps the translator read יְסֻפְּרוּ.

Ver. 19. *My God, my God.* Heb., *my strength.*

Ver. 20. *My unity*, ܝܚܝܕܘܬܝ. Heb., יְחִידָתִי, translated, *my darling*. Some have supposed that the translator understood the expression, *my unity*, in the mouth of our Lord, as referring to the union of two natures in his divine person.

Ver. 21. *My humility from the horn that is exalted*, ܡܢ ܩܪܢܐ ܪܡܬܐ. A. V. *For thou hast heard me from the horns of the unicorns*, וּמִקַּרְנֵי רֵמִים עֲנִיתָנִי. For עֲנִיתָנִי, *thou hast heard me*, the translator read עֲנָוָתִי *my gentleness or humility.* And so the LXX. have τὴν ταπείνωσίν μου; for רֵמִים, *unicorns*, רָמוֹת or רָמִים.

25. My praise is before thee in the great congregation; my vows will I pay before them that fear him.

26. The poor shall eat and be satisfied, and they shall praise the Lord that seek him; their heart shall live forever.

27. All the ends of the earth shall remember and turn unto the Lord, and all the families of the nations shall worship before him.

28. For the kingdom is the Lord's, and he is ruler over the Gentiles.

29. All the hungry of the earth shall eat and worship before the Lord, and all that go down into the dust shall kneel before him; my soul liveth unto him.

30. The seed that serveth him shall declare his generation unto the Lord.

31. They shall come and shew his righteousness to a people that shall be born, whom the Lord shall make.

Ver. 26. *Their heart.* Heb., *your heart.*

Ver. 29. *All the hungry of the earth,* ܟܠ ܟܦܢܝ̈ ܐܪܥܐ. A. V. *All they that be fat upon earth,* כָּל־דִּשְׁנֵי־אֶרֶץ. The root דָּשֵׁן means both *fatness* and *ashes.* It was understood in the second sense by the translator, as spoken of the poor who live in the dust and ashes of the earth.

My soul liveth unto him, ܢܦܫܝ ܠܗ ܚܝܐ. Heb., נַפְשׁוֹ לֹא חִיָּה, *none can keep alive his own soul.* The translator may have read נַפְשִׁי לוֹ חָיָה.

Ver. 30. *The seed that serveth him shall declare his generation unto the Lord.* Heb., as rendered in the common version, *a seed shall serve him; it shall be accounted to the Lord for a generation.* It is difficult to reconcile the two texts. The Syriac seems to be rather a gloss than a translation.

PSALM XXIII.

A Psalm of David—concerning his royal table; and, as respects ourselves, spiritually applied to Christian nations in a new way.

1. The Lord shall feed me, nor shall he suffer anything to be lacking to me.
2. He shall make me to dwell in rich pastures, and shall lead me beside the still waters.
3. He hath converted my soul, and led me in the paths of truth.
4. For thy Name's sake, though I walk through the valleys of the shadows of death, I will fear no evil, for thou *art* with me; thy rod and thy staff they comfort me.
5. Thou hast prepared a table before me against mine enemies; thou hast anointed my head with oil, and my cup inebriateth like wine.
6. Thy mercy and loving kindness have followed me all the days of my life, that I may dwell in the house of the Lord forever.

Ps. XXIII. Ver. 2. *Rich pastures,* ܟ̈ܣܝܐ ܘܚܣܝܢܐ, literally, *pastures of strength.* Heb., *green pastures.*

Ver. 4. *For thy name's sake,* ܫܡܟ ܡܛܠ. Heb., *for his name's sake,* and construed with the third verse.

Ver. 5. *My cup inebriateth like wine,* ܟܣܝ ܐܝܟ ܚܡܪܐ ܪܘܝ. A. V. *My cup runneth over;* literally, *my cup is abundance,* כּוֹסִי רְוָיָה. The Syriac verb is the same, but in conjugation Aphel signifies *to inebriate.* LXX., καὶ τὸ ποτήριόν σου μεθύσκον ὡς κράτιστον.

Ver. 6. *That I may dwell.* Heb., *and I will dwell.*

PSALM XXIV.

A Psalm of David—concerning the first day when God began the work of creation.

1. The earth is the Lord's with the fulness thereof; the world and all that dwell therein;
2. For he hath laid its foundations in the sea, and established it in the floods.
3. Who shall ascend into the hill of the Lord? and who shall stand in his holy mountain?
4. He that hath clean hands and a pure heart, and sweareth not falsely by himself, and sweareth not deceitfully.
5. This one shall receive a blessing from the Lord, and righteousness from God our Saviour.
6. This is the generation that seeketh and waiteth for thy face, O God of Jacob.
7. Lift up your heads, O ye gates, and be ye lift up, ye everlasting gates; the King of glories shall come in.
8. Who is this King of glories? The Lord strong and mighty; the Lord mighty and warlike.

Ps. XXIV. Ver. 3. *In his holy mountain.* Heb., *in his holy place*.

Ver. 4. *Sweareth not falsely by himself,* ܠܐ ܝܡܐ ܒܢܦܫܗ ܕܓܠܐܝܬ. A. V. *Hath not lifted up his soul unto vanity,* לֹא־נָשָׂא לַשָּׁוְא נַפְשׁוֹ. The diversity is not so great as at first sight appears, since the Hebrew words were a common formula for false swearing, as in Exod. xx. 7., Deut. v. 11.

Ver. 6. *That seeketh and waiteth for thy face, O God of Jacob.* The Hebrew is substantially the same, though the address is to Jacob, and not to the God of Jacob. The version of the LXX. has the same peculiarity, ζητούντων τὸ πρόσωπον τοῦ θεοῦ Ἰακώβ.

9. Lift up your heads, O ye gates, and be ye lift up ye everlasting gates; the King of glories shall come in.

10. Who is this King of glories? The Lord Almighty; he is the King *that shall be* glorified forever.

(LAUD, AND THE BEGINNING OF THE GRADE.)

PSALM XXV.

A Psalm of David. — Instruction *in the duty* of thanksgiving.

1. Unto thee, O Lord, have I lift up my soul;

2. My God, in thee have I put my trust; let me not be ashamed; let not mine enemies triumph over me;

3. And also let none of them that put their trust in thee be ashamed; *but* let the wicked be ashamed in their vanity.

4. Shew me thy ways, O Lord, and teach me thy paths.

5. Lead me in thy truth, and teach me, for thou art my God and my deliverer; and for thee have I waited all the day.

6. Remember, O Lord, thy loving kindnesses, which *were* of old, and thy mercies.

7. Remember not against me the offences of my youth; but according to the abundance of thy lov-

---

Ver. 10. *The Lord Almighty,* ܠܡܳܪܝܳܐ ܚܰܝܠܬܳܢܳܐ. This is the ordinary Syriac translation of יְהוָה צְבָאוֹת, *the Lord of Hosts.*

He is the king that shall be glorified forever. Heb., *he is the king of glory.*

Ps. xxv. Ver. 3. *In their vanity,* ܒܣܪܺܝܩܘܬܗܘܢ. A. V. *Without cause,* רֵיקָם. But the root רִיק expresses the idea of *emptiness* or *vanity.*

ing kindnesses remember me for thy goodness' sake, O God.

8. The Lord is good and just; therefore he directeth sinners in the way;

9. And guideth the humble in judgment, and teacheth the poor his way.

10. All the ways of the Lord *are* mercy and truth unto them that keep his covenant, and his testimonies.

11. For thy Name's sake, O Lord, purge me from mine iniquity, for it is great.

12. What man is he that feareth the Lord? him shall he teach the way that he hath chosen.

13. His soul also shall dwell at ease, and his seed shall inherit the earth.

14. The thought of the Lord *is* about them that fear him; and he hath shewn them his covenant.

15. Mine eyes *look* always unto the Lord, for he delivereth my feet from the net.

16. Turn unto me, and have mercy upon me; for I am solitary and in misery.

17. The sorrows of my heart are enlarged, but bring thou me out of my troubles.

18. Consider my subjection and my toil, and forgive me all my sin.

19. Consider also that mine adversaries are many, and hate me with an unjust hatred.

20. Preserve my soul and deliver me, for I have put my trust in thee.

Ver. 14. *The thought of the Lord*, ܠܒܗ ܕܡܪܝܐ. A. V. *The secret of the Lord*, סוֹד יְהֹוָה.

Ver. 20. There seems to have been an omission in this verse of the words *let me not be ashamed*, which are expressed in the Hebrew.

21. Perfect and righteous men have attached themselves unto me, because I have waited for thee.

22. Deliver Israel, O God, from all his oppressors.

PSALM XXVI.

A Psalm of David. — When his friends turned away from him in his flight. — As respects ourselves, the supplication of the man that progresseth in virtue before God.

1. Judge me, O Lord, for I have walked in mine integrity; I have put my trust in the Lord, *therefore* I shall not be moved.

2. Examine me, O Lord, and prove me; try my reins and my heart.

3. For thy loving kindnesses *are* before mine eyes, and I have walked in the truth.

4. I have not sat with evil men, neither have I entered in with the foolish.

5. I have hated the congregation of evil doers, and I have not sat with the wicked.

6. I have purely washed my hands, and *so* have I compassed thine altar, O Lord;

7. That I might publish the voice of thy praise, and tell of all thy wondrous works.

Ver. 21. *Perfect and righteous men.* Heb., *integrity and uprightness.* Concrete for the abstract: so also the LXX., ἄκακοι καὶ εὐθεῖς. *Have attached themselves unto me,* ܠܝ ܩܦܘ. A. V. *Let them preserve me,* יִצְּרוּנִי. LXX., ἐκολλῶντο μοι.

Ps. XXVI. Ver. 3. *The truth.* Heb., *thy truth.*

Ver. 6. *Purely.* Heb., *in innocency.*

Ver. 7. *That I might publish the voice of thy praise.* Heb., *That I may publish with the voice of thanksgiving.*

8. Lord, I have loved the ministry of thy house, and the place where thine honour dwelleth.

9. Destroy me not with sinners, nor my life with blood-thirsty men;

10. In whose hands *is* deceit, and their right hand *is* full of gifts.

11. But I have walked in mine integrity; deliver me and have mercy upon me.

12. My foot standeth in righteousness, and I will bless the Lord in the congregation.

PSALM XXVII.

A Psalm of David. — On account of the infirmity that fell upon him.

1. The Lord is my light and my salvation; whom shall I fear? The Lord is the strength of my life; of whom shall I be afraid?

2. When the wicked approached me to eat up my flesh, *even* mine adversaries and my foes, they were overthrown together and fell.

3. If an army should encamp against me, my heart will not fear; if war should arise against me, in this will I be confident;

Ver. 8. *The ministry of thy house,* ܘܟܐܢܐ ܕܒܝܬܟ.
A. v. *The habitation of thy house,* מְעוֹן בֵּיתֶךָ.

Ver. 9. *Destroy me not with sinners,* ܠܐ ܬܘܒܕܢܝ ܥܡ ܚܛܝܐ.
A. v. *Gather not my soul with sinners,* אַל־תֶּאֱסֹף עִם־חַטָּאִים נַפְשִׁי. The Hebrew verb means both *to gather* and *to destroy;* the translator took it in the latter sense.

4. That one *thing* I have desired of the Lord, and after it will I seek; that I may dwell in the house of the Lord all the days of my life, and that I may behold the beauty of the Lord and visit his temple.

5. For he shall hide me in his secret place in the evil day, and in the shadow of his tabernacle shall he hide me, and set me up upon a rock.

6. From henceforth shall my head be lifted up above mine adversaries that have compassed me about: I will offer in his tabernacle the sacrifices of praise; I will sing and speak praises unto the Lord.

7. Hear my voice, O Lord, when I cry unto thee; have mercy upon me, and hear me.

8. My heart talketh with thee, and my face seeketh thy face.

9. Turn not away thy face from me, O Lord, nor in anger afflict thy servant; O Lord, be thou my helper; cast me not away, neither forsake me, O my God, and my deliverer.

10. For my father and mother have forsaken me, but the Lord hath taken me up.

11. Teach me thy way, O Lord, and lead me in thy righteous paths;

Ps. XXVII. Ver. 4. *That one thing,* شَيْءٌ. אַחַת, *one thing.*

Ver. 8. *My heart talketh with thee, and my face seeketh thy face,* جى إذ اخذ جب دخذنى إقب لاطىب. A. V. *When thou saidst, seek ye my face; my heart said unto thee, thy face, Lord, will I seek,* לְךָ אָמַר לִבִּי בַּקְּשׁוּ פָנָי אֶת־פָּנֶיךָ יְהֹוָה אֲבַקֵּשׁ. If we suppose the translator to have read בְּקֻשׁוּ instead of בַּקְּשׁוּ and to have overlooked the words יְהֹוָה אֲבַקֵּשׁ, we can account for the peculiarity of his version.

Ver. 9. *Afflict.* Heb., *put away.*

12. And deliver me not to mine adversaries, for false witnesses have risen up against me, and have spoken wickedness.

13. But I believe that I shall see the good things of the Lord in the land of the living.

14. Put your trust in the Lord, and your heart shall be confirmed; put your trust in the Lord.

PSALM XXVIII.

A Psalm of David.—Prayer and supplication; and that we should implore aid.

1. Unto thee, O Lord, have I cried: my God, be not silent to me; lest, *if* thou be silent to me, I become like them that go down into the pit.

2. Hear the voice of my supplication, when I cry unto thee, and when I lift up my hands towards thy holy temple.

3. Number me not with the wicked, and with evil doers, which speak peace with their neighbours, while evil *is* in their heart.

Ver. 12. *Speak wickedness.* Heb., *breathe out cruelty.*

Ver. 13. *But I,* לוּלֵי. The Hebrew here is לוּלֵא, *unless,* which requires that previous words be supplied, as in the common version.

Ver. 14. *Your heart shall be confirmed.* What corresponds to this in the Hebrew is rendered in the common version, *be of good courage, and he shall strengthen thine heart.*

Ps. XXVIII. Ver. 3. *Number me not.* Heb., *draw me not away.*

4. Recompense them according to their deeds, and according to their wickedness.

5. Because they have not considered the works of the Lord, nor the work of his hands, he shall cast them down, and shall not build them up.

6. Blessed is the Lord, who hath heard the voice of my supplication.

7. The Lord *is* my helper, and my supporter; in whom my heart trusteth; my flesh also exulteth, and in song will I praise him.

8. The Lord is the strength of his people, and the defender and deliverer of his Anointed.

9. Save thy people, and bless thine inheritance; feed them, and guide them forever.

Ver. 4 is more copiously expressed in the Hebrew.

Ver. 7. *My flesh also exulteth, and in song will I praise him,* ܚܕܝ ܒܣܪܝ ܘܒܬܫܒܘܚܬܝ ܐܘܕܐ ܠܗ. There is an unaccountable difference between this and the Hebrew, which, as translated in the common version, is, *and I am helped; therefore my heart greatly rejoiceth and with my song will I praise him.* The Septuagint is similar to the Syriac, ἀνέθαλεν ἡ σάρξ μου, καὶ ἐκ θελήματός μου ἐξομολογήσομαι αὐτῷ. I have rendered ܚܕܝ, *exulteth;* literally, it means, *to grow, to germinate, to flourish.*

Ver. 8. *The strength of his people,* ܥܘܫܢܗ ܕܥܡܗ. A. V. *Their strength,* עֹז־לָמוֹ. The translator seems to have read עֹז לְעַמּוֹ.

PSALM XXIX.

A Psalm of David — *concerning the oblation.*

1. Bring young rams unto the Lord; offer unto the Lord praise and glory.
2. Ascribe unto the Lord the honour *due* unto his Name; worship the Lord in the court of his holiness.
3. The voice of the Lord *is* upon the waters; the glorious God thundereth; the Lord *is* upon many waters.
4. The voice of the Lord *is* powerful; the voice of the Lord *is* full of majesty.
5. *It is* the voice of the Lord that breaketh the cedar-trees; yea, the Lord breaketh the cedars of Lebanon.
6. He breaketh them in pieces also like a calf; Lebanon, and Sirion, like young unicorns.

Ps. XXIX. Ver. 1. *Bring young rams unto the Lord,* اِبْلٌ0 كَفِّدْنَا حَنْبَ وَحَزْ. A. V. *Give unto the Lord, O ye mighty,* הָבוּ לַיהוָֹה בְּנֵי אֵלִים. The translator probably read בְּנֵי אֵילִים, *young rams.* The LXX. combined both readings, and hence the version of the Book of Common Prayer: *Bring unto the Lord, O ye mighty; bring young rams unto the Lord.*

Ver. 2. *In the court of his holiness,* ܚܙܘܿܠ ܘܡܥܘܼܡܗ. A. V. *In the beauty of holiness,* בְּהַדְרַת־קֹדֶשׁ. The reading here was doubtless בְּחַדְרַת־קֹדֶשׁ, *in the chamber, inner apartment, or penetralia of holiness.* So the LXX., ἐν αὐλῇ ἁγίᾳ αὐτοῦ.

Ver. 6. *He breaketh them in pieces also,* اِنْقَ وَأَقْصَم0. A. V. *He maketh them also to skip,* וַיַּרְקִידֵם. LXX., καὶ λεπτυνεῖ αὐτάς. The translator and the LXX. seem to have read יְדִיקֵם.

7. *It is* the voice of the Lord that divideth the flame of fire.

8. *It is* the voice of the Lord that shaketh the wilderness; yea, the Lord shaketh the wilderness of Kadesh.

9. *It is* the voice of the Lord that maketh the hinds to tremble, and rooteth up the forests; and in his temple doth every man speak praise.

10. The Lord hath reduced the water flood; the Lord sitteth a King forever.

11. The Lord shall give strength to his people; the Lord shall bless his people with peace.

PSALM XXX.

A Psalm of David. — Prophecy and thanksgiving.

1. I will extol thee, O Lord, for thou hast lifted me up, and hast not made my foes to rejoice over me.

2. O Lord, my God, I have made my supplication unto thee, and thou hast healed me.

Ver. 9. *Maketh the hinds to tremble,* ܡܚܝܠ ܐܝܠܬܐ. A. V. *Maketh the hinds to calve,* יְחוֹלֵל אַיָּלוֹת. A variation not difficult of explanation; the verb חול, in another conjugation, meaning *to shake,* or *cause to tremble.*

Ver. 10. *The Lord hath reduced the water flood,* ܡܪܝܐ ܡܚܣܢ ܛܘܦܢܐ. A. V. *The Lord sitteth upon the flood,* יְהוָה לַמַּבּוּל יָשָׁב. The translator for יָשָׁב, *sitteth,* seems to have read יָשִׁיב, *turneth back.* Perhaps an allusion may have been supposed to the Deluge.

3. Thou hast also brought up my soul out of hell, and hast kept me alive from them that go down into the pit.

4. Sing unto the Lord, O ye his elect, and give thanks for the remembrance of his holiness.

5. For *there is* rebuke in his wrath, but in his favour *there is* life: weeping may endure for a night, but joy *cometh* in the morning.

6. I said in my prosperity that I should never be moved.

7. O God, in thy favour thou hast established strength upon my glory; *but* thou didst turn away thy face, and I was troubled.

8. I cried unto thee, O Lord, and unto thee, my Lord, did I make supplication.

9. What profit is there in my blood, that I should go down to destruction? The dust cannot give thanks unto thee, neither can it declare thy truth.

10. Hear, O Lord, and have mercy upon me; O Lord be thou my helper.

Ps. xxx. Ver. 3. *From them that go down into the pit.* The unpointed Hebrew text will bear this meaning.

Ver. 5. *Rebuke in his wrath,* ܒܠܘܙܐ ܚܣܡܐ ܕܐܠܗܐ. A. V. *His anger endureth but a moment,* רֶגַע בְּאַפּוֹ. The translator may have read רֹגֶז בְּאַפּוֹ. The LXX. have ὀργὴ ἐν τῷ θυμῷ αὐτοῦ.

Ver. 7. *Thou hast established strength upon my glory,* ܐܩܝܡܬ ܫܘܦܪܐ ܠܚܣܢܝ ܟܠܗ. A. V. *Thou hast made my mountain to stand strong,* הֶעֱמַדְתָּה לְהַרְרִי עֹז. The translator may have read לְהַדְרִי for לְהַרְרִי as did doubtless the LXX., who have παρέσχου τῷ κάλλει μου δύναμιν.

Ver. 9. *To destruction.* Heb., *to the pit.* The Hebrew word שַׁחַת has both meanings.

11. For thou hast turned my mourning into joy; thou hast put off my sackcloth, and girded me with gladness.

12. For this cause will I sing praise unto thee, and will not be silent; O Lord, my God, I will give thanks unto thee forever.

PSALM XXXI.

A Psalm of David. — Confession and continual supplication to God.

1. In thee, O Lord, have I put my trust; let me never be ashamed, but deliver me in thy righteousness.

2. Incline thine ear unto me, and hear me speedily; O God, be thou my helper and my refuge, and save me.

3. For thou art my strength, and my refuge, comfort me, O Lord, for thy Name's sake;

4. And take me out of this net which they have privily laid for me, for thou art my defender.

5. Unto thee have I committed my spirit, and thou hast redeemed me, O Lord God of truth.

6. Thou hatest all them that regard vain superstitions, but I have put my trust in thee, O Lord.

Ver. 12. *For this cause will I sing praise unto thee.* Heb., *To the end that my glory may sing praise to thee.*

Ps. xxxi. Ver. 3. *Comfort me,* كلبك. A. V. *Lead me and guide me,* תַּנְחֵנִי וּתְנַהֲלֵנִי. We may conjecture that for תְּנַחֲמֵנִי, תַּנְחֵנִי was the reading here.

Ver. 5. *Unto thee.* Heb., *into thy hand.*

Ver. 6. *Thou hatest.* Heb., *I have hated.*

7. I will be glad, and rejoice in thy mercy; for thou hast seen my humility, and hast known the affliction of my soul;

8. And thou hast not delivered me into the hands of mine enemies; thou hast set my feet in a large room.

9. Have mercy upon me, O Lord, for I am in trouble: mine eye is disquieted through indignation; and my soul and my belly.

10. For my life is consumed with grief, and my years with mourning; my strength hath become weak through poverty, and my bones are vexed on account of all mine enemies:

11. I was a reproach also to my neighbours, and a terror to them that know me; and they that saw me without fled from me.

12. I am forgotten, as a dead man out of mind, and I am like a broken vessel.

13. For I have heard the slander of many, while they took counsel together against me, and devised that they might take my life.

Ver. 7. *My humility,* ܡܘܟܟܘܬܝ. A. V. *My trouble,* עָנְיִי; for which the translator seems to have read עֲנָוְתִי.

Ver. 9. *Mine eye is disquieted through indignation.* Heb., *mine eye is consumed with grief.*

Ver. 10. *Through poverty,* ܒܡܣܟܢܘܬܐ. A. V. *Because of mine iniquity,* בַּעֲוֹנִי. The true reading, however, may be בְּעָנְיִי; this was evidently adopted by the translator.

Ver. 10, 11. *My bones are vexed on account of all mine enemies: I was a reproach also to my neighbours.* Heb., *and my bones are consumed. I was a reproach among all mine enemies, but especially among my neighbours.*

Ver. 13. There is an omission of the words, translated, *fear was on every side.*

14. But I have put my trust in thee, O Lord; I have said, O Lord, thou *art* my God;

15. And the times are in thy hands; deliver me from mine enemies, and from them that persecute me.

16. Make thy face to shine upon thy servant, and deliver me in thy mercy.

17. O Lord, let me not be ashamed, for I have called upon thee; let the wicked be ashamed, and go down to the grave;

18. And let the lips of the wicked be closed, which speak falsehood and folly against the righteous.

19. O how many are thy mercies, which thou keepest for them that fear thee, *and* for them that put their trust in thee before the sons of men!

20. Thou shalt conceal them in the secret of thy presence from the disturbance of men; thou shalt hide them in thy tabernacle from contention.

21. Blessed is the Lord, which hath chosen the elect for himself, *and placed them* in a strong city.

22. I said in my haste that I had perished from before thine eyes; but thou heardest the voice of my supplication when I cried unto thee.

Ver. 15. *The times.* Heb., *my times.*

Ver. 17. *Go down to the grave.* Heb., *be silent in the grave.*

Ver. 18. *Which speak falsehood and folly.* Heb., *which speak grievous things proudly and contemptuously.*

In ver. 19. the Hebrew word, translated, *thou hast wrought,* is omitted.

Ver. 20. *From the disturbance.* Heb., *from the pride.*

Thy tabernacle. Heb., *a pavilion.*

Ver. 21. *Chosen the elect for himself and placed them in a strong city,* ܐܠܝܐ ܟܡܝܗܐ ܚܣܢܐ ܚܕ ܚܘܐ. A. V. *Shewed me his marvellous kindness in a strong city,* הִפְלִיא חַסְדּוֹ לִי בְּעִיר מָצוֹר. The translator may have read לוֹ הִפְלִיא חֲסִידָיו.

23. O love the Lord, all ye his saints ; the Lord preserveth the faithful, and requiteth their deeds to the wicked.

24. Be strong, and let your heart be confirmed, all ye that put your trust in the Lord.

PSALM XXXII.

A Psalm of David — concerning the offence of Adam, who presumptuously sinned; and a prophecy of the Messiah, through whom *we* are delivered from Gehenna.

1. Blessed is he whose unrighteousness is forgiven, and whose sins are covered.
2. Blessed is the man to whom the Lord will not impute his sin, and in whose heart there is no guile.
3. For when I kept silence, my bones waxed old, while I was groaning all the day.
4. For thy hand was heavy upon me day and night, and grief was stirred up in my breast to destroy me.

Ver. 23. *Requiteth their deeds to the wicked.* Heb., *plentifully rewardeth the proud doer.*

Ps. xxxii. Ver. 4. *Grief was stirred up in my breast to destroy me,* ܘܐܣܬܚܦ ܚܫܝ ܠܩܐܛܐ ܠܡܡܝܬܢܝ. A. V. *My moisture is turned into the drought of summer,* נֶהְפַּךְ לְשַׁדִּי בְּחַרְבֹנֵי קַיִץ. The following explanation of this difference has been suggested: for קַיִץ, *summer,* קוֹץ was read, meaning *thorn,* and, metaphorically, *suffering.* For בְּחַרְבֹנֵי, *into the drought of,* בְּחָרְבְנִי, with signification borrowed from חֶרֶב, *a sword,* and with regard to the word לְשַׁדִּי, *my moisture,* the ל was thought to be a servile letter, so that the word would mean, *to,* or *in my breast.*

5. I acknowledged my sins unto thee, and mine offences have I not hid from thee; I said I will make confession concerning mine offences unto the Lord, and thou forgivest me all my sins.

6. For this shall every one that is chosen of thee make his prayer unto thee in an acceptable time; but the flood of great waters shall not come nigh unto him.

7. Do thou protect me, and preserve me from mine enemies; compass me about with praise and deliverance, that I may give heed unto thee.

8. I will teach thee the way wherein thou shalt go, and I will fix mine eyes upon thee.

9. Be ye not like horse and mule, which are without understanding; whom *men* restrain with the bridle from their youth, nor do they come nigh unto him.

Ver. 6. *Chosen of thee.* Heb., *Godly.*

Ver. 7. *Do thou protect me, and preserve me from mine enemies; compass me about with praise and deliverance.* With verbal differences, the Hebrew is substantially the same.

That I may give heed unto thee, ܐܙܕܗܪ ܒܟ. A. V. *I will instruct thee,* אַשְׂכִּילְךָ; construed with succeeding words.

Ver. 8. *I will fix mine eyes upon thee.* Heb., *I will guide thee with mine eye.*

Ver. 9. *Whom men restrain with the bridle from their youth, nor do they come nigh unto him,* ܘܟܕ ܥܠܝܡܝܢ ܡܚܣܡܝܢ ܠܗܘܢ ܒܦܓܘܕܬܐ: ܠܐ ܢܬܩܪܒܘܢ ܠܦܘܡܗ. A. V. *Whose mouth must be held in with bit and bridle, lest they come near unto thee,* בְּמֶתֶג־וָרֶסֶן עֶדְיוֹ לִבְלוֹם בַּל קְרֹב אֵלֶיךָ. The word עֶדְיוֹ, *his mouth,* the translator probably derived from an Arabic root signifying *youth.* It is difficult to account for the rendering of the latter part of the sentence, *nor do they come nigh unto him,* and it is not very obvious what meaning was attached to the expression.

10. Many are the troubles of the unrighteous; but he that putteth his trust in the Lord, mercy shall compass him about.

11. Be glad, ye righteous, and rejoice in the Lord; and praise him, all ye that are true of heart.

PSALM XXXIII.

A Psalm of David. — In its literal sense, concerning those whom he appointed over the ministry of the Lord; and spiritually, as respects ourselves, a discourse concerning the glory of Deity.

1. Praise the Lord, O ye righteous, and *truly* praise is comely to the upright.
2. Give thanks unto him with the harp, and sing unto him with an instrument of ten strings.
3. Praise him in a new song; sing skilfully with the voice.
4. For the word of the Lord is right, and all his works *are done* in truth.
5. He loveth righteousness and judgment; the earth is full of the goodness of the Lord.
6. By the word of the Lord were the heavens made, and all the hosts of them by the breath of his mouth.

Ver. 11. *Praise him.* Heb., *shout for joy.*

Ps. xxxiii. Ver. 2. *With an instrument of ten strings,* ܒܟܢܪܐ ܘܒܩܝܬܪܐ. A. V. *With the psaltery and an instrument of ten strings,* בְּנֵבֶל עָשׂוֹר.

Ver. 3. *Sing skilfully with the voice.* Heb., *play skilfully with a loud noise.*

7. He gathered the waters of the seas, as it were into bottles, and laid up the deeps in storehouses.

8. Let all the earth fear the Lord, and let all the inhabitants of the world tremble before him.

9. For he spake, and they were; and he commanded, and made *it* steadfast.

10. The Lord bringeth the counsel of the heathen to nought, and the Lord maketh the devices of the people of none effect.

11. The counsel of the Lord endureth forever, and the purpose of his heart throughout all generations.

12. Blessed is the people, whose God is the Lord; *even* the people whom he hath chosen to himself for an inheritance.

13. The Lord looketh down from heaven, and beholdeth all the children of men;

14. And from his seat he looketh upon all the inhabitants of the earth;

15. Whose heart he fashioneth alike, and considereth all their works.

16. There is no king saved by great power; neither is any mighty man delivered by the greatness of his strength.

17. An horse is a vain thing for safety; neither can he deliver his rider by his great strength.

Ver. 7. *As it were into bottles,* ܐܝܟ ܙܩܐ. A. V. *As an heap,* כַּנֵּד. For נֵד, heap, the translator read נֹאד, or נאד, *bottle.* The LXX. have ὡσεὶ ἀσκόν.

Ver. 9. *And they were,* ܘܗܘܘ. A. V. *And it was done,* וַיֶּהִי. LXX., καὶ ἐγενήθησαν.

Ver. 14. *From his seat.* Heb., *From the place of his dwelling.*

Ver. 17. *His rider,* ܠܪܟܒܗ. There is nothing corresponding to this in the Hebrew.

18. The eyes of the Lord *are* over the righteous which wait for his mercy;

19. That he may deliver their souls from death, and preserve them alive in the *time of* drought.

20. But our soul waiteth for the Lord; for he is our helper and protector;

21. And in him our heart shall rejoice; for we have hoped in his holy Name.

22. Let thy mercy be upon us, O Lord, according as we have put our trust in thee.

PSALM XXXIV.

A Psalm of David;—when he goeth into the house of the Lord, and giveth the first fruits to the priests.

1. I will bless the Lord at all times, and his praises *shall be* always in my mouth.

2. My soul shall glory in the Lord; the poor shall hear *thereof*, and be glad.

3. O magnify the Lord with me, and let us exalt his Name together.

4. I sought the Lord, and he heard me; and delivered me from all mine afflictions.

5. Look unto him, and put your trust in him, and your faces shall not be ashamed.

Ps. xxxiv. Ver. 4. *Mine afflictions.* Heb., *my fears.*

Ver. 5. This verse in the Hebrew is not in the imperative form as in the Syriac, and the noun has the suffix of the third person instead of the second.

The ninth verse of the Hebrew is wanting in the Syriac; translated, *O fear the Lord, ye his saints; for there is no want to them that fear him.*

6. This is the poor man that called upon him, and he heard him, and delivered him from all his afflictions.

7. The camp of the angels of the Lord is round about them that fear him, and delivereth them.

8. O taste, and see that the Lord is good; and blessed are all that put their trust in him.

10. The rich do lack, and suffer hunger; but they that seek the Lord shall not want any good thing. Diapsalma.

11. Come, ye children, hearken unto me; and I will teach you the fear of the Lord.

12. What man is he that desireth life, and would fain see good days?

13. Keep thy tongue from evil, and thy lips, that they speak no guile.

14. Depart from evil, and do good; seek peace and pursue it.

15. The eyes of the Lord *are* over the righteous, and his ears *are open* to hear them;

16. *But* the countenance of the Lord *is* against the evil, that he may destroy the remembrance of them from the earth.

Ver. 10. *The rich*, كَفِيرٌ. A. V. *The lions*, כְּפִירִים. This was doubtless regarded as used metaphorically for the proud and arrogant. So the LXX. have πλούσιοι.

Diapsalma, ܦܳܣܽܘܩܳܐ. This is the Greek διάψαλμα, which is a translation of the Hebrew סֶלָה, *Selah*. It is thought to denote a variation either in the modulation of the voice, or in the subject matter of the Psalm. The places in which the word, or its equivalent, occurs, do not always correspond in the different versions.

17. The righteous cry, and the Lord heareth them, and delivereth them.

18. The Lord is nigh unto them that are of a broken heart, and he saveth them that are of an humble spirit.

19. Many are the evils of the righteous, but the Lord delivereth him out of them all;

20. And keepeth all his bones, so that not one of them is broken.

21. Evil slayeth the wicked, and they that hate the righteous shall be consumed.

22. The Lord shall deliver the souls of his servants; and all they that put their trust in him shall not be condemned.

PSALM XXXV.

A Psalm of David;—literally referring to his pursuit of the Edomites; also, the supplication of the righteous.

1. Judge my cause, O Lord, and fight against them that fight against me.

2. Lay hold of armour and shield, and stand up for my help.

Ver. 17. *The righteous.* This word exists in the Syriac, but is supplied in the common versions of the Hebrew, being wanting in the original.

Ver. 21. *Shall be consumed.* Heb., *shall be desolate.*

Ver. 22. *Shall not be condemned.* Heb., *shall be desolate.*

Ps. xxxv. Ver. 1. *Judge my cause,* ܕܘܢ ܕܝܢܝ. A. V. *Plead my cause with them that strive with me,* רִיבָה אֶת־יְרִיבָי. The translator seems to have read רִיבָה אֶת רִיבִי.

Ver. 2. *Armour.* Heb., *shield.*

3. Draw the sword, and brandish *it* against my persecutors; and say unto my soul, I am thy Saviour.

4. Let them be ashamed, and confounded, that seek after my soul; let them turn backward, and be put to confusion, that imagine evil against me.

5. Let them be as the dust before the wind, and let the angel of the Lord pursue them.

6. Let their way be dark, and let there be slippery places in it; and let the angel of the Lord pursue them.

7. For they have hid snares for me, and spread a net for my soul.

8. Let evil come upon them suddenly, and let the net which they have spread *for me* catch them; and let them fall into the pit which they have digged.

9. But my soul shall be joyful in the Lord, and rejoice in his salvation;

10. And all my bones shall say, O Lord, who is like unto thee, thou that deliverest the miserable from his enemy; and the poor and miserable from him that spoileth him by violence?

11. False witnesses did rise up, and laid to my charge things that I knew not.

12. They requited me evil for good, and destroyed my soul from among men.

Ver. 3. *Sword.* Heb., *spear.* *Brandish it.* Heb., *stop the way.*

Ver. 7. The Hebrew as translated is, *For without cause have they hid for me their net in a pit, which without cause they have digged for my soul.*

Ver. 8. *Suddenly,* ܠܐ ܝܕܥ. Heb., לֹא יֵדָע, translated, *at unawares.*

Ver. 12. *Destroyed my soul from among men.* Heb., *to the spoiling of my soul.*

13. But in their sickness I put on sackcloth, and humbled my soul with fasting, and my prayer returned into mine own bosom.

14. I behaved myself like a friend and a brother; and I was afflicted like one that sitteth in mourning.

15. But in my sufferings, they assembled themselves together, and rejoiced over me; they were assembled together against me for a long time, and I knew *it* not.

16. In their pride and derision, they gnashed upon me with their teeth.

17. O my Lord thou hast seen enough; rescue my soul from their sedition, and my unity from the lions.

18. I will give thee thanks in the great congregation, and I will praise thee among much people.

19. Let not my perfidious enemies rejoice over me, that hate me without a cause; that wink with their eyes;

Ver. 14. *I was afflicted like one that sitteth in mourning.* Heb., *I bowed down heavily as one that mourneth for his mother.*

Ver. 15. *They were assembled against me for a long time,* ܐܟܢܫܘ ܥܠܝ ܢܟܐܐ. A. V. *The abjects gathered themselves together against me,* נֶאֶסְפוּ עָלַי נֵכִים. It has been plausibly conjectured, however, that for ܢܟܐܐ the reading should be ܢܟܐܐ, *smitings,* thus corresponding to the Hebrew נֵכִים, though rendered *abjects* in the common version, and the Greek of the Septuagint, μάστιγες. The words, *they did tear me and ceased not,* forming part of this verse in the Hebrew, are not given in the Syriac.

Ver. 16. *In their pride and derision,* ܒܚܘܢܦܗܘܢ ܘܒܡܘܝܩܗܘܢ. A. V. *With hypocritical mockers in feasts,* בְּחַנְפֵי לַעֲגֵי מָעוֹג.

Ver. 17. *Thou hast seen enough.* Heb., *how long wilt thou look on?*

20. And speak not peace, but imagine deceit against the humble of the earth.

21. They opened their mouth against me, and said, aha! aha! our eye hath seen *his desire* upon him.

22. *This* thou hast seen, O God; keep not silence, O my Lord, and be not thou far from me.

23. Awake to my judgment, my God, and my Lord, and consider mine oppression.

24. Judge me, O Lord, according to thy righteousness, that they may not rejoice over me;

25. Nor say in their heart, our soul is satisfied, and we have devoured him.

26. Let them be ashamed, and confounded together, that wish for my hurt, and let them be clothed with shame, that magnify themselves against me.

27. Let them rejoice and be glad, that wish for my triumph; and let them say always, the Lord is great, which hath pleasure in the prosperity of his servant.

28. And my tongue shall confess thy righteousness, and thy praises, all the day long.

Ver. 21. *Our eye hath seen his desire upon him.* The preposition with the pronominal suffix, בלו, not in Hebrew, seems to require the translation which I have given.

PSALM XXXVI.

A Psalm of David,—while Saul was pursuing him; *signifying* to us the rebuke of our enemies, and, moreover, containing a discourse concerning Deity.

1. The ungodly man imagineth wickedness in his heart, because there is no fear of God before his eyes.
2. For it is abominable in his eyes, that he should forsake his sins, and hate them.
3. The word of his mouth *is* sorrow and deceit, and he loveth not to do good.
4. He deviseth sorrow upon his bed, and walketh in the way that is not good, that he may commit wickedness.
5. Thy loving kindnesses, O Lord, *are* in the heavens; and thy truth *reacheth* to the heaven of heavens.

Ps. xxxvi. Ver. 1. *The ungodly man imagineth wickedness in his heart,* ܚܫܰܒ݂ ܚܰܛܳܝܳܐ ܒ݁ܠܶܒ݁ܶܗ ܘܶܐܡܰܪ. A. V. *The transgression of the wicked saith within my heart,* נְאֻם־פֶּשַׁע לָרָשָׁע בְּקֶרֶב לִבִּי. The translator seems to have read, נְאֻם־פֶּשַׁע רָשָׁע בְּקֶרֶב לִבּוֹ.

Ver. 2. *For it is abominable in his eyes that he should forsake his sins and hate them,* ܡܶܛܽܠ ܕ݁ܰܡܣܰܢܶܐ ܒ݁ܥܰܝܢܰܘܗ̱ܝ ܘܢܶܫܒ݁ܽܘܩ ܥܰܘܠܶܗ ܘܢܶܣܢܶܐ ܐܶܢܽܘܢ. A. V. *For he flattereth himself in his own eyes, until his iniquity be found to be hateful,* כִּי־הֶחֱלִיק אֵלָיו בְּעֵינָיו לִמְצֹא עֲוֺנוֹ לִשְׂנֹא. A very obscure passage. The Syriac version is rather a gloss than a translation.

Ver. 4. *That he may commit wickedness.* Heb., *he abhorreth not evil.*

6. Thy righteousness *is* like the mountains, O God, and thy judgments *are* like the great deep; O Lord, thou preservest men and beasts.

7. How many are thy mercies, O God! therefore the children of men shall be covered in the shadow of thy wings.

8. They shall be satisfied with the fatness of thine house; and thou shalt make them drink of thy pleasant river.

9. For with thee is the fountain of life, and in thy light do we see light.

10. Preserve thy loving kindnesses to them that are near thee, and thy righteousness to the upright in heart.

11. Bring not against us the arrogant foot, and let not the hands of the wicked disturb us.

12. For there are they fallen, all the workers of falsehood; they are cast down, and are not able to rise.

(LAUD, AND THE BEGINNING OF THE GRADE.)

PSALM XXXVII.

A Psalm of David;—concerning them that say, wherefore doth not the Lord take vengeance upon the insolent?

1. Be not jealous of the wicked, neither be thou envious against the workers of iniquity.

Ver. 6. *The mountains, O God,* ܛܘܪܐ ܕܐܠܗܐ. Heb., הַרְרֵי־אֵל, *the great mountains*, literally, *the mountains of God*. But to have this meaning, the Syriac should be, ܛܘܪܐ ܕܐܠܗܐ.

Ver. 7. *How many*. Heb., *How excellent*.

Ver. 10. *Them that are near thee.* Heb., *them that know thee.*

Ver. 11. *Bring not against us the arrogant foot.* Heb., *Let not the foot of pride come against me.*

2. For they dry up quickly like the stubble, and wither like the green herb.

3. Trust in the Lord, and be doing good; dwell in the land, and seek after truth.

4. Trust in the Lord, and he shall give thee the desire of thine heart.

5. Make thy way direct before the Lord, and trust in him, and he will bring *it* to pass;

6. And bring forth thy righteousness like the light, and thy judgments like the noonday.

7. Seek the Lord, and incline unto him; and be not envious against the man that doeth evil and prospereth *in* his way.

8. Cease from wrath, and let go displeasure, and be not emulous to do evil.

9. For the wicked shall be consumed; but they that put their trust in the Lord shall inherit the earth.

10. In a little time thou shalt seek for the wicked, and he shall not be; thou shalt look for his place, and it shall not be found.

11. But the poor shall inherit the earth, and be solaced with abundant peace.

Ps. xxxvii. Ver. 2. *For they dry up quickly.* Heb., *For they shall soon be cut down.*

Ver. 3. *Seek after truth,* ܚܝܒ ܟܦܫܐܝܠ. A. V. *Verily thou shalt be fed,* רְעֵה אֱמוּנָה; but literally, *feed upon truth,* which is not very different from the Syriac, though בְּעָה might have been the reading.

Ver. 5. *Make thy way direct before the Lord.* Heb., *Commit thy way unto the Lord.*

Ver. 7. *Seek the Lord and incline unto him.* Heb., *Rest in the Lord, and wait patiently for him.* The latter part of this verse in the original, translated, *because of the man who bringeth wicked devices to pass,* is omitted in the Syriac.

12. The wicked is angry with the righteous, and gnasheth upon him with his teeth.

13. But the Lord shall laugh at him; for he knoweth that his day is coming.

14. The wicked draw the sword, and bend the bow, that they may slay the poor and humble, and them whose ways *are* upright.

15. Their sword shall pierce their own heart, and their bows shall be broken.

16. A little that the righteous hath is better than the great possessions of the wicked.

17. For the arms of the wicked shall be broken; *but* the Lord upholdeth the righteous;

18. And the Lord knoweth the days of the perfect ones, and their inheritance shall endure forever.

19. They shall not be ashamed in the evil hour, and in the days of dearth they shall be satisfied.

20. For the wicked shall perish, and the pampered enemies of the Lord shall fail; and like smoke shall they consume away.

21. The wicked borroweth, and payeth not again; but the righteous is merciful and giveth.

Section.

22. For they that are blessed of the Lord shall in-

Ver. 12. *Is angry*, ܐܬܚܡܬ. A. v. *Plotteth*, זֹמֵם. זָקַם may have been the reading.

Ver. 16. *The great possessions of the wicked.* In the Hebrew the adjective is construed with the second substantive: *the riches of many wicked.*

Ver. 20. *Pampered*, ܡܕܩܠܝ. A. v. *Shall be as the fat of lambs*, or, *as the glory of the fields*, בִּיקַר כָּרִים. *Like smoke.* Heb., *into smoke*, בֶעָשָׁן, unless this should be read בְּעָשָׁן.

herit the earth; and they that are cursed of him shall be consumed.

23. The steps of a *good* man are ordered by the Lord, and he directeth his way.

24. For though he falleth, he is not harmed, for the Lord holdeth his hand.

25. I have been young, and am old, and *yet* never saw I the righteous to have been forsaken, nor his seed to have begged their bread.

26. But all the day he is merciful and lendeth, and his seed is blessed.

27. Depart from evil, and do good; *and* rest forevermore.

28. For the Lord loveth judgment, and forsaketh not his saints, but preserveth them forever; but he destroyeth the seed of the wicked.

29. The righteous also shall inherit the earth, and dwell therein forever.

30. The mouth of the righteous meditateth wisdom; and his tongue talketh of judgment.

31. The law of the Lord *is* in his heart; and his footsteps shall not slide.

32. The wicked waiteth for the righteous, and seeketh to slay him.

33. The Lord will not leave him in his hands, but he will condemn him in judgment.

34. Trust in the Lord, and keep his way, and he

Ver. 23. *And he directeth his way.* Heb., *and he delighteth in his way.*

• Ver. 33. *But he will condemn him.* Heb., *nor condemn him.* For וְלֹא, *nor*, the Syriac has ܐܠܐ, *but*. The reference, of course, in the latter, is to the wicked; while in the former it is to the righteous.

shall exalt thee to inherit the earth; when the wicked are consumed thou shalt see *it*.

35. For I have seen the wicked who were in great prosperity, and exalted like the trees of the forest.

36. When I passed by, he was not; and I sought him, and could not find him. Diapsalma.

37. Keep innocency, and choose righteousness; for there is a good end to men of peace.

38. But sinners shall be consumed together; and the end of the wicked *shall be* destruction.

39. The Lord *is* the deliverer of the saints, and helpeth them in times of trouble.

40. The Lord helpeth them, and delivereth them; and rescueth them from the wicked, and saveth them, because they put their trust in him.

Ver. 36. *When I passed by,* ܟܚܢܐ ܟ݁ܡ. Heb., וַיַּעֲבֹר, *yet he passed away.*

Ver. 37. *Keep innocency and choose righteousness, for there is a good end to men of peace,* ܢܳ ܐܶܬ݂ܢܰܛ݁ܰܪ ܥܰܟ݁ܶܐ ܘܰܚܙܺܝ ܠܐܘܪܚܳܐ. ܡܶܛܽܠ ܕ݁ܐܝܬ݂ ܥܢܶܐ ܠܓ݂ܰܒ݂ܪܳܐ ܫܰܝܢܳܐ ܘܣܳܓ݂ܕ݁ܳܐ. A. V. *Mark the perfect man, and behold the upright; for the end of that man is peace,* שְׁמָר־תָּם וּרְאֵה יָשָׁר כִּי־אַחֲרִית לְאִישׁ שָׁלוֹם. There is not much difference here, however, if we suppose יָשָׁר and תָּם to be abstract instead of concrete, and take אִישׁ to be in the construct state before שָׁלוֹם. The LXX. have φύλασσε ἀκακίαν καὶ ἴδε εὐθύτητα, ὅτι ἐστὶν ἐγκατάλειμμα ἀνθρώπῳ εἰρηνικῷ. Hence the version in the Book of Common Prayer.

PSALM XXXVIII.

A Psalm of David;—when the Philistines said to Achish the king, this is David that killed Goliath, we will not that he go with us against Saul;—moreover, now, as respects ourselves, instruction *in the duty of* confession.

1. O Lord, rebuke me not in thine anger; neither correct me in thy displeasure;
2. For thine arrows are fixed in me, and thy hand resteth *heavily* upon me.
3. There is no health in my flesh, because of thine anger; and there is no rest in my bones, because of my sins.
4. For mine offences are gone over my head, and like a heavy burden are oppressive to me.
5. My wounds stink, and are corrupt;
6. And by reason of mine offences I am sore troubled; I go in mourning all the day long.
7. For mine ankle bones are full of trembling, and there is no health in my flesh.
8. I am troubled, and grievously afflicted; and I have roared on account of the disquietude of my heart.
9. O Lord, all my desire is before thee, and my groanings are not hid from thee.

Ps. xxxviii. Ver. 6. *By reason of mine offences.* This forms part of the fifth verse, and in the Hebrew is construed with the preceding words. I have ventured to change the position of the words to avoid awkwardness.

Ver. 7. *Mine ankle bones are full of trembling.* Heb., *my loins are filled with a loathsome disease.*

10. My heart is agitated, and my strength faileth me, and the light of mine eyes is gone from me.

11. My lovers and my friends did stand aloof from my sorrow, and my kinsmen stood afar off.

12. They also that seek my soul, and wish for my hurt, have laid hold upon me, and spoken falsehood and deceit; and all the day long have meditated *evil against me.*

13. But I, as a deaf man, heard not; and like a dumb man I opened not my mouth;

14. And I was like a man that heareth not, and in whose mouth there is no reproof.

15. For I have put my trust in thee, O Lord, and thou hast answered me, O Lord my God.

16. For I said, *hear me,* lest they rejoice over me; and lest, when my feet slip, they be lifted up against me.

17. For I am ready to suffer, and my sorrow is always before me.

18. For I will declare mine offences unto thee, and *so* shall I be purified from my sins. Diapsalma.

19. Mine enemies are mighty, and behold *me;* and they that hate me wrongfully are many in number.

Ver. 10. *Is agitated,* ܢܶܬܗܦܶܟ, literally, *is subverted.* Heb., סְחַרְחַר, *panteth.*

Ver. 12. *Have laid hold upon me,* ܐܶܚܰܕܘ. A. V. *Lay snares for me,* יְנַקְשׁוּ.

Ver. 17. *To suffer,* ܠܚܰܫܳܐ. A. V. *To halt,* לְצֶלַע.

Ver. 18. *And so shall I be purified from my sins.* Heb., *I will be sorry for my sin.*

Ver. 19. *And behold me,* ܚܳܐܶܝܢ. Heb., חַיִּים, *are lively.* Did not the translator read חֹזִים?

20. They rewarded me evil for good, and hate me, because I seek *the thing that* good *is*.

21. Forsake me not, O Lord my God, and be not thou far from me;

22. But continue to help me and deliver me.

PSALM XXXIX.

To Jeduthun. — A supplication; also a commandment to keep the tongue from impure conversation, and the sight, and all the senses.

1. I said that I will take heed to my way, and will not sin with my tongue; I will keep my mouth from iniquity, on account of the wicked that are before me.

2. I was dumb, and sorrowful; and I was afflicted, *so that I enjoyed* no peace, and my sorrow was stirred.

Ver. 22. *Deliver me.* Heb., *O Lord, my salvation.*

Ps. xxxix. Title. *To Jeduthun,* ܠܝܕܘܬܘܢ. This may either mean *to* Jeduthun or *of* Jeduthun; but the Hebrew expressly calls this a Psalm of David, which determines the translation here. LXX., τῷ Ἰδιθοὺν ᾠδὴ τῷ Δαυίδ.

Ver. 1. *From iniquity,* ܡܢ ܥܘܠܐ. A. V. *With a bridle,* מַחְסוֹם. It has been conjectured that the reading was מֵחֲמֹס, *from envying;* with the signification of the Syriac verb.

On account of. Heb., *while.*

Ver. 2. *And I was afflicted so that I enjoyed no peace,* ܘܚܫܬ ܡܢ ܛܒܬܐ. A. V. *I held my peace even from good,* הֶחֱשֵׁיתִי מִטּוֹב. The translator might have derived the verb from חָשַׁשׁ, with the meaning of the Syriac verb, *to suffer,* and read וְהָחֲשׁוֹתִי.

3. My heart was hot within me, and fire was kindled in my body; *then* I spake with my tongue;

4. Lord, make me to know mine end, and the measure of my days, what it is, that I may know for what *purpose* I continue.

5. For lo! thou hast given *me* my days by measure, and my continuance is even as nothing before thee; for all men in their stay are like a vapour.   Diapsalma.

6. For man walketh in a vain shew, and disappeareth like a vapour; he layeth up treasures, and knoweth not for whom he gathereth them.

7. Now what is my hope but thee, O Lord?

8. Deliver me from all mine offences, and make me not a reproach to the wicked.

9. I was dumb, and I opened not my mouth, because thou didst *it*.

10. Remove thy stroke away from me, and *take* from me the smiting of thy hands.

11. I am consumed with reproof on account of my sins; thou chastenest man, and makest his lusts to pass away like the stubble; and *truly* all men are like a vapour.

Ver. 3. *In my body,* ܒܗܓܝܢܝ. A. V. *In my musing,* בַּהֲגִיגִי, or, *while I mused.*

Ver. 4. *For what purpose I continue.* Heb., *how frail I am.*

Ver. 5. *In their stay.* Heb., *at his best state.*

Vapour. Heb., *vanity.*

Ver. 6. *Disappeareth like a vapour,* ܐܝܟ ܓܘܢܐ ܡܬܦܫܪ, literally, *becometh warm like a vapour which is dissipated by the heat.* Heb., אַךְ־הֶבֶל יֶחֱמָיוּן. *Surely they are disquieted in vain.* The translator may have read, כְּהֶבֶל יֵחַמּוּ.

Ver. 11. *Makest his lusts to pass away like the stubble.* Heb., *makest his beauty to consume away like a moth.* For עָשׁ, *a moth*, the translator read קַשׁ, *stubble.*

12. Hear my prayer, O Lord, and my supplication, and incline unto *the voice of* my weeping, and hold not thy peace; for I am a stranger with thee, and a sojourner, as all my fathers *were*.

13. Deliver me, that I may be refreshed, before I go hence and be no more.

PSALM XL.

A Psalm of David; — in its literal sense *understood to have been composed* when Shemaiah brought to him the names of them that ministered in the house of the Lord; and, spiritually, thanksgiving to God from the ministers and the Church.

1. In the Lord have I truly put my trust, who hath turned unto me, and heard my supplication;

2. And brought me up out of the pit of adversity, and out of the mire of corruption; he hath set my feet upon a rock, and established my goings.

3. He hath put a new song in my mouth, *even* praise to God, that many might see *it* and rejoice, and put their trust in the Lord.

4. Blessed is the man that trusteth in the Name of

Ver. 13. *Deliver me.* Heb., *Spare me.*

Ps. XL. Ver. 4. *Trusteth in the Name of the Lord,* ܟܠ ܡܣܒܪ ܒܫܡܐ ܕܡܪܝܐ. A. V. *That maketh the Lord his trust,* אֲשֶׁר־שָׂם יְהוָה מִבְטָחוֹ. שֵׁם יְהוָה, the name of the Lord, was doubtless the reading. LXX., οὐ ἔστι τὸ ὄνομα κυρίου ἐλπὶς αὐτοῦ.

To vanity, ܠܚܡܣܢܝܢ. A. V. *Unto the proud,* אֶל־רְהָבִים. LXX., εἰς ματαιότητας. *To false speaking,* ܠܡܡܠܠܝ. Heb., שָׂטֵי כָזָב, *such as turn aside unto lies.* LXX., μανίας ψευδεῖς.

the Lord, and turneth not *aside* unto vanity, nor to false speaking.

5. Many are the things that thou hast done, O Lord, our God, thy wondrous works, and thy thoughts *which are* to us-ward, and there is no one like unto thee; thou hast declared *them*, and spoken *of them*, and they are more than can be numbered.

6. In sacrifices and offerings thou hast had no pleasure, but mine ears hast thou opened; and whole burnt sacrifices for sins thou hast not required.

7. Then said I, Lo, I come; for in the beginning of the Scriptures it is written of me;

8. I delight to do thy will, O God, and thy law *is* within my heart.

9. I have proclaimed thy righteousness in the great congregation, and I have not refrained my lips.

10. O Lord, thou knowest that I have not hid thy righteousness within my heart, but I have declared thy salvation and thy truth; neither have I concealed thy mercy and thy truth from the great congregation.

Ver. 5. *There is no one like unto thee,* ܠܡܕ ܐܚܛܒܝ. Heb., אֵין עֲרֹךְ אֵלֶיךָ; translated, *they cannot be reckoned up in order unto thee.* The words, however, may be rendered so as to correspond with the Syriac. LXX., οὐκ ἔστι τίς ὁμοιωθήσεταί σοι.

Thou hast declared them and spoken of them. Heb., *if I would declare and speak of them.*

Ver. 6. *Whole burnt sacrifices for sins.* Heb., *burnt offering and sin offering.*

Ver. 7. *In the beginning of the Scriptures,* ܚܢܝܣ ܕܟܬܒܐ.

A. V. *In the volume of the Book,* בִּמְגִלַּת־סֵפֶר. LXX., ἐν κεφαλίδι βυβλίου.

Ver. 10. *O Lord, thou knowest.* These words belong to verse 9th, but I have changed their position, because in the Syriac version they are connected with the words that follow.

11. And thou, also, O Lord, withhold not thy loving kindnesses from me; but let thy loving kindnesses and thy truth alway preserve me.

12. For innumerable evils have compassed me about, and my sins have taken hold of me, so that I am not able to look up; and they are more than the hairs of my head, and my heart hath failed me.

13. Be pleased, O Lord, to deliver me; O Lord continue to help me.

14. Let them be ashamed and confounded that seek to destroy my soul; let them turn back, and be put to confusion, that wish for my evil.

15. Let them be overwhelmed with a twofold confusion, that say of me, aha! aha!

16. Let all them that seek thee, be glad in thee; and let them that love thy salvation, say alway, the Lord is great.

17. But I am poor and in misery; O my Lord, they have imagined *evil* against me: thou art my helper and my deliverer; make no tarrying, O my God!

Ver. 15. *Let them be overwhelmed with a twofold confusion,* ܬܐܡܗܘܢ ܚܐܢܐ ܘܒܐܦܠܗܘܢ; literally, *Let them be amazed in the repetition of their shame.* Heb., יָשֹׁמּוּ עַל־עֵקֶב בָּשְׁתָּם, *Let them be desolate for a reward of their shame.* The root שָׁמַם, however, has the signification, *to be amazed* or *astonished*, which the translator adopted. It is difficult to explain the other variation.

Ver. 17. *They have imagined evil against me.* Heb., *the Lord thinketh upon me.*

PSALM XLI. ⁴/ /

A Psalm of David; — when he appointed stewards to care for the poor; also a prophecy concerning Christ, and concerning Iscariot.

1. Blessed is he that considereth the poor, for the Lord will deliver him in the time of trouble.
2. The Lord will preserve him, and keep him alive, and bless him upon the earth; nor will he deliver him to his enemies.
3. The Lord will support him upon his bed of pain; yea, he maketh all his bed in his sickness.
4. I have said, thou art my Lord; have mercy upon me, and heal my soul, for I have sinned against thee.
5. Mine enemies speak evil against me, *saying*, when shall he die, and his name perish?
6. When they come to see me, they speak falsehood, and imagine evil in their heart; they go forth into the street and tell *it*.
7. All they that hate me whisper together against me, and imagine evil against me.
8. They meditate upon a thing of evil; *they say* now that he lieth, he shall rise up no more.

Ps. XLI. Ver. 6. *Imagine evil in their heart.* Heb., *his heart gathereth iniquity to itself.*

Ver. 8. *They meditate upon a thing of evil,* ܚܫܒܘ ؟ وكما ܢܐܡܪܘܢ ܠܗ. A. V. *An evil disease, say they, cleaveth fast unto him,* דְּבַר־בְּלִיַּעַל יָצוּק בּוֹ. For יָצוּק, the translator may have read יָצוּרוּ, from צוּר, *to frame, to imagine.*

9. Yea, even mine own familiar friend, in whom I trusted, which did eat of my bread, in whom I trusted, hath dealt very deceitfully with me.

10. But thou, O Lord, be merciful unto me; raise me up, that I may requite them.

11. By this I know that thou favourest me, because mine enemy doth not afflict me.

12. But thou upholdest me in mine integrity, and settest me up before thee forever.

13. Blessed is the Lord God of Israel, from everlasting to everlasting. Amen and Amen.

Ver. 9. *The words, in whom I trusted,* are not repeated in the Hebrew.

Hath dealt very deceitfully with me. Heb., *hath lifted up his heel against me.*

Ver. 11. *Afflict,* مخجام. Heb., יָרִיעַ, *triumph.* This verb was doubtless supposed to be Hiphil of רָעַע or רוּעַ, with the sense of bringing affliction or evil upon another.

END OF THE FIRST BOOK.

THE SECOND BOOK.

PSALM XLII.

A Psalm of the sons of Korah; — Supplication of the prophets; and *a Psalm* which David sang, during his persecution, and when he desired to return to Jerusalem.

1. Like the hart which crieth for the water brooks, so also crieth my soul after thee, O Lord.
2. My soul thirsteth for thee, the living God; when shall I come and see thy face?
3. O God, my tears have been *my* meat, by day and by night, while they were continually saying unto me, Where is thy God?
4. These things I remember, and my soul is troubled; for I would go under thy strong protection to the

---

Ps. XLII. Ver. 1. *Crieth*, خَـرّ. A. v. *Panteth*, תַּעֲרֹג. The Jewish commentators, however, make the word to denote the cry of the deer.

Ver. 2. *See thy face*, اسرا اقـمـي. A. v. *Appear before*, אֵרָאֶה פְּנֵי. Perhaps אֶרְאֶה was read.

Ver. 3. *O God*, construed in Hebrew with the preceding verse.

Ver. 4. *My soul is troubled.* Heb., *I pour out my soul in me.* For I would go under thy strong protection, ܘܐܕܟ ܬܚܝ ܚܦܓܘܝ ܟܡܝܢܐ. A. v. *For I had gone with the multitude; I went with them*, כִּי אֶעֱבֹר בַּסָּךְ אֶדַּדֵּם. The reading seems to

house of God, *when* with the voice of praise and thanksgiving the multitude rejoice.

5. Why art thou troubled, O my soul, and why art thou amazed? Hope thou in God; for I will yet give him thanks, *who is* the helper of my countenance, and my God.

6. My soul is troubled within me; therefore have I remembered thee from the land of Jordan, from Hermon, and from the little hill.

7. Deep calleth unto deep, and voice unto voice of thy water courses; all thy storms and waves are gone over me.

8. *Yet* the Lord will command his mercies in the daytime, and his praises in the night season; with me *shall be* my prayer unto the living God.

9. I said unto God, Why hast thou forgotten me, and why go I mournfully, because of the oppression of the enemy?

10. *As* with the breaking of my bones mine enemies

have been כִּי אֶעֱבֹר בַּסָּךְ אֶדַּדֵּם, which the LXX. adopted, ὅτι διελεύσομαι ἐν τόπῳ σκηνῆς θαυμαστῆς.

Rejoice. Heb., *kept holy day.*

Ver. 5. *Who is the helper of my countenance and my God.* Heb., *for the help of his countenance.* In the original, the words, *my God*, are construed with the next verse.

Ver. 7. *Voice unto voice of thy water courses.* Heb., *at the voice of thy water spouts.*

Ver. 8. *And his praises in the night season; with me shall be my prayer unto the living God.* Heb., *And in the night his song shall be with me, and my prayer unto the God of my life.* The two texts correspond in the main; the difference arises from the position of the accent in the Hebrew.

Ver. 10. *As with the breaking of my bones.* Heb., *As with a sword in my bones;* more literally, *For a wounding in my bones,* with which the Syriac agrees.

reproach me, while they continually say unto me, Where is thy God?

11. Why art thou troubled, O my soul, and why art thou amazed? Hope thou in God; for I will yet give him thanks, *who is* the helper of my countenance, and my God.

PSALM XLIII. 43

A Psalm of David;—when Jonathan made known to him that Saul sought to slay him; moreover, the supplication of the prophets; *wherein also the Psalmist* casts reproach upon the Jews.

1. Judge my cause, O God, and avenge me of an unmerciful people, and deliver me from unjust and deceitful men;

2. For thou art the God of my strength; and wherefore hast thou forgotten me? and why go I mournfully, because of the oppression of the enemy?

3. O send out thy light and thy truth, and they shall comfort me, and bring me to thy holy hill, and to thy dwelling.

4. And I will go to the altar of God, even to the God that giveth joy to my youth; upon the harp will I praise thee, O God, my God.

Ps. XLIII. Ver. 1. *Avenge me.* Heb., *plead my cause.*

Ver. 3. *They shall comfort me,* ܢܒܝܐܘܢܝ. A. V. *Let them lead me,* יַנְחוּנִי. Probably יְנַחֲמוּנִי was the reading.

Ver. 4. *Giveth joy to my youth,* ܚܕܘܬܐ ܕܛܠܝܘܬܝ. A. V. *My exceeding joy,* שִׂמְחַת גִּילִי. The version of the LXX. corresponds with the Syriac; τὸν εὐφραίνοντα τὴν νεότητά μου. גִּיל

5. Why art thou troubled, O my soul, and why art thou amazed? Hope thou in God; for I will yet give him thanks, *which is* the helper of my countenance, and my God.

PSALM XLIV. 44

A Psalm of the sons of Korah, which the people sang at Horeb with Moses; *containing*, moreover, the supplication of the prophets, of David and the rest; and *signifying* to us triumph and victory over them that fight *against us.*

1. O God, we have heard with our ears, and our fathers have also narrated unto us, what thou didst in their days, in the days of old.

2. Thy hand destroyed the heathen, but thou plantedst them; thou didst afflict the kingdoms, and establish them.

3. For they gat not the land in possession by their own sword, neither did their own arm deliver them; but thy right hand, and thine arm, and the light of thy countenance, because thou hadst a favour unto them.

4. Thou art God, my King, that hast given commandment concerning the deliverance of Jacob.

in Arabic has the meaning of youth, which may account for the rendering of the word in this place.

Ps. XLIV. Ver. 2. *And establish them*, ܐܰܬܩܶܢ ܐܶܢܽܘܢ. A. V. *And cast them out,* וַתְּשַׁלְּחֵם. It will be seen that the Syriac preserves the parallelism of the two clauses of the verse; though perhaps ܐܰܬܩܶܢ should be read for ܐܰܬܩܶܢ.

Ver. 4. *That hast given commandment concerning the deliverance of Jacob.* This clause in the original is in the imperative form.

5. Through thee, will we transfix our enemies, and for thy Name will we trample upon them that hate us.

6. For we trust not in our own bows; neither in our own armour that it should deliver us.

7. It is thou that hast delivered us from them that hate us, and put our enemies to shame.

8. We praise thee, O God, all the day; and we will give thanks unto thy Name forever.

9. *But* now thou hast forgotten us, and put us to shame, and thou goest not forth with our armies.

10. But thou hast made us to turn backward, and our enemies spoil us.

11. Thou hast given us like sheep *appointed* for meat, and hast scattered us among the heathen.

12. Thou hast sold thy people without price, and hast lightly esteemed their exchange.

13. Thou hast made us a reproach to our neighbours, and a mockery and derision to them that are round about us.

14. Thou hast made us a proverb among the heathen, and a shaking of the head among the people.

15. All the day long my shame is before me, and the shame of my face hath covered me;

16. For the voice of him that reproacheth and blasphemeth, and by reason of the enemy that avengeth.

17. All these things have happened unto us, and yet we have not forgotten thee; nor have we dealt falsely in thy covenant;

Ver. 10. *Spoil us.* Heb., *spoil for themselves.*

Ver. 12. *And hast lightly esteemed their exchange,* ܘܠܐ ܐܣܓܝܬ ܒܡܘܗܒܬܗܘܢ; literally, *and hast not increased their exchange.* Heb., *and dost not increase thy wealth by their price.*

18. Neither have we turned backward, nor perverted our paths from thy way.

19. For thou hast humbled us in the place of dragons, and covered us with the shadows of death.

20. But we have not forgotten the Name of our God, nor stretched forth our hands to strange gods.

21. God searcheth this out, for he knoweth the thoughts of the heart.

22. For thy sake are we killed all the day long, and are counted as sheep for the slaughter.

23. Awake, and sleep not, O Lord; remember us, and forget us not;

24. And turn not away thy face from us, and forget not our humiliation and oppression.

25. For our soul lieth in the dust, and our belly cleaveth to the ground.

26. Arise, help us, and deliver us, for thy mercies' sake.

Ver. 19. *In the place of dragons.* The Syriac is كلاڑ اِبلْتا, which yields no tolerable sense. كلاڑ ڑالْتَتا has been suggested as the true reading.

In verses 20th and 21st, a peculiarity of construction will be noted.

Ver. 23. *Remember us and forget us not.* Heb., *arise, cast us not off forever.*

(LAUD, AND THE BEGINNING OF THE GRADE.)

PSALM XLV. 45

Written by the sons of Korah, in the days of Moses; the manifestation of the Messiah; also concerning the Church, and concerning the glorious power of God.

1. My heart is overflowing with good matters, and I will speak of the things which I have made touching the King; my tongue *is* the pen of a ready writer.

2. *He is* fairer in his appearance than the children of men; mercies are poured out upon thy lips, wherefore God hath blessed thee forever.

3. Gird the sword upon thy thighs, O thou most mighty;

4. Thy majesty and thy glory shall triumph. Ride

Ps. XLV. Ver. 2. *He is fairer in his appearance.* Heb., *Thou art fairer.*
Mercies. Heb., *grace.*
Ver. 4. *Thy majesty and thy glory shall triumph. Ride on upon the word of truth and the meekness of righteousness,* ܘܗܕܪܝ ܘܫܘܒܚܝ ܐܩܪ: ܘܪܟܒ ܥܠ ܦܬܓܡܐ ܘܡܟܝܟܐ ܘܙܕܝܩܐ. A. V. *With thy glory and thy majesty; and in thy majesty ride prosperously because of truth and meekness and righteousness,* הוֹדְךָ וַהֲדָרֶךָ: וַהֲדָרְךָ צְלַח רְכַב עַל־דְּבַר־אֱמֶת וְעַנְוָה־צֶדֶק. The translator seems to have read, הוֹדְךָ וַהֲדָרֶךָ .צְלַח: רְכַב עַל־דְּבַר־אֱמֶת וְעַנְוַת־צֶדֶק.
Thy law is in the fear of thy right hand, ܢܡܘܣܟ ܒܕܚܠܬܐ ܕܝܡܝܢܟ. A. V. *And thy right hand shall teach thee terrible things,* וְתוֹרְךָ נוֹרָאוֹת יְמִינֶךָ. It is quite evident that the translator read, וְתוֹרָתְךָ בְּיִרְאַת יְמִינֶךָ.

on, upon the word of truth, and the meekness of righteousness; thy law *is* in the fear of thy right hand.

5. Thine arrows are sharp, and the heathen shall fall under thee, in the midst of the King's enemies.

6. Thy throne, O God, *is* forever and ever; a right sceptre *is* the sceptre of thy kingdom.

7. Thou hast loved righteousness, and hated iniquity; wherefore God, thy God, hath anointed thee with the oil of gladness above thy fellows.

8. All thy garments smell of myrrh, cassia, and stacte; out of the principal palace and from my house they have made thee glad.

9. The King's daughter standeth in glory; and on thy right hand *is* the queen, in clothing of the gold of Ophir.

10. Hearken, O my daughter, and consider; and incline thine ear; forget also thine own people, and thy father's house;

11. That the King may greatly desire thy beauty, for he is thy Lord; worship him.

Ver. 8. *Out of the principal palace and from my house,* ܡܢ ܗܝܟܠܐ ܕܢܓܦܐ ܕܫܢܐ ܕܟܣܦܐ. A. V. *Out of the ivory palaces whereby,* מִן־הֵיכְלֵי שֵׁן מִנִּי. In the word מִנִּי the translator took the Yodh paragogic for the pronominal suffix.

Ver. 9. *The King's daughter standeth in glory; and on thy right hand is the queen,* ܒܪܬ ܡܠܟܐ ܩܡܬ ܒܫܘܒܚܐ ܘܡܠܟܬܐ ܥܠ ܝܡܝܢܟ. A. V. *Kings' daughters were among thy honourable women: upon thy right hand did stand the queen,* בְּנוֹת מְלָכִים בְּיִקְּרוֹתֶיךָ נִצְּבָה שֵׁגַל לִימִינְךָ. We can only account for this difference by supposing the translator to have read בַּת־מֶלֶךְ בְּיָקָר נִצְּבָה וְשֵׁגַל לִימִינְךָ.

12. And the daughter of Tyre shall worship him; the rich, *also,* among the people, shall seek thy face with offerings.

13. All the glory of the King's daughter *is* within, and her clothing is adorned with fine gold.

14. With offerings shall she come to the King, and after her shall they bring the virgins, her companions;

15. And they shall come with joy and gladness, and enter into the King's palace.

16. Instead of thy fathers, shall be thy children; make them rulers in all the earth;

17. That thy Name may be remembered throughout all generations. Therefore shall the heathen praise thee forever and ever.

Ver. 12. The construction is varied from the Hebrew, and the words, *shall worship him,* seem to be supplied to complete the sense.

Ver. 13. *All the glory of the King's daughter is within,* ܦܓܗ ܡܘܚܢܐ ܘܟܠܗ ܟܕܕܐ ܡܢ ܠܓܘ. A. V. *The King's daughter is all glorious within,* כָּל־כְּבוּדָּה בַת־מֶלֶךְ פְּנִימָה. The translator read, perhaps, כְּבוֹד in the construct state before בַת־מֶלֶךְ.

Her clothing is adorned with fine gold. Heb., *her clothing is of wrought gold.*

Ver. 14. *With offerings shall she come.* Heb., *She shall be brought in raiment of needle-work.*

PSALM XLVI. 46

A Psalm of the sons of Korah; — in which David sings concerning the affliction that happened to the people. — As respects prophecy, the preaching of the Apostles is mystically represented.

1. Our God, *thou art* our strong refuge, and thou art always found by us to be our helper in times of affliction.

2. Therefore will we not fear, when the earth is moved, and the mountains are moved in the midst of the seas;

3. Though the waters thereof be troubled and agitated, and though the mountains be shaken by his power. Diapsalma.

4. Streams of rivers shall rejoice in the city of our God; holy is the dwelling-place of the Most High.

5. God is in the midst of her, she shall not be moved; God shall help her, and that right early.

6. The heathen were tumultuous, and the kingdoms were moved; he lifted up his voice, and the earth did tremble.

Ps. XLVI. Ver. 1. *Thou art always found by us to be our helper.* Heb., *a very present help.* But the Hebrew may be more literally rendered, *found exceedingly a help.*

Ver. 3. *By his power,* ܚܒܡܠܘܬܗ. A. V. *With the swelling thereof,* בְּגַאֲוָתוֹ. LXX., ἐν τῇ κραταιότητι αὐτοῦ.

Ver. 4. *Streams of rivers shall rejoice in the city of our God.* Heb., *There is a river, the streams whereof shall make glad the city of God.*

Ver. 6. *Did tremble,* ܢܕ. A. V. *Melted,* תָּמוּג. LXX., ἐσαλεύθη.

7. The Lord Almighty *is* with us; and the God of Jacob *is* our helper.

8. Come and see the works of God, which doeth wonders in the earth;

9. And maketh wars to cease from the borders of the earth; breaking the bows, and knapping the spears in sunder, and burning the chariots in the fire.

10. Turn ye, and know that I am God; I am exalted among the heathen, and I am exalted in the earth.

11. The Lord Almighty *is* with us; the God of Jacob *is* our helper.

PSALM XLVII. מז

A Psalm of the sons of Korah; — concerning the glory of God on Mount Sinai; referring also to the calling of the Gentiles.

1. O clap your hands all ye people, and sing unto God with the voice of praise.

2. For the Lord *is* Most High, and to be feared; he is the great King over all the earth.

3. Which subdueth the heathen under us, and the nations under our feet.

4. He hath made us to choose the inheritance, and the glory of Jacob, whom he loved.

Ver. 7. *Almighty,* ܚܝܠܬܢܐ. The Syriac rendering of צְבָאוֹת, *of hosts.*

Our helper. Heb., *our refuge.*

Ver. 8. *Wonders,* ܬܕܡܪܬܐ. A. V. *Desolations,* שַׁמּוֹת. LXX., τέρατα.

Ver. 10. *Turn ye.* Heb., *Be still.*

Ps. XLVII. Ver. 4. *He hath made us to choose the inheritance.* Heb., *He shall choose our inheritance for us.*

5. God hath gone up with praise, and the Lord with the sound of the trump.

6. O sing unto God with praise; sing unto our King.

7. Since God is King over all the earth, sing praises unto him.

8. God reigneth over the heathen; God sitteth upon his holy seat.

9. Ye rulers of the Gentiles, turn ye unto the God of Abraham; for to God belong all the powers of the earth, and he is very high exalted.

PSALM XLVIII.

Written by the sons of Korah, against the pride of the Gentiles.— A hymn of the Church to God.— The destruction of the persecutors.

1. Great is our Lord, and greatly to be praised in the city of our God, and upon his holy and glorious mount.

Ver. 9. *Turn ye unto the God of Abraham,* ܘܐܦܢܘ ܠܘܬ ܐܠܗܗ ܕܐܒܪܗܡ. A. V. *Are gathered together, even the people of the God of Abraham,* נֶאֶסְפוּ עַם אֱלֹהֵי אַבְרָהָם. For עַם, the translator seems to have read עִם. The LXX. translate the word μετά.

The powers of the earth, ܣܢܐܓܪ̈ܝ ܐܪܥܐ. *The shields of the earth,* מָגִנֵּי־אָרֶץ. LXX., οἱ κραταιοὶ τῆς γῆς.

Ps. XLVIII. Ver. 1. *Glorious,* ܡܫܒܚܐ. This would seem to be a translation of יְפֵה נוֹף, *beautiful for situation,* construed with the succeeding words.

2. A joy in the whole earth *is* mount Zion, which *is* upon the sides of the north; it is the city of the great King.

3. God in her palaces maketh known his power.

4. For lo! kings prepared themselves, and came, and have passed by together.

5. They saw *it*, and were astonished and troubled; and trembling took hold upon them, and pains, as of a woman in travail.

7. The ships of Tarshish shall be broken with a strong wind.

8. Like as we have heard, so have we seen in the city of the Lord Almighty, in the city of our God; God shall establish her forever. Diapsalma.

9. We have waited, O God, for thy mercy, in the midst of thy temple.

10. According to thy Name, O God, so are thy praises unto the ends of the earth; thy right hand is full of thy righteousness.

11. Let the mount Zion rejoice, and let the daughters of Judah be glad, because of thy judgments, O Lord.

12. Walk about Zion, and go round about her; and number the towers thereof.

13. Mark ye well her power, and overthrow *if ye*

Ver. 3. *Maketh known his power.* Heb., *is known for a refuge.*

Ver. 4. *Prepared themselves, and came,* ܐܬܛܝܒܘ. A. V. *Were assembled,* נוֹעֲדוּ. The Syriac verb ܛܝܒ, in conjugation ethpaal, signifies *to depart, to go, to come;* strictly, *to prepare and gird one's self for a journey.*

Ver. 7. *Shall be broken with a strong wind.* Heb., *thou breakest with an east wind.*

Ver. 13. *Her power,* ܣܘܪܗ̇. Heb., חֵילָהּ, *her bulwarks.*

can her palaces, that ye may declare to another generation,—Diapsalma—

14. That this is God, our God, forever and ever; he shall be our guide unto death.

PSALM XLIX. 49

A Psalm of the sons of Korah;—a prophecy concerning the power of the Gentiles; and the doctrine of the Divine judgment.

1. Hear this, all ye people; attend, all ye inhabitants of the earth;
2. Low and high, *both* rich and poor together.
3. My mouth shall speak of wisdom, and the meditation of my heart *shall be* of understanding.
4. I will incline mine ears unto parables, and I will utter my dark sayings upon the harp.
5. I will not fear in the evil days; *when* the wickedness of mine enemies compasseth me about;

The two words have the same root-meaning, but the Hebrew form here used has a restricted and technical sense.

Overthrow if ye can, ܘܣܡܗܘܢ. A. V. *Consider*, פַּסְּבוּ. The Hebrew verb used here in Chaldee and Syriac means *to destroy*. LXX., καταδύλεσθε.

Ps. XLIX. Ver. 2. *Low and high*, ܚܬܢ ܐܙܟܪ ܡܚܝܬܢܠܗܠ; literally, *Sons of earth and sons of men*. The words correspond to the Hebrew בְּנֵי־אִישׁ גַּם־בְּנֵי אָדָם גַּם, and I have assumed that they have the same idiomatic meaning.

Ver. 5. *Of mine enemies*, ܐܚܟܕܟܒ. A. V. *Of my heels*,

6. All they that trust in their power, and boast themselves in the abundance of their riches.

7. A brother delivereth not; and a man shall not pay to God *the price of* his own redemption;

8. *For* the redemption of their soul is precious.

9. Labour eternally, that thou mayest live forever, and mayest not see corruption;

10. Yet shalt thou see wise men die; likewise fools perish, and they that want understanding, and leave their possessions to others.

עֲקֵבַי. If we consider this word, as we may, a participle or participial noun from the verb עָקַב, *to supplant*, there is no substantial variation between the two texts.

Ver. 7. *A brother delivereth not, and a man shall not pay to God the price of his own redemption*, اِنَا لَا فَتَهَ ס ܣܚܕ ܠܐ : ܢܬܗ ܠܐܚܐ ܢܦܪܩܝܘܗܝ. A. V. *None of them can by any means redeem his brother, nor give to God a ransom for him*, אָח לֹא־פָדֹה יִפְדֶּה אִישׁ לֹא־יִתֵּן לֵאלֹהִים כָּפְרוֹ. There is a close correspondence here between the two texts; but the translation will depend upon the division of the sentence.

Ver. 9. *Labour eternally*, لَاتَ لــجـجـم, construed with the succeeding words, and I have accordingly changed their position. Heb., וַיֶּחְדַּל לְעוֹלָם, *and it ceaseth forever;* construed with the preceding words, and forming part of the eighth verse. The version of the LXX. resembles the Syriac; καὶ ἐκοπίασεν εἰς τὸν αἰῶνα.

That thou mayest live forever and mayest not see corruption, ܘܢܐܬܐ ܠܚܝܐ ܚܠܦܝܢ : ܘܠܐ ܢܚܙܐ ܚܒܠܐ. A. V. *That he should still live forever and not see corruption*, וִיחִי־עוֹד לָנֶצַח לֹא יִרְאֶה הַשָּׁחַת. According to the English version this verse is construed with the 7th, the 8th being regarded as parenthetical.

Ver. 10. *Yet shalt thou see.* Heb., *For he seeth.*

11. Their sepulchres *are* their perpetual abodes, and their dwelling-places throughout all generations; and *yet* they call the land *by their own* names.

12. Man in his honour hath no understanding, but is delivered to the beasts, and made like unto them.

13. This is the way of them, a snare to their soul; and in the end they shall feed with their mouth like sheep. Diapsalma.

Ver. 11. *Their sepulchres are their perpetual abodes,* ܩܒܪ̈ܝܗܘܢ ܠܥܠܡ ܒ̈ܬܝܗܘܢ. A. V. *Their inward thought is,* (literally, *their heart is,*) *that their houses shall continue forever,* קִרְבָּם בָּתֵּימוֹ לְעוֹלָם. For קִרְבָּם, the translator read קִבְרָם, and also the LXX., who have καὶ οἱ τάφοι αὐτῶν.

Ver. 12. *In his honour.* Heb., *being in honour.*

Hath no understanding, בְּלִי־יָלִין לא ܐܣܬܟܠ. A. V. *Abideth not.* The translator doubtless read יָבִין, as in the last verse, as did the LXX., who have οὐ συνῆκε.

Is delivered, ܘܐܫܬܠܡ. A. V. *He is like,* נִמְשַׁל. For this the translator read נִשְׁלַם. The other variation in the second hemistich of this verse arises from the word נִדְמוּ. It may be derived from דָּמָה, *to be like,* or דָּמָה, *to destroy.* The English translator adopted the latter derivation, the Syriac translator the former; the LXX. also, who have καὶ ὡμοιώθη αὐτοῖς.

Ver. 13. *A snare to their soul,* ܘܬܘܩܠܐ ܠܢܦܫܗܘܢ. A. V. *Is their folly,* כֵּסֶל לָמוֹ. LXX., σκάνδαλον αὐτοῖς. Both translators for כֵּסֶל read מֹקֵשׁ.

And in the end they shall feed with their mouth like sheep. ܘܒܚܪܬܐ ܕܦܘܡܗܘܢ ܬܪܥܐ ܐܝܟ ܥܢܐ. A. V. *Yet their posterity approve their sayings,* וְאַחֲרֵיהֶם בְּפִיהֶם יִרְצוּ. For יִרְצוּ, we may suppose the translator to have read יִרְעוּ. In the original כַּצֹּאן, *like sheep,* is connected with the words following.

14. They shall be consigned to the grave, and death shall feed upon them; and the righteous shall have dominion over them in the morning; and the grave shall consume their beauty, and from their prosperity shall they be cast out.

15. *But* God shall deliver my soul, and rescue me from the power of hell.

16. Be not thou afraid, when one is made rich, and when the glory of his house is increased;

17. For when he dieth, he shall carry nothing away; neither shall his glory descend after him.

18. For while he lived, he blessed his soul; and *a man* will praise thee when thou doest well unto him;

19. But thou shalt bring him to the generation of his fathers, *and* he shall never see light.

20. Man in his honour hath no understanding, but is delivered to the beasts, and made like unto them.

Ver. 14. *They shall be consigned to the grave.* Heb., *They are laid in the grave.*

And the grave shall consume their beauty and from their prosperity shall they be cast out. Heb., *and their beauty shall consume in the grave from their dwelling.*

Ver. 15. *But God shall deliver my soul and rescue me from the power of hell.* Heb., *But God will redeem my soul from the power of the grave; for he shall receive me.*

Ver. 18. *And a man will praise thee when thou doest well unto him.* Heb., *and men will praise thee when thou doest well to thyself.*

PSALM L. 50

Written by Asaph the prophet, concerning the legal sacrifices of the covenant of Moses, and their abrogation. *In which also God warns us, that, if we do not keep his commandments, we shall be reprobate before Him, for this reason, that we have contemned the inspired scriptures.*

1. The God of gods, the Lord, hath spoken, and called the earth, from the rising of the sun unto the going down thereof.
2. Out of Zion, a glorious crown, hath God appeared.
3. God shall come, and shall not keep silence; a fire shall devour before him, and rage exceedingly round about him.
4. He shall call the heavens from above, and the earth, that he may judge his people.
5. Be gathered unto him, O ye saints of his, which have established a covenant with him by sacrifice.
6. The heavens shall declare his righteousness, for God is the Judge. Diapsalma.
7. Hear, O my people, and I will speak unto thee, and Israel, I will take thee to witness; I am God, *even* thy God.

Ps. L. Ver. 2. *A glorious crown, hath God appeared,* ܚܒܝܠ ܢܘܗ ܐܓܕܐ ܚܡܚܣܢܐ. A. V. *The perfection of beauty, God hath shined,* מִכְלַל־יֹפִי אֱלֹהִים הוֹפִיעַ. The root כָּלַל, meaning *to make perfect,* in Syriac, means *to crown.*

Ver. 7. *Unto thee,* ܠܟ. This is wanting in the original.

I will take thee to witness, ܐܣܗܕܟ. One version has ܐܣܗܕ ܒܟ, which would agree with the Hebrew.

8. I will not reprove thee for thy sacrifices; and thy burnt offerings are always before me.

9. I will take no bullocks out of thine house, nor he-goats out of thy flock.

10. For all the beasts of the field are mine, and the cattle that *are* upon the mountains, and the bullocks.

11. I know all the fowls of the air; and the beasts of the field are mine.

12. If I were hungry, I would not tell thee; for the world is mine, with the fulness thereof.

13. I will not eat the flesh of calves, nor drink the blood of goats.

14. Offer unto God thanksgiving, and pay thy vows unto the most High;

15. And call upon me in the day of trouble; I will strengthen thee, and thou shalt praise me. Diapsalma.

16. As for the sinner, God saith unto him, What hast thou to do with the writings of my command-

---

Ver. 10. *And the cattle that are upon the mountains, and the bullocks*, ܘܬܘܪ̈ܐ ܕܚܩܠܬܐ ܘܛܘܪ̈ܐ. A. V. *And the cattle upon a thousand hills*, בְּהֵמוֹת בְּהַרְרֵי־אָלֶף. The translators regarded אֶלֶף as a collective noun, meaning *oxen* or *bullocks*, and not as an adjective of number. The LXX. translate in the same way, καὶ βόες.

Ver. 11. *Of the air*. Heb., *of the mountains*.

Ver. 15. *I will strengthen thee*, اكمني. Secondarily, however, this verb means *to aid* or *assist*, and thus approaches nearer to the meaning of the Heb., אֲחַלְּצֶךָּ.

Ver. 16. *What hast thou to do with the writings of my commandments?* ܡܐ ܠܟ ܕܬܟܬܘܒ ܦܘܩܕܢ̈ܝ. A. V. *What hast thou to do to declare my statutes?* מַה־לְּךָ לְסַפֵּר חֻקָּי. The translator evidently read לְסֵפֶר.

ments, that thou hast taken my covenant in thy mouth?

17. But thou hast hated my correction, and hast cast my words behind thee.

18. When thou sawest a thief, thou consentedst with him, and hast cast in thy lot with the adulterer.

19. Thy mouth hath spoken evil things, and thy tongue hath uttered deceit.

20. Thou didst sit, and meditate against thy brother, and hast mocked thine own mother's son.

21. All these things hast thou done, and I kept silence concerning thee; thou thoughtest, O thou evil doer, that I was like thyself; but I will reprove thee, and set these things in order before thine eyes.

22. Consider this, all ye that forget God, lest he tear you in pieces, and there be none to deliver.

23. Whoso offereth praise, he honoureth me; and there will I shew him the way of the salvation of our God.

Ver. 21. *Concerning thee,* بِكَ, not expressed in the original.

O thou evil doer, كَظَالِمٍ, not expressed in the original.

Ver. 23. *And there will I shew him the way of the salvation of our God,* ܘܬܡܢ ܐܘܪܚܐ ܐܚܘܝܘܗܝ ܘܢܦܩܬܗ ܕܐܠܗܢ. A. V. *And to him that ordereth his conversation aright, will I shew the salvation of God,* וְשָׂם דֶּרֶךְ אַרְאֶנּוּ בְּיֵשַׁע אֱלֹהִים. For וְשָׂם, the reading was undoubtedly וְשָׁם, which the LXX. also adopted, who have, καὶ ἐκεῖ ὁδὸς ᾗ δείξω αὐτῷ τὸ σωτήριον θεοῦ.

PSALM LI.

A Psalm of David, — when he sinned, and killed Uriah; and, as respects ourselves, containing instruction, and *inculcating the duty of* confession.

1. Have mercy upon me, O God, according to thy loving-kindness; and, according to the multitude of thy tender mercies, blot out mine offences.

2. Wash me throughly from mine iniquity, and cleanse me from my sins.

3. For I acknowledge my transgressions, and my sins are ever before me.

4. Against thee only have I sinned, and done evils in thy sight; for thou shalt be justified in thy saying, and be clear in thy judgments.

5. For I was begotten in iniquity, and in sin did my mother conceive me.

6. But thou hast pleasure in truth, and hast made known to me the hidden things of thy wisdom.

7. Sprinkle me with hyssop, and I shall be clean; wash me with it, and I shall be whiter than snow.

Ps. LI. Ver. 5. *I was begotten.* Heb., *I was shapen.*

Ver. 6. In the first hemistich of this verse, the word בַּטֻּחוֹת, *in the inward parts*, is not translated.

And hast made known to me the hidden things of thy wisdom, ܘܟܣܝܬܐ ܚܟܡܬܟ ܐܘܕܥܬܢܝ. A. V. *And in the hidden part thou shalt make me to know wisdom,* וּבְסָתֻם חָכְמָה תוֹדִיעֵנִי. The LXX., like the Syriac, τὰ ἄδηλα καὶ τὰ κρύφια τῆς σοφίας σου ἐδήλωσάς μοι.

Ver. 7. *Sprinkle me.* Heb., *Purge me.*

8. O satisfy me with thy joy and thy gladness, and my bones *that are* humbled shall rejoice.

9. Turn away thy face from my sins, and blot out all mine iniquities.

10. Create in me a clean heart, O God, and renew a right spirit within me.

11. Cast me not away from thy presence, and take not thy holy Spirit from me.

12. But restore to me thy joy and thy salvation, and let thine excellent spirit sustain me;

13. That I may teach thy way unto the wicked, and sinners may be converted unto thee.

14. Deliver me from blood-guiltiness, O my God, the God of my salvation, and my tongue shall praise thy righteousness.

15. O Lord, open thou my lips, and my mouth shall sing thy praises.

16. For thou hast no pleasure in sacrifices, neither art thou appeased with whole burnt offerings.

17. The sacrifices of God are a humble spirit; a contrite heart, God will not despise.

18. Do good in thy good pleasure unto Zion, and build thou the walls of Jerusalem.

With it, בָּהּ. This is not in the original.

Ver. 8. *Satisfy me*, اَسْمِعْني. A. V. *Make me to hear*, תַּשְׁמִיעֵנִי. Did not the translator read תַּשְׂבִּיעֵנִי?

My bones that are humbled. Heb., *the bones which thou hast broken.* LXX., ὀστᾶ τεταπεινωμένα.

Ver. 16. In connection with the first hemistich of this verse, the Hebrew has וְאֶתֵּנָה, *else would I give it*, which is not translated.

Neither art thou appeased. Heb., *thou delightest not.*

19. Then shalt thou be pleased with the sacrifices of truth, and with whole burnt offerings; then shall bullocks be offered upon thine altar.

PSALM LII. 52

A Psalm of David;—in which he reproveth every evil temper, and *sheweth* the end thereof.

1. Wherefore dost thou glory in mischief, O mighty man? even against the innocent all the day long
2. Thy tongue deviseth iniquity; and like a sharp razor thou hast executed deceit.
3. Thou hast loved evil more than good;—Diapsalma—and falsehood more than the words of righteousness;—Diapsalma—
4. Thou hast loved all them that speak iniquity; and deceitful tongues.
5. Wherefore God shall root thee out, and cast thee out forever from thy dwelling, and thy root from the land of the living;—Diapsalma—

Ps. LII. Ver. 1. *Even against the innocent all the day long*, ܟܠܗ ܡܢܫܢܐ ܠܚܣܡܝ. A. V. *The goodness of God endureth continually*, חֶסֶד אֵל כָּל־הַיּוֹם. We may conjecture the reading to have been עַל חָסִיד כָּל־הַיּוֹם.

Ver. 4. *All them that speak iniquity*, ܟܠ ܕܡܡܠܠܝܢ ܒܝܫܐ. A. V. *All devouring words*, כָּל־דִּבְרֵי־בָלַע. Perhaps the translator read כָּל־דִּבְרֵי־בְרָע.

And deceitful tongues. Heb., *O thou deceitful tongue.*

Ver. 5. *And thy root,* ܘܫܪܫܟ O. A. V. *And root thee,* וְשֵׁרֶשְׁךָ. LXX., καὶ τὸ ῥίζωμά σου. Both translators read וְשָׁרְשְׁךָ.

6. That the righteous may see *it*, and rejoice, and put their trust in the Lord, and say;

7. This is the man that made not God his confidence, but trusted in the abundance of his riches, and was lifted up by his possessions.

8. But I *am* like an excellent olive tree, in the house of God; I trust in the mercy of God forever and ever.

9. I will praise thee forever, because thou hast done *it*; and I will proclaim thy Name throughout all generations before thy saints.

PSALM LIII.

Concerning Ahitophel, that counselled Absalom to pursue David his father, and slay him; and his wickedness returned upon his own head and he died. — Also disclosing to us the revelation of a Saviour, and deliverance from the people that are without God.

1. The wicked man saith in his heart, there is no God: They are corrupt, and become abominable in their wickedness, and there is none that doeth good.

2. God looked down from heaven upon the chil-

Ver. 6. *And rejoice and put their trust in the Lord.* Heb., *and fear and shall laugh at him.*

And say, ܘܢܐܡܪܘܢ. This is wanting in the original.

Ver. 7. *And was lifted up by his possessions.* Heb., *and strengthened himself in his wickedness.*

Ver. 9. *I will proclaim thy name throughout all generations before thy saints.* Heb., *and I will wait on thy name; for it is good before thy saints.*

dren of men, to see if there were any that would understand, and seek after God.

3. They are all gone out of the way together, and become abominable, and there is none that doeth good, no, not one.

4. And they have no knowledge, all the workers of iniquity, that have eaten up my people, as if they would eat bread; neither have they called upon God.

5. There were they in fear, where no fear was, because God hath scattered their bones; for they that please men are brought to shame, because God hath rejected them.

6. O that salvation *were come* to Israel out of Zion; when the Lord bringeth back the captivity of his people, Jacob shall rejoice, and Israel shall be glad.

Ps. LIII. Ver. 5. *Because God hath scattered their bones; for they that please men are brought to shame,* ܟܙܢ̈ܝ: ܐܠܗܝܢ ܘܠܗܢ ܕܚܒܝܬܢܦܐ ܚܠܦܘ.
A. V. *For God hath scattered the bones of him that encampeth against thee: Thou hast put them to shame,* כִּי־אֱלֹהִים פִּזַּר עַצְמוֹת חֹנָךְ הֱבִישֹׁתָה, a wide variation. For חֹנָךְ, *encampeth against thee*, the translator seems to have read חָנֵף, *a hypocrite or man-pleaser.* The LXX. adopted the same reading, ὁ θεὸς διεσκόρπισεν ὀστᾶ ἀνθρωπαρέσκων.

Ver. 6. *O that,* ܡܢ ܢܬܠ. I have translated this according to the idiom of the Hebrew equivalent, מִי יִתֵּן.

PSALM LIV. 54

A Psalm of David, — when he sent Joab and his army to fight with Absalom; and signifying to us the victory, and the prayer of him that is preserved of God.

1. Save me, O God, by thy Name, and judge me by thy strength.
2. Hear my prayer, O God, and hearken unto the words of my mouth.
3. For strangers are risen up against me, and mighty ones seek after my soul, and have not thought upon thee, O God. Diapsalma.
4. O God, my helper, O Lord, the upholder of my soul,
5. Bring evil upon mine adversaries, and put them to silence in thy truth;
6. And I will freely sacrifice unto thee, and praise thy Name, O Lord, for it is good.
7. For thou hast delivered me out of all afflictions; and mine eye hath seen *his desire* upon mine enemies.

Ps. LIV. Ver. 3. *Mighty ones.* Heb., *oppressors.*

Ver. 4. *The upholder of my soul.* Heb., *with them that uphold my soul.*

Ver. 5. *Bring evil.* Heb., *He shall reward evil.*

Ver. 6. *Freely,* ܚܣܕܝܒܐܝܬ. Michaëlis translates, *Spontanea separatione sacrificabo tibi.* Walton, *Et ego maturo cum judicio sacrificabo tibi.*

PSALM LV. נה

A Psalm of David, — when he mourned for Absalom his son, who had been slain; also a prophecy concerning them that sinned presumptuously against the Messiah.

1. Hearken unto my prayer, O God, and turn not away from my supplication.
2. Hear me, and answer me, and turn thee unto my cry, and hear me;
3. Because of mine enemies, and because of the oppression of the wicked.
4. For the wicked have laid *snares* for me, and hated me;
5. And fear hath fallen upon me,
6. And the shadows of death have covered me. I said, O that I had wings like a dove, and had fled away, and been at rest;
7. And had gone afar off, and fled away, and dwelt in the wilderness; — Diapsalma —

Ps. LV. Ver. 2. *And turn thee unto my cry and hear me.* Heb., *I mourn in my complaint and make a noise.*

Ver. 4. *For the wicked have laid snares for me,* וְגָּבוּ ܚܓܕ ܟܡܢ. A. V. *For they cast iniquity upon me,* כִּי־יָמִיטוּ עָלַי אָוֶן. For אָוֶן the translator seems to have read פְּעֲלֵי־אָוֶן.

Ver. 5, 6. *And fear hath fallen upon me, and the shadows of death have covered me.* This is rather a paraphrase than a translation of the original, in which the same general meaning is differently expressed. In the remainder of the 6th verse, and in verses 7th and 8th, the preterite form of the verbs seems to require the translation which I have given.

8. And had waited for him that delivereth me from the tempestuous wind.

9. Restrain, O my Lord, the conversation of their tongues; for I have seen contention and strife in the city.

10. Day and night, they go about the walls thereof; iniquity and falsehood are in the midst of it;

11. Oppression also; and deceit and guile depart not from her streets.

12. For it was not mine enemy that reproached me, that I might have borne *it*; neither was he that hated me lifted up against me, that I might have hid myself from him:

13. It was thou, a man like myself, my neighbour and my friend.

14. We ate bread together in the house of God, while we were walking in harmony.

15. Bring destruction upon them, and let them go down quick into hell, for evil is in the midst of them.

Ver. 8. *And had waited for him that delivereth me,* ܠܡܦܨܝ ܠܝ. A. V. *I would hasten my escape,* אָחִישָׁה מִפְלָט לִי. For אָחִישָׁה, it seems probable that אֹחִילָה was read, and for מִפְלָט, מְפַלֵּט. LXX., προσεδεχόμην τὸν σώζοντά με.

Ver. 9. *Restrain, O my Lord, the conversation of their tongues.* Heb., *Destroy, O Lord, and divide their tongues.*

Ver. 13. *A man like myself, my neighbour, and my friend.* Heb., *A man mine equal, my guide, and mine acquaintance.*

Ver. 14. *We ate bread together in the house of God, while we were walking in harmony.* Heb., *We took sweet counsel together and walked unto the house of God in company.* The principal variation here arises from the word סוֹד, counsel, for which the translator seems to have read צֵידָה or סָעוֹד. The LXX. also translate it by the word ἐδέσματα.

16. But I will cry unto God, and God shall deliver me.

17. In the evening, and in the morning, and at noon, will I meditate, and speak, and cause my voice to be heard.

18. Deliver my soul from them that know me, for through contention they were with me.

19. God shall hear, and humble them; he that was before the worlds; *because* they know no change, therefore they fear not God.

20. They have stretched forth the hand against their friend, and have profaned his covenant.

21. They were troubled at the indignation of his countenance, and by reason of the anger of his heart; his words were softer than oil, yet they *were* arrows.

Ver. 18. *Deliver my soul from them that know me, for through contention they were with me,* ܩܪܒܐ ܕܝܠܗܘܢ ܥܡ ܐܢܝܢ. A. V. *He hath delivered my soul in peace from the battle that was against me, for there were many with me,* פָּדָה בְשָׁלוֹם נַפְשִׁי מִקְּרָב־לִי כִּי־בְרַבִּים הָיוּ עִמָּדִי. For מִקְּרָב־לִי כִּי־בְרַבִּים, we may conjecture that the translator read מְקָרוֹב לִי כִּי־בְרִיבִים. The Syriac partially agrees with the version of the LXX. who have ἀπὸ τῶν ἐγγιζόντων μοι.

Ver. 21. *They were troubled at the indignation of his countenance, and by reason of the anger of his heart,* ܐܬܬܙܝܥܘ ܡܢ. A. V. *The words of his mouth were smoother than butter, but war was in his heart,* חָלְקוּ מַחְמָאֹת פִּיו וּקְרָב־לִבּוֹ. The translator understood חָלְקוּ to mean *they were divided,* and thence *troubled,* and for מַחְמָאֹת read מֵחֲמַת. So also the LXX., διεμερίσθησαν ἀπὸ ὀργῆς

22. Cast thy care upon the Lord, and he shall sustain thee; nor will he ever suffer his saints to be moved.

23. But do thou, O God, bring them down into the pit of destruction, the men that are shedders of blood, and deceitful, and let them not bring their days to an end; but I will put my trust in thee.

(LAUD, AND THE BEGINNING OF THE GRADE.)

PSALM LVI. 56

A Psalm of David.— Thanksgiving of the righteous man because he was delivered from the enemy, and from the hand of Saul; also concerning the Jews, and concerning the Messiah.

1. Have mercy upon me, O God, for man trampleth upon me; all the day long, the warrior hath oppressed me.

2. Mine enemies have trampled upon me all the day; for a multitude of the warlike are lifted up against me.

τοῦ προσώπου αὐτοῦ. It will be observed, of course, that this verse in the Syriac conveys a meaning widely different from the ordinary rendering of the Hebrew.

Ps. LVI. Ver. 1. *Trampleth upon me,* ܫܐܦܢܝ. A. V. *Would swallow me up,* שְׁאָפַנִי. The verb may have been derived from שׁוּף. The LXX. have κατεπάτησέ με.

Ver. 2. *For a multitude of the warlike are lifted up against me,* ܣܓܝܐܐ ܘܣܩܝܠܐ ܕܡܬܚܫܒܢ ܠܠܘܩܒܠܝ ܣܓܝ. A. V. *For there be many that fight against me, O thou most High,* פְּרִידְבַּים לֹחֲמִים לִי מָרוֹם.

But מָרוֹם may be taken adverbially with the prefix בְּ, and this would justify the translation.

3. *Yet* in the day time will I not be afraid, for I put my trust in thee.

4. In God will I glory; in God have I put my trust; I will not fear what man doeth unto me.

5. All the day long they were taking counsel against me, and imagining evil against me.

6. They hide themselves, and abide, and mark my steps, as if they waited for my soul;

7. And they say, he hath no deliverer: do thou judge them in the wrath of the heathen.

8. O God, I have made my confession unto thee; put my tears before thee, and in thy book.

Ver. 3. *Yet in the day time will I not be afraid.* Heb., *What time I am afraid.*

Ver. 4. *In God will I glory.* Heb., *In God I will praise his word.*

Ver. 5. *They were taking counsel against me, and imagining evil against me.* Heb., *they wrest my words; all their thoughts are against me for evil.*

Ver. 6. *And abide,* ܢܬܚܒܐܘܢ. A. V. *They gather themselves together,* יָגוּרוּ. The root גור, however, means *to abide,* and *dwell,* as well as *to assemble.* The LXX. have παροικήσουσι.

Ver. 7. *And they say, he hath no deliverer.* Heb., *Shall they escape by iniquity?*

Do thou judge them in the wrath of the heathen, ܒܚܡܬܐ ܕܥܡܡܐ ܕܘܢ ܐܢܘܢ. A. V. *In thine anger cast down the people, O God,* בְּאַף עַמִּים הוֹרֵד אֱלֹהִים. The translator seems to have considered אַף as in the construct state before עַמִּים. אֱלֹהִים was translated in connection with the succeeding words.

Ver. 8. *I have made my confession unto thee,* ܐܘܕܝܬ ܠܟ. A. V. *Thou tellest my wanderings,* נֹדִי סָפַרְתָּה. For נֹדִי the translator may have read לְדִי, *my light,* and figura-

9. Then shall mine enemies turn backward, and I shall know that God is for me.

10. I will praise the word of God.

11. In God, put I my trust; I will not fear what man doeth unto me.

12. To thee, O God, will I pay my vows, and sacrifice unto thee with thanksgiving.

13. For thou hast delivered my soul from death, and my feet from falling, that I may be well pleasing before thee, O God, in the land of the living.

PSALM LVII.

A Psalm of David; — when Saul turned to pursue him; also thanksgiving, and the calling of the Gentiles to the Faith.

1. Have mercy upon me, O God, for my soul trusteth in thee; and in the shadow of thy wings will I find protection, until trouble be overpast.

tively, *my life*, as if the expression were נַרִי סָפַרְתִּי in accordance with the version of the LXX.; τὴν ζωήν μου ἐξήγγειλά σοι.

Before thee, عِنْدَكَ. A. V. *Into thy bottle*, בְנֹאדֶךָ. The translator read לְנֶגְדֶּךָ.

Ver. 9. The words בְּיוֹם אֶקְרָא, in the original, *when I cry unto thee*, are not translated.

Ver. 10. *I will praise the word of God.* Heb., *In God will I praise his word; in the Lord will I praise his word.*

Ver. 13. *That I may be well pleasing before thee, O God,* ارضَ مَعَكَ جَـٰدًا. A. V. *That I may walk before God,* לְהִתְהַלֵּךְ לִפְנֵי אֱלֹהִים. LXX., τοῦ εὐαρεστῆσαι ἐνώπιον τοῦ θεοῦ.

2. I will cry unto God, most High, even unto God my deliverer, — Diapsalma —

3. Who hath sent from heaven, and delivered me, and cast reproach upon mine adversaries. Diapsalma. God hath sent forth his mercy and truth,

4. And hath delivered my soul from the dogs; for I lay as one dead when I was *so* troubled *among them, even* men whose teeth *are* spears and arrows, and their tongue like a sharp sword.

5. Be thou exalted, O God, above the heavens, and *let* thy glory be above all the earth.

6. They have prepared a net for my feet, and have digged a pit for my soul, and have fallen into the midst of it *themselves.* Diapsalma.

7. My heart is fixed, O God, my heart is fixed; I will give praise, and sing with my glory.

Ps. LVII. Ver. 2. *My deliverer.* Heb., *that performeth all things for me.*

Ver. 3. *And cast reproach upon mine adversaries,* ܘܚܣܕ ܠܡܚܣܕܢܝ. A. V. *From the reproach of him that would swallow me up,* חֵרֵף שֹׁאֲפִי. This, however, may be rendered according to the Syriac version with which the LXX. partly agree, ἔδωκεν εἰς ὄνειδος τοὺς καταπατοῦντάς με.

Ver. 4. *And hath delivered my soul from the dogs, for I lay as one dead when I was so troubled among them,* ܘܦܨܐ ܢܦܫܝ ܡܢ ܟܠܒܐ. ܕܡܟܬ ܘܐܬܚܪܒܬ ܟܕ ܚܒܝܫ ܐܢܐ. A. V. *My soul is among lions; and I lie even among them that are set on fire,* נַפְשִׁי בְּתוֹךְ לְבָאִם אֶשְׁכְּבָה לֹהֲטִים. The versions of the LXX. and the Syriac translator correspond; καὶ ἐρρύσατο τὴν ψυχήν μου ἐκ μέσου σκύμνων, ἐκοιμήθην τεταραγμένος.

Ver. 6. *And have digged a pit for my soul.* Heb., *my soul is bowed down; they have digged a pit before me.*

Ver. 7. *With my glory,* ܒܐܝܩܪܝ. This expression is not in the original.

8. Awake up, my harp; awake, psaltery and harp; I also myself am awakened right early.

9. I will praise thee, O God, among the heathen; I will sing unto thy Name among the nations;

10. For thy mercy is exalted unto the heavens, and thy truth unto the heaven of heavens.

11. Be thou exalted, O God, above the heavens; and *let* thy glory *be* above all the earth.

PSALM LVIII.

A Psalm of David;—when Saul was angry with the Priests, because they did not reveal to him concerning David, that they knew where he was; also unfolding to us the doctrine of the just judgment of God.

1. Ye do indeed speak righteousness, and judge the thing that is right, O ye sons of men!

2. Lo! ye do all speak wickedness in the earth, and your hands are entangled in iniquity.

Ver. 8. *My harp.* Heb., *my glory.*

Ps. LVIII. Ver. 1. *Ye do indeed speak righteousness,* ܐܝܢ ܙܳܕܩܳܐܝܺܬ ܐܳܡܪܺܝܢ ܐܢܬܘܢ. A. V. *Do ye indeed speak righteousness, O congregation?* הַאֻמְנָם אֵלֶם צֶדֶק תְּדַבֵּרוּן. For אֵלֶם perhaps אוּלָם was read. ܐܝܢ is a particle of affirmation. In the Syriac version, the clause seems to be a strong affirmation by which the contrary is implied.

Ver. 2. *Lo! ye do all speak wickedness in the earth, and your hands are entangled in iniquity,* ܗܳܐ ܟܽܠܟܽܘܢ ܟܡܺܐܢ ܡܡܰܠܠܺܝܢ ܐܢܬܘܢ ܒܐܪܥܐ. ܟܐܦܐ. ܐܺܝܕܰܝܟܽܘܢ ܒܥܰܘܠܳܐ ܐܶܬܚܰܠܛ. A. V. *Yea, in heart ye work wickedness: ye weigh the violence of your hands in the*

3. The unrighteous are a separate people from the womb; and they go astray as soon as they are born, they that speak lies.

4. Their poison *is* like the venomous serpent, and like that of the deaf asp that stoppeth her ears,

5. That she may not hear the voice of the enchanter, the exorcist, and the wizard.

6. God shall break their teeth in their mouth; root out also the great teeth of the young lions, O Lord.

7. Let them be cast away, as waters that are poured forth; and let him shoot out his arrows until they are consumed.

8. Let them be destroyed, like wax that melteth and falleth away before the fire. The fire fell, and they saw *it* not, neither did they perceive the sun.

earth, אַף־בְּלֵב עוֹלֹת תִּפְעָלוּן בָּאָרֶץ חֲמַס יְדֵיכֶם תְּפַלֵּסוּן. A wide variation. For the Hebrew תְּפַלֵּסוּן, and the Syriac ܡܚܒܠܝܢ, the LXX. have συμπλέκουσιν.

Ver. 3. *Are a separate people*, ܐܠܝܨܝܐ. I have rendered this freely to avoid awkwardness. The Hebrew is זֹרוּ, *are estranged*.

Ver. 5. *The voice of the enchanter, the exorcist, and the wizard.* The Syriac is rather a free translation of the original.

Ver. 7. *Let them be cast away*, ܢܬܕܚܩܘܢ. A. V. *Let them melt away*, יִמָּאֲסוּ. But the word will also bear the Syriac rendering.

That are poured forth. Heb., *which run continually.*

And let him shoot out his arrows until they are consumed. Heb., *when he bendeth his bow to shoot his arrows, let them be as cut in pieces.*

Ver. 8. *Let them be destroyed, like wax that melteth and falleth away before the fire,* ܐܝܟ ܫܥܘܬܐ ܕܦܫܪܐ ܘܢܦܠܐ ܡܢ ܩܕܡ ܢܘܪܐ ܬܬܢܬܦܘܢ. A. V. *As a snail which melteth, let every one*

9. Let their thorns be sharp and noxious, and let indignation vex them.

10. The righteous shall rejoice, because he seeth the recompense; and he shall wash his hands in the blood of the wicked.

11. So that a man shall say, There is indeed fruit to the righteous, and there is a God that shall judge them in the earth.

שַׁבְּלוּל. But for כְּמוֹ שַׁבְּלוּל תֶּמֶס יַהֲלֹךְ, *of them pass away,* the LXX. have κηρός.

The fire fell and they saw it not, neither did they perceive the sun, ܐ. v. *Like the untimely birth of a woman that they may not see the sun,* נֵפֶל אֵשֶׁת בַּל־חָזוּ שָׁמֶשׁ. The translator would seem to have read נֵפֶל אֵשׁ (taking the word יָבִינוּ from the succeeding verse) בַּל־חָזוּ וְשֶׁמֶשׁ לֹא יָבִינוּ. The LXX. adopt a similar translation; ἔπεσε πῦρ καὶ οὐκ εἶδον τὸν ἥλιον. An allusion is supposed to have been made here to the destruction of Sodom and Gomorrah.

Ver. 9. *Let their thorns be sharp and noxious, and let indignation vex them,* ܐ. v. *Before your pots can feel the thorns, he shall take them away as with a whirlwind, both living and in his wrath,* בְּטֶרֶם יָבִינוּ סִּירֹתֵיכֶם אָטָד כְּמוֹ־חַי כְּמוֹ־חָרוֹן יִשְׂעָרֶנּוּ. The word סִיר, however, may mean *thorn* as well as *pot,* and so the LXX. have τὰς ἀκάνθας. The translator evidently makes the sense to turn upon the antithesis between סִיר, and אָטָד which is a prickly shrub of a noxious character. I have rendered the passage somewhat freely, and do not pretend to explain all its differences from the original.

Ver. 10. *His hands.* Heb., *his feet.*

Ver. 11. *That shall judge them.* Heb., *that judgeth.*

PSALM LIX.

David sang it when he heard that Saul had slain the priests; and it unfolds to us the turning of the Gentiles to the Faith, and the reprobation of the Jews.

1. Deliver me from mine enemies, O God, and defend me from them that rise up against me.
2. Deliver me from the workers of falsehood, and save me from men *that are* shedders of blood.
3. For they lie in wait for my soul, and have confirmed their malice against me, not for mine offences, and not for my sins, O my Lord.
4. *For* without *mine* offence they run against me, and prepare themselves against me; O Lord God Almighty, awake thou, and behold.
5. Do thou, O God of Israel, awake, and visit all the heathen, and be not merciful to any of the wicked. Diapsalma.
6. In the evening they will return, and howl like dogs, and go round about the city.

Ps. LIX. Ver. 3. *And have confirmed their malice against me,* ܐܫܪܘ ܒܝܫܬܗܘܢ ܥܠܝ. A. V. *The mighty are gathered against me,* יָג֥וּרוּ עָלַ֗י עַזִּ֥ים.

Ver. 4. The word ܥܠܝ, *against me,* twice repeated in this verse, is not in the original.

O Lord God Almighty. This forms part of verse 5, but in the Syriac is connected with verse 4. I have therefore changed the position of the words.

Awake thou. Heb., *awake to help me.*

7. The word of their mouth *is* a sword in their lips; and they say, Who doth hear?

8. But do thou, O Lord, laugh at them, and have all the heathen in derision.

9. I will praise thee, O God, for thou art my refuge.

10. O God, let thy mercy prevent me; shew me, O God, *my desire* upon mine enemies.

11. Slay them not, lest *men* forget my people; but remove them by thy power, and disquiet them, O Lord my hope.

12. *For* the sin of their mouth, *which* their lips have spoken, let them be taken in their pride; for they have spoken cursing and lies.

13. Destroy them in thy wrath, destroy them, and let them not be found; that they may know that God is ruler over Jacob, and over the ends of the earth. Diapsalma.

14. In the evening they will return, and howl like dogs, and go round about the city.

15. They will seek for food; neither will they be satisfied, nor tarry through the night.

Ver. 7. *The word of their mouth is a sword in their lips.* Heb., *Behold they belch out with their mouth: swords are in their lips.*

Ver. 9. *I will praise thee, O God, for thou art my refuge.* Heb., *Because of his strength will I wait upon thee, for God is my defence.*

Ver. 11. *Lest men forget my people,* ܠܐ ܬܢܫܐ ܠܥܡܝ. A. V. *Lest my people forget,* פֶּן־יִשְׁכְּחוּ עַמִּי. It will be seen, however, that the Hebrew is capable of both meanings.

Ver. 15. *They will seek for food; neither will they be satisfied, nor tarry through the night,* ܢܒܥܘܢ ܠܡܐܟܠܐ ܘܠܐ ܢܣܒܥܘܢ ܘܠܐ ܢܒܘܬܘܢ. A. V. *Let them wander up and down for meat, and*

16. But I will praise thy power, and give praise unto thy mercy in the morning; for thou art to me a place of refuge, and a deliverer in the day of affliction.

17. Unto thee, O God, will I sing, for thou art the God of my refuge, and the God of my mercy.

PSALM LX.

David sang it, *when he said*, if I fall into the hands of Saul, I die; and he sought for safety in flight, and also they that were with him. Moreover it maketh known to us the conversion of the Gentiles, and the termination of the Jewish Dispensation.

1. O God, thou hast forgotten us, and rejected us, and thou art displeased with us.

2. Thou hast made the earth to tremble, and hast opened it; heal the breach thereof, for it is weakened.

3. Thou hast shewed thy people hard things, and hast given them a feculent wine to drink.

grudge if they be not satisfied, הֵמָּה יְנוּעוּן לֶאֱכֹל אִם־לֹא יִשְׂבָּעוּ. וַיָּלִינוּ. The Hebrew verb לוּן means both *to murmur* and *to lodge over night.*

Ps. LX. Ver. 1. *Thou hast forgotten us, and rejected us, and thou art displeased with us.* Heb., *thou hast cast us off, thou hast scattered us, thou hast been displeased; O turn thyself to us again.* These latter words are not translated.

Ver. 3. *A feculent wine,* ܚܡܪܐ ܕܥܟܪܐ. A. V. *The wine of astonishment,* יַיִן תַּרְעֵלָה.

4. Thou hast given a sign to them that fear thee, that they flee not before the bow.

5. Wherefore, that thy beloved may be armed, save me with thy right hand, and hear me.

6. God hath spoken in his holiness; I will be strong, and will divide Shechem, and mete out the valley of Succoth.

7. Gilead is mine and Manasseh is mine; Ephraim also is the strengthener of my head; Judah *is* my king,

8. And Moab *is* the washing of my feet; upon Edom will I unloose my shoes, and over Philistia will I triumph.

Ver. 4. *That they flee not before the bow,* ܘܠܐ ܬܚܙܡܘܢ. ܡܛܠ ܩܘܫܬܐ. A. V. *That it may be displayed because of the truth,* לְהִתְנוֹסֵס מִפְּנֵי קֹשֶׁט. This variation is not difficult of explanation. For קֹשֶׁט, the translator read קֶשֶׁת, and the verb was derived from נוּס, and not from נָסַס. The version of the LXX. corresponds: τοῦ φυγεῖν ἀπὸ προσώπου τόξου.

Ver. 5. *Wherefore, that thy beloved may be armed,* ܕܢܬܚܦܛ. ܘܢܬܦܨܘܢ ܢܓܝܒܝܟ. A. V. *That thy beloved may be delivered,* לְמַעַן יֵחָלְצוּן יְדִידֶיךָ.

Ver. 6. *I will be strong,* ܐܬܢܨܚ ܐܢܐ. A. V. *I will rejoice,* אֶעְלֹזָה. The translator seems to have confounded the verbs עָלַז and עָזַז.

Ver. 7. *Strengthener of my head.* Heb., *strength of my head.*

My King, ܡܠܟܝ. A. V. *My lawgiver,* מְחֹקְקִי. LXX., βασιλεύς μου.

Ver. 8. *The washing of my feet.* Heb., *my washpot.*

Will I unloose, ܐܫܪܐ, unless the reading should be ܐܪܡܐ, which would correspond more nearly with the Hebrew אַשְׁלִיךְ *will I cast out.*

9. Who will lead me into Edom, and who will bring me into the strong city?

10. For lo! thou, O God, hast forgotten us, and goest not forth with our armies.

11. O give us help against our enemies, for vain is the help of man.

PSALM LXI.

A Psalm of David;—when Jonathan made known to him the purpose of Saul, who was seeking his destruction; and, spiritually, signifying supplication with thanksgiving.

1. Hear my prayer, O God, and attend unto my supplication.

2. From the ends of the earth will I cry unto thee, in the tribulation of my heart; for thou hast set me up upon a rock, and hast comforted me.

3. For thou hast been a house of refuge for me, and a high tower from mine enemies;

Over Philistia will I triumph. Heb., *Philistia, triumph thou because of me.*

In verse 10 a slight difference of construction will be observed between the Hebrew and Syriac.

Ver. 11. *Against our enemies.* Heb., *from trouble.*

Ver. 12 of the Hebrew is wanting in the Syriac, translated; *Through God we shall do valiantly: for he it is that shall tread down our enemies.*

Ps. LXI. Ver. 2. *For thou hast set me up upon a rock, and hast comforted me,* ܘܟܠ ܩܐܦ ܐܘ ܒܥܚܒܣ ܘܟܬܠܒܣ. A. V. *Lead me to the Rock that is higher than I,* בְּצוּר־יָרוּם מִמֶּנִּי תַנְחֵנִי. The reading was, undoubtedly, בְּצוּר תְּרוֹמְמֵנִי תְנַחֲמֵנִי.

4. That I might dwell in thy tabernacle forever, — Diapsalma — and find protection in the shadow of thy wings.

5. For thou, O God, hast heard my vows, and hast given an inheritance to them that fear thy Name.

6. Thou hast prolonged the King's life, and his years throughout all generations;

7. That he may be established before God forever: mercy and truth, who shall preserve them?

8. So will I sing praise unto thy Name forever, while I daily perform my vows.

Ver. 5. *And hast given an inheritance to them that fear thy name.* Heb., *thou hast given me the heritage of those that fear thy name.*

Ver. 7. *Mercy and truth, who shall preserve them?* ܠܚܣܕ݂ܐ ܘܩܘܫܬܐ ܡܢܘ ܢܛܪ ܐܢܘܢ. A. V. *O prepare mercy and truth which may preserve him,* מָן חֶסֶד וֶאֱמֶת יִנְצְרֻהוּ. מָן is regarded as imperative, Piel of מָנָה. The translator considered it an interrogative pronoun. The LXX. fell into the same error, if it be one, though they give a more intelligible meaning to the passage: ἔλεος καὶ ἀλήθειαν αὐτοῦ τίς ἐκζητήσει αὐτῶν;

PSALM LXII.

Written by Jeduthun the Psalmist. — In its literal sense, it is said to contain an allusion to the following narrative: When the young men of Abner and the young men of David were playing together, and slew each other, one of them that pertained to Abner slew the youngest brother of the sons of Zeruiah, *namely,* the brother of Joab. And Joab kept it *in mind* a long time, and slew Abner, a mighty man in the time of Saul. And, *in its spiritual sense,* it indicates to us now the doctrine of the forgiveness of sin, if we repent and confess.

1. My soul waiteth upon God; for from him is my salvation.

2. And he is my God, and my deliverer, and my great refuge, so that I shall not be moved.

3. How long will ye be provoked against a man, that ye may slay *him,* like a wall that tottereth, and like a hedge that is broken down?

4. Yea, even from his honour they purpose to cast him down; and they run with lies; they bless with their mouth, but they curse with their heart. Diapsalma.

Ps. LXII. Ver. 2. *My great refuge.* Heb., *my defence.* The word *great,* in the original, is used adverbially.

Ver. 3. *That ye may slay him,* ܬܩܛܠܘܢܝ. A. V. *Ye shall be slain all of you,* תְּרָצְּחוּ כֻלְּכֶם. In the remainder of the verse, the supplied words in the common version of the Hebrew convey a different meaning from what the construction of the verse in the Syriac would seem to require.

Ver. 4. *They run,* ܪܗܛܘ. A. V. *They delight,* יִרְצוּ. The translator probably read יָרוּצוּ. The LXX. have ἔδραμον.

5. My soul, wait thou upon God; for from him is my salvation;

6. And he is my God, and my deliverer, and my refuge, so that I shall not be moved.

7. In God is my deliverance and my glory; God is my strength, my helper, and my hope.

8. Trust in him at all times, ye people; and pour out your heart before him, for God is our protection. Diapsalma.

9. And like a vapour are all deceitful men, which are fraudulent in the balance, and altogether vain.

10. Trust not in oppression, and love not robbery; when riches increase, let not your heart rejoice in them.

11. There is one thing which God hath spoken, and these two things have I heard, for power is of God;

12. And to thee, O Lord, *belongeth* mercy; for thou requitest every man according to his works.

Ver. 5. *My salvation.* Heb., *my expectation.*

Ver. 7. *God is my strength, my helper, and my hope.* Heb., *the rock of my strength and my refuge is in God.*

Ver. 9. *And like a vapour are all deceitful men.* Heb., *Surely men of low degree are vanity, and men of high degree are a lie.*

Which are fraudulent in the balance and altogether vain, ܘܲܕ݂ܓ̇ܛܠܘܢ ܡܚܕܟܝܢ ܡܣܝܩܝܢ ܐܩܣܪܐ. This passage has been also rendered, *which are raised or weighed in the balance.* The sense will depend upon the meaning given to conjugation Aphel of the verb ܟܝ. The LXX. translate it by ἀδικῆσαι. The Hebrew is בְּמֹאזְנַיִם לַעֲלוֹת הֵמָּה מֵהֶבֶל יָחַד, *to be laid in the balance they are altogether lighter than vanity.*

Ver. 10. *Love not robbery.* A. V. *Become not vain in robbery,* אַל־תֶּהְבָּלוּ. LXX., ἐπὶ ἁρπάγματα μὴ ἐπιποθεῖτε. Both translators seem to have read אַל־תִּבְהָלוּ.

Ver. 11. *For.* Heb., *that,* which gives a better sense.

PSALM LXIII.

A Psalm of David;—literally, when he said to the king of Moab, my father and my mother abode with thee when they fled from the face of Saul; and, in like manner, I have fled unto thee. And by us, now, it is understood *to be* the thanksgiving of the man *that is* perfect before God, in the spirit. *Blessed are they that thirst after righteousness, etc.*

1. My God, thou *art* my God, I will wait for thee; my soul thirsteth for thee, and my flesh longeth for thee.

2. Like a dry and languishing land that needeth water, so have I looked for thee in truth, that I might behold thy power and glory.

3. For thy loving kindnesses *are* better than life, and my lips shall praise thee.

4. Thus will I bless thee while I live, and I will lift up my hands in thy Name.

5. My soul shall be anointed, as *it were with* marrow and fatness, and my mouth shall sing unto thee, with lips of praise.

6. I have remembered thee upon my bed, and meditated upon thee in the night-season.

7. For thou art my helper, and in the shadow of thy wings will I glory.

Ps. LXIII. Ver. 1. *I will wait for thee.* Heb., *early will I seek thee.*

Ver. 2. *Like a dry and languishing land that needeth water, so have I looked for thee in truth, that I might behold thy power and glory.* Heb., *In a dry and thirsty land where no water is; to see thy power and thy glory, so as I have seen thee in the sanctuary.*

Ver. 5. *Shall be anointed.* Heb., *shall be satisfied.*

Ver. 7. *Will I glory,* ܐܫܬܒܗܪ. One version has ܐܣܬܬܪ, *will I be protected.* Heb., *will I rejoice.*

8. My soul goeth after thee, and thy right hand hath upholden me.

9. They have sought to destroy my soul, but they shall go into the lower parts of the earth.

10. They shall be delivered to the sword, and shall be food for foxes.

11. But the King shall rejoice in God, and every one that sweareth by him shall glory; for the mouth of the deceitful shall be stopped.

PSALM LXIV.

Composed by David, when Gad the prophet warned him, *saying*, abide not in the hold, for Saul seeketh to kill thee; and, as respects ourselves, *in a spiritual sense*, the triumph of the Agonists, and the instruction of them that fear God, and victory in battle.

1. Hear my voice, O God, when I make supplication unto thee, and preserve me from the fear of mine enemies.

2. Hide me from the evil of the wicked, and from the conversation of the workers of iniquity.

3. Which have whet their tongue like a sword, and their words like an arrow;

4. That they may privily shoot at him that is per-

Ps. LXIV. Ver. 1. *Preserve me.* Heb., *preserve my life.*

Ver. 2. *From the evil of the wicked.* Heb., *from the secret counsel of the wicked.*

Conversation. Heb., *insurrection.*

Ver. 3. *And their words like an arrow.* Heb., *and bend their bows to shoot their arrows, even bitter words.*

Ver. 4. *Nor will they be seen,* ܠܐ ܢܬܚܙܘܢ. A. V. *And fear not* וְלֹא יִירָאוּ. The translator read וְלֹא יֵרָאוּ.

fect; suddenly will they shoot at him, nor will they be seen.

5. And they strengthen *themselves in* their mischief, and purpose privily to lay snares; and they say, Who seeth us?

6. The unrighteous imagine *evil*, and are consumed in searching out iniquity, each one from his inward *thought*, and the deep of his heart.

7. God shall be exalted, and shall shoot at them suddenly *with* an arrow;

8. And their tongues shall languish, and all they that see them shall fear.

Ver. 6. *The unrighteous imagine evil, and are consumed in searching out iniquity, each one from his inward thought and the deep of his heart,* ܐܬܚܫܒܘ ܟܠܗܘܢ ܥܘܠܐ܂ ܘܓܡܪܘ ܒܥܩܒܐ ܕܥܘܠܐ܂ ܘܐܬܒܨܝܘ ܓܒܪ ܒܬܪܥܝܬܗ ܘܒܠܒܐ ܥܡܝܩܐ. A. v. *They search out iniquities; They accomplish a diligent search: both the inward thought of every one of them and the heart is deep,* יַחְפְּשׂוּ־עוֹלֹת תַּמְנוּ חֵפֶשׂ מְחֻפָּשׂ וְקֶרֶב אִישׁ וְלֵב עָמֹק. The Hebrew תַּמְנוּ is rendered ܘܓܡܪܘ, *are consumed,* a meaning which the word will bear, and which is given to it by the LXX. who have ἐξέλιπον. There is a wide difference in meaning otherwise between the Hebrew and Syriac, which I do not pretend to explain.

Ver. 7. *Shall be exalted,* ܢܬܬܪܝܡ. A. v. *But (God) shall shoot at them,* וַיֹּרֵם. The translator seems to have read וְיֻרַם with the LXX. who have καὶ ὑψωθήσεται. But it will be seen that the Syriac text combines the two readings.

In this verse the Hebrew הָיוּ מַכּוֹתָם, *they shall be wounded,* is not translated.

Ver. 8. *And their tongues shall languish.* Heb., *So they shall make their own tongues to fall upon themselves.*

Shall fear. Heb., *shall flee away.*

9. And all men shall be afraid, and shall shew forth the works of God, and shall consider the work of his hands.

10. The righteous shall rejoice in the Lord, and put their trust in him; and all they that are true of heart shall praise him.

PSALM LXV.

A Psalm of David;—literally, when he brought up the Ark of God to Zion; and, as respects ourselves, spiritually, containing an allusion to the preaching of the Apostles, who converted the Gentiles by the proclamation of the Gospel.

1. To thee, O God, praise is becoming in Zion; and unto thee shall the vow be performed.

2. Hear my prayer; to thee shall all flesh come.

3. The words of the wicked prevail against me; but *as for* my sins, thou shalt purge them away.

4. Blessed is the man in whom thou delightest, and whom thou causest to approach *unto thee;* that he may dwell in thy courts, and be satisfied with the good

---

Ver. 10. *Shall praise him.* Heb., *shall glory.*

Ps. LXV. Ver. 1. *Is becoming,* نَعِمَ. A. V. *Waiteth,* דֻּמִיָּה. LXX., πρέπει.

Ver. 2. *Hear my prayer.* Heb., שֹׁמֵעַ תְּפִלָּה, *O thou that hearest prayer.* The translator must have read שָׁמַע תְּהִלָּתִי. LXX., εἰσάκουσον προσευχῆς μου.

Ver. 3. *The words of the wicked,* خَلَلٍ وَكَفَلٍ. A. V. *Iniquities,* דִּבְרֵי עֲוֺנֹת. LXX., λόγοι ἀνόμων.

Ver. 4, 5. *And be satisfied with the good things of thy house, and with the holiness of thy Temple, and with thy fearful righteousness. Hear me, O God, our Saviour.* Heb., *we shall be satisfied*

things of thy house, and with the holiness of thy temple, and with thy fearful righteousness.

5. Hear me, O God, our Saviour, *that art* the hope of all the ends of the earth, and of the nations *that are* afar off.

6. *Which* by his strength setteth fast the mountains, and by his power doeth mighty things.

7. *Which* stilleth the storms of the seas, and the noise of their waves.

8. The heathen shall be moved, and the inhabitants of the earth shall be afraid at thy tokens, and at the outgoings of the morning and evening.

---

with the goodness of thy house, even of thy holy temple. By terrible things in righteousness, wilt thou answer us, O God of our salvation. There is a wide difference here in the construction. Of the words, *and with thy fearful righteousness*, corresponding to the Hebrew *by terrible things in righteousness*, and forming part of the 5th verse, I have changed the position, in order to bring them into the connection which their construction requires.

Ver. 5. *Of the nations that are afar off.* Heb., *of them that are afar off upon the sea.*

Ver. 6. *And by his power doeth mighty things.* Heb., *being girded with power.*

Ver. 8. *The heathen shall be moved*, ܬܐܙܝܥ ܥܡ̈ܡܐ.

A. V. *And the tumult of the people,* וַהֲמוֹן לְאֻמִּים. LXX., ταραχθήσονται τὰ ἔθνη. Both translators seem to have read יֶהֱמוּן. These words form part of verse 7, but I have changed their position.

And the inhabitants of the earth shall be afraid at thy tokens, and at the outgoings of the morning and evening, ܘܢܣܬܒ̈ܗܠܘܢ ܥܡܘܪ̈ܝܗ ܕܐܪܥܐ ܡܢ ܐܬܘ̈ܬܟ ܘܡܢ ܡܦܩܢܐ ܕܨܦܪܐ ܘܕܪܡܫܐ.

A. V. *They also that dwell in the uttermost parts are afraid at thy*

9. In glory thou hast remembered the earth; thou hast given it rest, and enriched it with abundance; the rivers of God are full of water; thou preparest their food, when thou hast *so* provided for it.

10. Thou waterest her furrows, that her fruits may be increased; her seed shall be nourished and blessed with the drops of rain.

11. Bless the crown of the year with thy goodness, and thy calves shall be satisfied with pasture.

tokens: thou makest the outgoings of the morning and evening to rejoice, וַיֵּרְדוּ יֹשְׁבֵי קְצָוֹת מֵאוֹתֹתֶיךָ מוֹצָאֵי בֹקֶר וָעֶרֶב תַּרְנִין. The translator seems to have read וּמוֹצָאֵי בֹקֶר וָעֶרֶב, rendering the word תַּרְנִין, *thou shalt cause to rejoice,* by ܚܣܚܢܠ, *in glory,* connected with the following verse with which I have placed it.

Ver. 9. *Thou hast remembered the earth, and given it rest, and enriched it with abundance.* Heb., *Thou visitest the earth and waterest it; thou greatly enrichest it.*

Ver. 10. *Thou waterest her furrows that her fruits may be increased; her seed shall be nourished and blessed with the drops of rain.* Heb., *Thou waterest the ridges thereof abundantly; thou settlest the furrows thereof; thou makest it soft with showers; thou blessest the springing thereof.*

Ver. 11. *Bless the crown of the year with thy goodness,* ܟܬܢ ܚܓܠܢ ܘܡܝܢܘ ܚܢܝܚܦܐܘ. A. V. *Thou crownest the year with thy goodness,* עִטַּרְתָּ שְׁנַת טוֹבָתֶךָ. The translator seems to have read עַטְּרָה, and to have borrowed the word תְּבָרֵךְ from the preceding verse. So the LXX., εὐλογήσεις τὸν στέφανον, κ. τ. λ.

And thy calves shall be satisfied with pasture, ܘܥܓܠܝܟ ܢܣܒܥܘܢ ܘܠܢ. A. V. *And thy paths drop fatness,* וּמַעְגָּלֶיךָ יִרְעֲפוּן דָּשֶׁן. The root עָגַל (Syr. ܥܓܠ) signifies *to roll*

12. They also shall be filled, whose dwellings are in the wilderness; the little hills shall be girded with praise,

13. And shall be clothed with the fatlings of the flocks; the valleys also shall be filled with corn, and shall rejoice and sing.

PSALM LXVI.

Uncertain;—concerning sacrifices and burnt offerings, and the incense of rams; and, spiritually, signifying to us the calling of the Gentiles and preaching.

1. O praise the Lord, all ye lands; sing unto the honour of his Name, sing unto the glory of his praise.

2. Say unto God, How terrible *are* thy works! through the greatness of thy power shall thine enemies submit themselves unto thee.

3. Throughout all the earth shall they worship thee,

Hence the derivative מַעְגָּל, *the track of a carriage* or *path;* and עֵגֶל, *a calf,* from its rapid motion. This partially explains the version of this passage.

Ver. 13. *And shall be clothed with the fatlings of the flocks,* ܢܬܚܡܨܢ ܡܪܥܝܬܐ ܘܚܠܒܐ. A. V. *The pastures are clothed with flocks,* לָבְשׁוּ כָרִים הַצֹּאן. The Hebrew כַּר, means both *pasture* and *fatling.*

Ps. LXVI. Ver. 1. *Sing unto the glory of his praise,* ܐܟܒܕܘ. ܫܘܒܚܗ ܘܐܫܬܒܚܘ A. V. *Make his praise glorious,* שִׂימוּ כָבוֹד תְּהִלָּתוֹ. For this the translator may have read שִׁירוּ כָבוֹד תְּהִלָּתוֹ.

sing unto thee, and praise thy Name forever; — Diapsalma —

4. And shall say, Come, see the works of God; for his wonders *are* many toward the children of men.

5. Which turned the sea into dry *land*, and they went through the flood on foot; then will we rejoice in him,

6. Who is ruler through his power forever: his eyes behold the nations, and the rebellious shall not be exalted forever. Diapsalma.

7. O bless God, ye heathen, and make the voice of his praise to be heard;

8. Which holdeth our soul in life, and suffereth not our feet to be moved.

9. For thou, O God, hast proved us, and hast tried us as they try silver.

10. Thou broughtest us into the net, and laidst affliction upon our loins;

11. And thou hast caused men to ride over our heads; thou didst make us go through fire and water; but thou broughtest us out into *a place of* refreshment.

12. I will enter thy house with honour, and will pay thee my vows;

13. Whatever my lips have uttered when my mouth spake in trouble.

Ver. 3. *Forever.* This is not expressed in the Hebrew.

Ver. 4. *And shall say.* This is not expressed in the Hebrew.
For his wonders are many. Heb., *he is terrible in his doing.*

Ver. 6. *And the rebellious shall not be exalted forever.* Heb., *let not the rebellious exalt themselves.*

Ver. 12. *With honour,* بِجَالِهِ. A. V. *With burnt offerings,* בְּעוֹלוֹת.

14. I will offer unto thee fat burnt sacrifices with the incense of rams; and I will offer bullocks and goats.

15. Come ye, *and* hear, and I will declare unto you, all ye servants of God, what he hath done for my soul.

16. I cried unto him with my mouth, and he answered me; and I extolled him with my tongue.

17. If thou seest iniquity in my heart, deliver me not, O Lord.

18. Then God heard the voice of my supplication.

19. Blessed is the Lord who hath not turned away my prayer, nor his mercy from me.

PSALM LXVII.

Of uncertain authorship;—the people sang it when they conducted David over the river Jordan; and to us, moreover, it is a prophetic intimation of the calling of the Gentiles, and the preaching of the Apostles, and the judgments of the Lord.

1. Our God be merciful unto us, *and* bless us, and cause his face to shine upon us;—Diapsalma—

2. That we may know his ways upon earth, and his saving health among all nations.

3. Let the people praise thee, O God; let all the people praise thee.

4. O let the kingdoms rejoice and sing; for thou judgest the people righteously, and governest the kingdoms upon earth. Diapsalma.

Ver. 16. *And he answered me.* This is not expressed in the Hebrew.

Ps. LXVII. Ver. 2. *That we may know his ways,* ܢܕܥ ܐܘܪܚܬܗ. A. V. *That thy way may be known,* לָדַעַת דַּרְכֶּֽךָ.

Ver. 4. *Kingdoms.* Heb., *nations.*

5. Let the people praise thee, O God; let all the people praise thee.

6. The earth hath yielded her fruits, *and* God, our God, shall bless us;

7. Yea, our God shall bless us, and all the ends of the earth shall fear him.

(LAUD, AND THE BEGINNING OF THE GRADE.)

PSALM LXVIII.

A Psalm of David; — when the kings made ready to fight with him; and, secondarily, a prophecy concering the Dispensation of the Messiah, and concerning the call of the Gentiles to the Faith.

1. Let God arise, and let all his enemies be scattered; let them also that hate him flee before him.

2. As smoke vanisheth, *so* let them vanish away; and as wax melteth before the fire, *so* let the wicked perish at the presence of God.

3. But let the righteous rejoice and prevail before God; yea, let them rejoice in his goodness.

4. Sing unto God and praise his Name; praise him that rideth in the west, the Lord is his Name; be strong before him,

Ps. LXVIII. Ver. 3. *And prevail,* ܢܶܬܥܰܫܢܽܘܢ. A. V. *Let them rejoice,* יַעֲלֹצוּ. The Hebrew עָלַץ and עָלָז seem to have been generally confounded by the translator with עָזַז.

Ver. 4. *Praise him that rideth in the west,* ܡܟܰܣܶܐ ܒܡܰܥܪܒܳܐ ܠܰܡܫܰܒܳܚܘ. A. V. *Extol him that rideth upon the heavens,* סֹלּוּ לָרֹכֵב בָּעֲרָבוֹת. The word עֲרָבוֹת, signifying *clouds,* or *heav-*

5. Who *is* a father of the fatherless, and a judge of the widows, *even* God in his holy habitation.

6. God maketh the solitary one to dwell in a family, and bringeth forth the prisoners into prosperity; but the rebels shall dwell among the tombs.

7. O God, when thou wentest forth before thy people; and when thou wentest through the wilderness, the earth trembled; — Diapsalma —

8. The heavens also dropped at the presence of God; this mount Sinai *was moved* at the presence of God, the God of Israel.

9. Thou, O God, gavest a gracious rain to thine inheritance; it was weakened, and thou didst confirm it;

10. And thy living creatures dwell therein; thou, O God, of thy goodness hast strengthened the poor.

11. The Lord shall give the word of the Gospel, with great power.

---

ens, and the word מַעֲרָבָה, meaning *west*, though derivatives from the same root, seem to have been confounded. The LXX, too, have τῷ ἐπιβεβηκότι ἐπὶ δυσμῶν.

The Lord is his name. Heb., *by his name Jah.*

Ver. 6. *The prisoners into prosperity,* ܐܦܩ ܚܒܝܫܐ. A. V. *Those which are bound with chains,* אֲסִירִים בַּכּוֹשָׁרוֹת. But the Hebrew may be rendered like the Syriac, perhaps more correctly.

But the rebels shall dwell among the tombs, ܘܡܪܘܕܐ ܢܥܡܪܘܢ ܒܝܬ ܩܒܪܐ. A. V. *But the rebellious dwell in a dry land,* אַךְ־סוֹרֲרִים שָׁכְנוּ צְחִיחָה. The LXX. have ἐν τάφοις.

Ver. 11. *The Lord shall give the word of the Gospel with great power,* ܡܪܝܐ ܢܬܠ ܡܠܬܐ ܕܐܘܢܓܠܝܘܢ ܒܚܝܠܐ ܪܒܐ. A. V. *The Lord gave the word; great was the company of those that published it.*

12. The kings of armies shall be assembled together, and the beauty of thy house shall divide the spoil.

13. Though ye have lien in the ashes, *yet shall ye be as* the wings of a dove that are covered with silver, and her feathers with pure gold. Diapsalma.

14. When God ordained the King thereon, it was *as white* as snow in Salmon, the hill of God.

15. O hills of Bashan! hills of summits!

Ver. 12. *Shall be assembled together,* ܢܬܟܢܫܘܢ. A. V. *Did flee apace,* יִדֹּדוּן יִדֹּדוּן. The Hebrew verb was derived, says Rosenmüller, from דּוֹד, *a friend,* and not from נָדַד, *to flee.*

The beauty of thy house, ܘܫܘܦܪܐ ܕܒܝܬܟ. A. V. *And she that tarried at home,* וּנְוַת בָּיִת. The translator derived נְוַת from נָאָה and not from בָּנָה, as did the LXX. who have καὶ ὡραιότητι τοῦ οἴκου.

Ver. 13. *In the ashes.* Heb., *among the pots.*

Pure. Heb., *yellow.*

Ver. 14. *When God ordained the king thereon, it was as white as snow in Salmon, the hill of God,* ܟܕ ܦܪܫ ܐܠܗܐ ܡܠܟܐ ܒܗ ܐܝܟ ܬܠܓܐ ܚܘܪܝܢ ܒܨܠܡܘܢ ܛܘܪܗ ܕܐܠܗܐ. A. V. *When the Almighty scattered kings in it, it was white as snow in Salmon,* בְּפָרֵשׂ שַׁדַּי מְלָכִים בָּהּ תַּשְׁלֵג בְּצַלְמוֹן. I have changed the position of the words, *the hill of God,* which in the Syriac are construed with this verse. ܦܪܫ, I have rendered *ordained,* more literally *separated,* corresponding to the Hebrew פָּרַשׁ. In the original the verb is פָּרַשׁ.

Ver. 15. *O hills of Bashan! hills of summits!* ܛܘܪܐ ܕܒܫܢ ܛܘܪܐ ܕܓܒܥܬܐ. A. V. *The hill of God is as the hill of Bashan; an high hill as the hill of Bashan,* הַר־אֱלֹהִים הַר־בָּשָׁן

16. What will ye, hills of Bashan, hills of summits? the hill that God hath chosen to dwell therein, the Lord will abide therein forever.

17. God rideth among the twenty thousands, and among the thousands of an host; the Lord *is* among them, *as in* Sinai, in his sanctuary.

18. Thou hast ascended up on high, and hast led captivity captive, and hast given gifts to men; and the rebellious also shall not dwell before God.

הַר גַּבְנֻנִּים הַר־בָּשָׁן. My translation of the Syriac here is entirely conjectural. The word ܓܒܢܬܐ which I have rendered *summits*, is in strictness of language a proper name. The word corresponding to the Hebrew גַּבְנֻנִּים, would be ܓܒܢܬܐ. It will be perceived, moreover, that while the two first words of the verse, as it stands in the Hebrew, are construed in the Syriac with the preceding verse, the two last are construed with the verse that follows.

Ver. 16. *What will ye?* ܚܢܠ ܓܒܐ ܘܢܐܦܘ. A. V. *Why leap ye?* לָמָּה תְרַצְּדוּן.

Ver. 17. *God rideth,* ܘܪܟܒ ܐܠܗܐ. A. V. *The chariots of God,* רֶכֶב אֱלֹהִים.

And among the thousands of an host, ܘܒܐܠܦܐ ܡܫܠܝ. A. V. *Even thousands of angels,* אַלְפֵי שִׁנְאָן. More correctly, perhaps, *thousands of repetition,* or *thousands many times repeated.*

Ver. 18. *And hast given gifts to men,* ܘܝܗܒܬ ܡܘܗܒܬܐ ܠܒܢܝܢܫܐ. A. V. *Thou hast received gifts for men,* לָקַחְתָּ מַתָּנוֹת בָּאָדָם. The LXX. have ἔλαβες δόματα ἐν ἀνθρώπῳ. The fact that St. Paul, Ephes. iv. 8., quotes apparently from the Syriac, and not from the Hebrew or the Septuagint, has led to much curious conjecture.

And the rebellious also shall not dwell before God. Heb., *yea, for the rebellious also, that the Lord God might dwell among them.*

19. Blessed is the Lord daily, who hath chosen us *to be* his inheritance. Diapsalma.

20. God *is* our Saviour; God *is* our deliverer: the Lord God *is* the Lord of death and the issues *thereof.*

21. But God shall cut off the head of his enemies, and the hairy scalps of such as go on still in their sins.

22. The Lord said, I will lead forth from among the teeth, and I will bring *my people* again from the depths of the sea.

23. For thy foot shall be dipped in blood, and the tongue of thy dogs *in the blood* of thine enemies.

24. They have seen thy goings, O God, *even* the going of my God, my holy King.

25. The princes went before, the singers *followed* after; among *them were* the damsels in companies striking the cymbals.

26. Blessed is the Lord God, from the fountains of Israel.

Ver. 19. *Who hath chosen us to be his inheritance.* Heb., *who loadeth us with benefits.*

Ver. 20. *The Lord God is the Lord of death and the issues thereof.* Heb., *and unto God the Lord belong the issues from death.*

Ver. 21. *Shall cut off.* Heb., *shall wound.*

Ver. 22. *From among the teeth,* ܡܶܢ ܒܶܝܬ ܫܶܢܶ̈ܐ. A. V. *From Bashan,* מִבָּשָׁן. The translator seems to have read מִבַּשָּׁנַיִם.

Ver. 24. *My holy King.* Heb., *my King in the sanctuary.*

Ver. 25. *Princes,* ܙܳܩܽܘ̈ܢܶܐ. A. V. *Singers,* שָׁרִים. שָׂרִים was the reading.

The singers. Heb., *the players on instruments.*

The words, *in companies,* ܟܰܕ ܣܳܦ̈ܩܳܢ, forming part of verse 26 in the Hebrew, are by the translator connected in mean-

27. There *is* little Benjamin in tranquillity; the princes of Judah and their rulers, the princes of Zebulun, and the princes of Naphtali.

28. Command, O God, thy strength, and strengthen, O God, that which thou hast prepared for us.

29. For thy temple's sake, to Jerusalem shall kings bring presents unto thee.

30. Rebuke the beast of the reeds, the multitude of the bulls, *and* the calves of the people that are covered with silver; scatter the people that delight in wars.

31. *Then* shall ambassadors come out of Egypt, and Ethiopia shall commit *her* hands unto God. Diapsalma.

ing with this verse, and I have therefore changed their position.

Ver. 27. *In tranquillity*, ܒܫܠܝܐ. A. V. *With their ruler*, לֹדָם. The translator derived this word from רָדָם and not from רָדָה, as did the LXX., who have ἐν ἐκστάσει.

And their rulers, ܘܡܫܠܛܢܝܗܘܢ. A. V. *And their council*, רִגְמָתָם. LXX., ἡγεμόνες αὐτῶν.

Ver. 28. *Command, O God, thy strength.* Heb., *Thy God hath commanded thy strength.*

Ver. 29. *To Jerusalem.* Heb., *at Jerusalem.*

Ver. 30. *The beast of the reeds*, ܚܝܘܬܐ ܕܩܢܝܐ. A. V. *The company of spearmen*, חַיַּת קָנֶה. The words, however, will bear the other meaning, by which we are to understand the crocodile as symbolical of Egyptian power.

That are covered with silver, ܕܡܟܣܝܢ ܒܣܐܡܐ. A. V. *Till every one submit himself with pieces of silver*, מִתְרַפֵּס בְּרַצֵּי־כָסֶף.

Ver. 31. *Ambassadors.* Heb., *princes.*
Shall commit. Heb., *shall soon stretch out.*

32. Praise God, O ye kingdoms of the earth; sing unto the Lord,

33. Which rideth upon the heaven of heavens; from the east he doth send out his voice, *and that* a mighty voice.

34. Give praise to God, and to Israel the excellency of beauty, whose strength *is* in the heaven of heavens.

35. O God, thou art terrible out of thy holy place; the God of Israel, he shall give strength and power to his people: Blessed is God.

PSALM LXIX.

A Psalm of David; — literally, when Sheba, the son of Bichri, sounded a trumpet, and the people desisted from following after David; understood also to be a prophecy concerning those things that the Messiah suffered, and concerning the reprobation of the Jews.

1. Save me, O God, for the waters are come in unto *my* soul.

2. I sink in deep mire, where there is no standing-place; I am come into deep waters, and the floods overflow me.

3. I am weary of my crying; my throat is dried, and mine eyes fail while I wait for my God.

Ver. 33. *From the east,* بِمَشْرِقٍ. A. V. *Which were of old,* קֶדֶם, in the construct state with שְׁמֵי, *the heavens.*

Ver. 34. *Give praise to God, and to Israel the excellency of beauty.* Heb., *Ascribe ye strength unto God; his excellency is over Israel.*

4. They that are mine enemies without cause, are more than the hairs of my head; and they that are mine enemies wrongfully are stronger than my bones: I restored that which I took not away.

5. O God, thou knowest mine offences, and my sins are not hid from thee.

6. Let not them that trust in thee, O Lord God Almighty, be ashamed for my sake; and let not them that seek thee be confounded for my sake, O God of Israel.

7. For thy sake have I received reproach, and shame hath covered my face.

8. I am even become a stranger unto my brethren, and an alien unto my mother's children.

9. For the zeal of thine house hath eaten me up, and the reproach of them that reproach thee hath fallen upon me.

10. I humbled my soul with fasting, and I became a reproach to them;

11. I made sackcloth my covering, and I became a proverb to them.

12. They also that sit in the gate meditate upon me, and the drunkards mutter against me.

13. But I have made my prayer before thee in an acceptable time; hear me, O God, in the abundance of thy mercy; and in the greatness of thy salvation,

---

Ps. LXIX. Ver 4. *Are stronger than my bones*, كمعضمـي. A. V. *They that would destroy me are mighty*, עָצְמוּ מַצְמִיתַי. The translator doubtless read עָצְמוּ מֵעַצְמוֹתַי.

Ver. 10. *I humbled my soul with fasting, and I became a reproach to them.* Heb., *When I wept and chastened my soul with fasting, that was to my reproach.*

Ver. 13. *In the greatness of thy salvation.* Heb., *in the truth of thy salvation.*

14. Take me out of the mire that I sink not; and let me be delivered from them that hate me, and from the deep waters;

15. That the waterflood do not overflow me, nor the deep swallow me up; and let not the pit shut her mouth upon me.

16. Hear me, O God, for thy loving-kindness is good, and turn unto me in the multitude of thy tender mercies;

17. And turn not away thy face from thy servant; hear me speedily, for I am in trouble.

18. Bring my soul nigh unto thy salvation; deliver me because of mine enemies.

19. Thou knowest my reproach, and my shame before all mine enemies.

Section.

20. Heal the breach of my heart and bind *it up;* I waited for some one that should grieve *for me*, but

Ver. 18. *Bring my soul nigh unto thy salvation.* Heb., *Draw nigh unto my soul and redeem it.*

Ver. 19. *Thou knowest my reproach, and my shame before all mine enemies,* ܐܢܬ ܝܕܥ ܐܢܬ ܚܣܕܝ : ܘܒܗܬܬܝ ܩܕܡܝܟܐ ܟܠܗܘܢ ܒܥܠܕܒܒܝ. A. V. *Thou hast known my reproach and my shame and my dishonour; mine adversaries are all before thee,* אַתָּה יָדַעְתָּ חֶרְפָּתִי וּבָשְׁתִּי וּכְלִמָּתִי נֶגְדְּךָ כָּל־צוֹרְרָי. The translator seems to have differently pointed the sentence, and to have read נֶגֶד כָּל־צוֹרְרָי.

Ver. 20. *Heal the breach of my heart and bind it up,* ܐܣܐ ܠܬܒܪܐ ܕܠܒܝ ܘܥܨܘܒܝܗܝ. A. V. *Reproach hath broken my heart and I am full of heaviness,* חֶרְפָּה שָׁבְרָה לִבִּי וָאָנוּשָׁה. The translation would require the Hebrew to be הַרְפֵּה שִׁבְרַת לִבִּי וַחֲבוֹשׁ, which we may conjecture to have been the reading.

That should grieve for me. Heb., *to take pity.*

there was none; and for a comforter, but I found none.

21. They gave *me* gall for my meat, and in my thirst they gave me vinegar to drink.

22. Let their table become a snare before them, and their recompense a means of offence.

23. Let their eyes be darkened that they see not, and let their back be bowed down alway.

24. Pour out thine indignation upon them, and let thy wrathful anger take hold of them.

25. Let their habitation be desolate, and let none dwell in their tents.

26. For they persecute him whom thou hast smitten, and they add to the sorrow of him that is slain.

27. Add iniquity unto their iniquity, and let them not come into thy righteousness.

28. Let them be blotted out of thy book of life, and not be written with the righteous.

29. But I am poor and sorrowful; thy salvation, O God, hath helped me.

Ver. 22. *And their recompense a means of offence,* ܘܦܘܪܥܢܗܘܢ ܠܬܘܩܠܐ. A. V. *And that which should have been for their welfare, let it become a trap,* וְלִשְׁלוֹמִים לְמוֹקֵשׁ. If for וְלִשְׁלוֹמִים we read וְשִׁלּוּמָם, the two texts would be coincident. The LXX. have εἰς ἀνταπόδοσιν.

Ver. 26. *And they add to the sorrow of him that is slain,* ܘܥܠ ܟܐܒܐ ܕܩܛܝܠܝܟ ܐܘܣܦܘ. A. V. *And they talk to the grief of those whom thou hast wounded,* וְאֶל־מַכְאוֹב חֲלָלֶיךָ יְסַפֵּרוּ. LXX., καὶ ἐπὶ τὸ ἄλγος τῶν τραυμάτων μου προσέθηκαν. Both translators, for יְסַפֵּרוּ, seem to have read יָסְפוּ.

Ver. 29. *Thy salvation, O God, hath helped me.* Heb., *let thy salvation, O God, set me up on high.*

30. I will praise the Name of God with a song, and will magnify him with thanksgiving.

31. I will be more pleasing to the Lord than oxen *and* fatlings that have horns and hoofs.

32. Behold, ye poor, and rejoice, and your heart shall live.

33. For the Lord heareth the poor, and despiseth not his prisoners.

34. Let heaven and earth praise him; and the seas and everything that moveth therein.

35. For God delivereth Zion, and buildeth the cities of Judah, that his servants may dwell there,

36. And have it in possession; and they that love his Name shall dwell therein.

PSALM LXX.

A Psalm of David; literally, when he sent Joab to seize Sheba, who had rebelled; and, secondarily, the supplication of the righteous, and of the Messiah.

1. Deliver me, O God; O Lord continue to help me.

2. Let them be ashamed and confounded that seek after my soul; let them turn backward and be put to shame that wish for my evil.

Ver. 31. *I will be more pleasing,* اَحَبّ. A. V. *This also shall please,* וְתִיטַב.

Ver. 32. *And your heart shall live.* Heb., *and your heart shall live, that seek God.*

3. Let them be overwhelmed with a twofold confusion, that say unto me, aha! aha!

4. Let all them that seek thee be glad in thee, and let them that love thy salvation say alway, God is great.

5. But I am poor and in misery; O God, look upon me: Thou *art* my helper and my deliverer; make no long tarrying, O my God.

PSALM LXXI.

Composed by David when Saul was fighting with the House of David; also a prophecy concerning the Passion, and the Resurrection of the Messiah.

1. In thee, O Lord, do I put my trust; let me never be put to confusion;

2. Deliver me in thy righteousness; incline thine ear unto me, and save me.

3. Be thou my habitation, whereunto I may continually resort; and give commandment to save me, for thou art my refuge and my castle.

4. Deliver me, O God, out of the hand of the wicked, and out of the hand of the unrighteous *and* evil man.

Ps. LXX. Ver. 3. *Let them be overwhelmed with a twofold confusion,* ܢܐܬܡܗܘܢ ܒܗܦܟܐ ܕܒܗܬܬܗܘܢ; literally, *Let them be amazed in the repetition of their shame.* Heb., יָשׁוּבוּ עַל־עֵקֶב בָּשְׁתָּם, *Let them be turned back for a reward of their shame.* (Vide notes to Ps. XL.)

Ps. LXXI. Ver. 2. The Hebrew וּתְפַלְּטֵנִי, *and cause me to escape,* forming part of this verse in the original, is not translated.

5. For thou art my hope, O Lord; *thou art* my trust, O God, from my youth.

6. For by thee have I been holden up from the womb; and thou art my confidence from my mother's bowels; and continually have I praised thee.

7. I am a wonder unto many, for thou art my strong confidence.

8. My mouth shall be filled *with* thy praise, and *with* thy majesty all the day.

9. Cast me not off in the time of old age, and forsake me not when my strength faileth.

10. For mine enemies speak against me, and they that lay wait for my soul take counsel together,

11. And say, God hath forsaken him; persecute him, and take him, for he hath no deliverer.

12. O God, be not thou far from me; O God, continue to help me.

13. Let them be ashamed and confounded that are adversaries to my soul; let them be covered *with* shame that wish for my evil.

14. But I will alway pray, and will praise thee more and more;

Ver. 6. *And thou art my confidence from my mother's bowels,* ܘܣܒܪܝ ܐܢܬ ܡܢ ܟܪܣܐ ܕܐܡܝ. A. V. *Thou art he that took me out of my mother's bowels,* מִמְּעֵי אִמִּי אַתָּה גוֹזִי. The Hebrew גוֹזִי, *he that took me out of,* may be derived from גָזָה, *to pass over,* taken in a transitive sense; or it may be derived from גָּמַל, *to recompense,* and would thus give a meaning more nearly approaching to the Syriac. The LXX. render it by σκεπαστής.

Ver. 13. *Shame.* Heb., *reproach and dishonour.*

Ver. 14. *I will pray.* Heb., *I will hope.*

15. And my mouth shall shew forth thy righteousness and thy praises all the day, for I know not the number *thereof*.

16. I will go in the strength of the Lord, and alone make mention of thy righteousness.

17. O God, *it has been* mine instruction from my youth, and until now, that I should declare thy wondrous works.

18. Forsake me not, even until gray hairs and old age; until I have shewed thy strength and thy power to the coming generation.

Ver. 15. *Thy praises.* Heb., *thy salvation.*

Ver. 15, 16. *For I know not the number thereof. I will go in the strength of the Lord, and alone make mention of thy righteousness,* ܛܢܗܐ ܕܠܐ ܬܘܟܠܐ ܡܣܬܒܪܢ: ܘܐܘܚܠܐ ܢܝܚܝܕܐܝܬ ܘܐܕܟܪ. ܘܐܚܘܐ ܘܐܘܣܦ ܟܣܘܣܝܗ. A. V. *For I know not the numbers thereof. I will go in the strength of the Lord God: I will make mention of thy righteousness, even of thine only,* כִּי לֹא יָדַעְתִּי סְפֹרוֹת: אָבוֹא בִּגְבֻרוֹת אֲדֹנָי יְהוִה אַזְכִּיר צִדְקָתְךָ לְבַדֶּךָ. The words ܛܢܗܐ ܕܠܐ ܬܘܟܠܐ ܡܣܬܒܪܢ, *for I know not the number thereof*, I have translated according to the common version of the Hebrew, כִּי לֹא יָדַעְתִּי סְפֹרוֹת. The Syriac ܡܣܬܒܪܢ, means literally, *writing*. The Hebrew סְפֹרוֹת, translated *numbers*, is a word not elsewhere occurring.

Ver. 17. *It has been mine instruction from my youth, and until now, that I should declare thy wondrous works.* Heb., *thou hast taught me from my youth, and hitherto have I declared thy wondrous works.*

Ver. 18. *Forsake me not, even until gray hairs and old age.* Heb., *Now, also, when I am old and gray-headed, O God, forsake me not.*

19. Thy righteousness, O God, *is* very high, and great things *are they* which thou hast done; O God who is like unto thee?

20. For thou hast shewed me great and sore trouble, but thou hast turned and quickened me; thou shalt also restore *me*, and bring me up from the depths of the earth.

21. Thou hast increased my greatness, and turned and comforted me.

22. I will also give thee thanks with the harp, and sing of thy truth; O God, I will sing unto thee with the harp, O thou holy One of Israel.

23. My lips shall rejoice, when I sing unto thee, and my soul which thou hast delivered;

24. And my tongue shall confess thy righteousness all the day long; for they shall be ashamed and confounded that wish for my evil.

PSALM LXXII.

A Psalm of David, when he made Solomon king; a prophecy, also, concerning the coming of the Messiah, and the calling of the Gentiles.

1. Give the King thy judgment, O God, and thy righteousness unto the King's son;

2. That he may judge thy people with righteousness, and thy poor with judgment.

3. The mountains shall bear peace to thy people, and the little hills thy righteousness.

Ps. LXXII. Ver. 3. *Thy righteousness,* زِنْ ܣܰܒܳܠ. A. V. *By righteousness,* בְּצְדָקָה.

4. For he shall judge the poor of the people, and shall save the children of the needy, and shall humble the oppressors.

5. They shall fear thee, as long as the sun and moon endure, throughout all generations.

6. He shall come down like rain upon the fleece, and as the drops that descend upon the earth.

7. In his days shall righteousness flourish, and abundance of peace until the moon pass away.

8. He shall have dominion from sea to sea, and from the rivers unto the ends of the earth.

9. *The inhabitants of* the islands shall bow before him, and his enemies shall lick the dust.

10. The kings of Tarshish and of the Isles shall bring presents unto him; the kings of Sheba and Seba shall offer him gifts.

11. All kings shall worship him, and all nations shall do him service.

12. For he shall deliver the needy from him that is stronger than he, and the poor that hath no helper.

13. He shall spare the poor and needy, and shall save the souls of the poor.

14. He shall deliver their souls from deceit and unrighteousness; precious is their blood in his sight.

15. He shall live, and unto him shall be given of the gold of Sheba; and we will pray for him continually, and daily will we bless him.

Ver. 6. *The fleece.* Heb., *the mown grass.*

Ver. 9. *The inhabitants of the islands,* ܠܓܙ̈ܪܢ. A. V. *They that dwell in the wilderness,* צִיִּים.

Ver. 12. *From him that is stronger than he,* ܡܢ ܡܢ ܕܥܫܝܢ ܡܢܗ. A. V. *When he crieth,* מְשַׁוֵּעַ. The translator read מֵעֹשֵׁק, as did the LXX., who have ἐκ δυνάστου.

16. He shall be like an abundance of corn in the earth; and upon the top of the mountains he shall make his fruit to flourish, like *the fruit* of Lebanon; and he shall cause *it* to grow out of his city, like the grass of the earth.

17. His Name shall endure forever; his Name, also, was before the sun; all nations shall be blessed in him, and all *men* shall praise him.

18. Blessed is the Lord God of Israel, who only doeth great wonders;

19. And blessed is his glorious Name forever, and let all the earth be filled with his glory. Amen. Amen.

Ver. 16. *He shall be like an abundance of corn in the earth, and upon the top of the mountains he shall make his fruit to flourish like the fruit of Lebanon*, ܢܗܘܐ ܐܝܟ ܣܘܓܐܐ ܕܥܒܘܪܐ ܟܐܪܥܐ. ܘܒܪܫܝ ܛܘܪܐ ܢܥܒܕ ܦܐܪܘܗܝ ܐܝܟ ܕܠܒܢܢ. A. V. *There shall be an handful of corn in the earth upon the top of the mountains; the fruit thereof shall shake like Lebanon*, יְהִי פִסַּת־בַּר בָּאָרֶץ בְּרֹאשׁ הָרִים יִרְעַשׁ כַּלְּבָנוֹן פִּרְיוֹ.

And he shall cause it to grow out of his city, ܘܢܘܥܘܢ ܡܢ ܡܕܝܢܬܗ. A. V. *And they of the city shall flourish*, וְיָצִיצוּ מֵעִיר.

What is called verse 20 in the Hebrew, translated, *The prayers of David the son of Jesse are ended*, is not in the Syriac.

END OF THE SECOND BOOK.

THE THIRD BOOK.

PSALM LXXIII.

Written by Asaph, the Recorder, concerning the death of Absalom; and, secondarily, a confession of human infirmity; *treating*, also, of the prosperity of the wicked, and the long suffering of God.

1. God *is* good to Israel, even to such as are of a clean heart.
2. But as for me, my feet were almost gone, and my steps had wellnigh slipped.
3. For I was envious at the unrighteous, when I saw the prosperity of the wicked.
4. For there is no end in their death, and their folly is great.
5. They are not in the labour of *other* men; neither are they plagued like *other* men.
6. Wherefore pride seizeth upon them, and they are covered *with* their iniquity and their wickedness;

Ps. LXXIII. Ver. 4. *End*, ܡܦܩܐ. A. V. *Bands*, חַרְצֻבּוֹת.

And their folly is great, ܣܓܝ ܗܘ ܘܫܛܝܘܬܗܘܢ. A. V. *But their strength is firm*, וּבָרִיא אוּלָם. אוּלָם seems to have been derived from אָיַל, *to be foolish*.

Ver. 6. *Seizeth upon them*. Heb., *compasseth them about as a chain*.

7. And their iniquity cometh out like fatness, and they do according to the counsel of *their* heart.

8. They imagine and speak evil, and utter calumny against the most High.

9. They set their mouth against the heavens, and their tongue walketh through the earth.

10. Therefore my people shall return hither, and shall fully discover for themselves;

And they are covered with their iniquity and their wickedness, ܘܐܬܟܣܝܘ ܒܥܘܠܗܘܢ ܘܒܥܘܠܗܘܢ. A. V. *Violence covereth them as a garment,* יַעֲטָף־שִׁית חָמָס לָמוֹ. LXX., περιεβάλοντο ἀδικίαν καὶ ἀσέβειαν αὐτῶν. For שִׁית, both translators may have read שֵׁת ; this is Schleusner's conjecture.

Ver. 7. *Their iniquity,* ܥܘܠܗܘܢ. A. V. *Their eyes,* עֵינֵמוֹ. The translator read עֲוֹנֵימוֹ. LXX., ἡ ἀδικία αὐτῶν.

And they do according to the counsel of their heart, ܘܥܒܕܘ ܐܝܟ ܡܘܠܟܢܐ ܕܠܒܗܘܢ. A. V. *They have more than heart could wish,* עָבְרוּ מַשְׂכִּיּוֹת לֵבָב. For עָבְרוּ, the translator read עָבְדוּ.

Ver. 8. *They imagine and speak evil, and utter calumny against the Most High,* ܐܣܬܠܝܘ ܘܡܠܠܘ ܒܝܫܐ ܒܐܠܗܢ. A. V. *They are corrupt and speak wickedly concerning oppression; they speak loftily,* יָמִיקוּ וִידַבְּרוּ בְרָע עֹשֶׁק מִמָּרוֹם יְדַבֵּרוּ. With a different punctuation, and reading בְּמָרוֹם for מִמָּרוֹם, there would be no substantial variation between the two texts.

Ver. 10. *My people.* Heb., *his people.*

And shall fully discover for themselves, ܘܡܟܢܘܬܐ ܬܡܠܐ ܠܗܘܢ. I translate this literally, though I cannot assign any very definite meaning to the words. The Hebrew is וּמֵי מָלֵא יִמָּצוּ

11. And shall say, How doth God know? and is their knowledge in the most High?

12. For lo! these wicked *are* prosperous in the world, and strong in power.

13. And I alone have cleansed my heart, and washed my hands in purity;

14. And all the day long have I been plagued, and chastened till the morning.

15. If I had said, I will do like them,

16. It would have been iniquity in mine eyes.

17. Until I went into the sanctuary of God, and considered their end.

18. According to their own craftiness, thou wilt deal with them, and cast them down when they are exalted.

לָמוֹ, *and waters of a full cup are wrung out to them;* for which the translator may have read יִמָּלְאוּ מִצָּאוּ לָמוֹ.

Ver. 13. *And I alone.* Heb., *Verily in vain.*

Ver. 15. In this verse and the one following there are wide variations from the Hebrew, portions of which do not seem to be translated at all.

If I had said, I will do like them. Heb., *If I say, I will speak thus; behold I should offend against the generation of thy children.*

Ver. 16. *It would have been iniquity in mine eyes.* Heb., *When I thought to know this, it was too painful for me.*

Ver. 18. *According to their own craftiness, thou wilt deal with them,* ܐܝܟ ܢܟܠܗܘܢ ܬܥܒܕ. A. V. *Surely thou didst set them in slippery places,* אַךְ בַּחֲלָקוֹת תָּשִׁית לָמוֹ. The Hebrew אַךְ, *surely,* is often translated ܐܝܟ, a word very similar, but with a different meaning, and corresponding to the Hebrew כְּ.

And cast them down when they are exalted, ܘܡܦܚܬ ܐܢܘܢ ܟܕ ܬܐܙܕܩܦܘܢ. A. V. *Thou castedst them down into destruc-*

19. How are they *brought* into amazement suddenly! They are utterly consumed with trouble.

20. As one is awakened when he hath seen a vision, thou, O Lord, in the city shalt despise their image.

21. And as for me, my heart was troubled, and my reins were changed *within me*.

22. So foolish was I, and ignorant: I was *as* a beast before thee.

24. Console me with thy counsel, and lead me after thy glory.

tion, הִפַּלְתָּם לְמַשּׁוּאוֹת. For לְמַשּׁוּאוֹת, the translator read, perhaps, לְמַשּׂוּאוֹת, from נָשָׂא, *to exalt.* The LXX. have ἐν τῷ ἐπαρθῆναι.

Ver. 20. *Thou, O Lord, in the city shalt despise their image,* ܚܙܢܐ ܟܡܝܐܠ ܟܚܣܘܡ ܐܡܗܝ. A. V. *O Lord, when thou awakest, thou shalt despise their image,* אֲדֹנָי בָּעִיר צַלְמָם תִּבְזֶה.

It is more natural, however, to translate בָּעִיר, *in the city,* than *when thou awakest,* as if it stood for בְּהָעִיר. The LXX. have ἐν τῇ πόλει σου. Hence the version in the Book of Common Prayer.

Ver. 21. *Were changed within me,* ܐܫܬܢܝ. A. V. *I was pricked,* אֶשְׁתּוֹנָן. This verb was derived by the translator from שָׁנָה, *to change.* LXX., ἠλλοιώθησαν.

Ver. 23 of the Hebrew, translated, *nevertheless I am continually with thee; thou hast holden me by my right hand,* is not in the Syriac version, though the latter clause forms part of the 24th verse.

Ver. 24. *Console me with thy counsel, and lead me after thy glory,* ܚܡܐܘܟܡܐܝ ܟܬܪܝܟ: ܚܙܐ ܐܝܗܢܝ ܘܟܢܝܫ. A. V. *Thou shalt guide me with thy counsel, and afterward receive me to glory,* בַּעֲצָתְךָ תַנְחֵנִי וְאַחַר כָּבוֹד תִּקָּחֵנִי. For תַּנְחֵנִי, the translator read תְּנַחֲמֵנִי, as elsewhere in several places.

25. Whom have I in heaven but thee? and whom have I desired upon earth *beside thee?* for thou hast holden *me by* my right hand.

26. My heart also faileth, and my flesh, and the strength of my heart; *but* in God is my portion forever.

27. For lo! they that are far from thee shall perish, and thou shalt destroy all them that do err from thee forever.

28. *But* I have desired to draw near unto God; acceptable is thy Name unto me, O Lord, my confidence, that I may tell of all thy wondrous works.

Ver. 26. *And the strength of my heart; but in God is my portion forever.* Heb., *but God is the strength of my heart and my portion forever.*

Ver. 28. *But I have desired to draw near unto God; acceptable is thy Name unto me, O Lord, my confidence, that I may tell of all thy wondrous works.* Heb., *But it is good for me to draw near to God: I have put my trust in the Lord God, that I may declare all thy works.*

PSALM LXXIV.

A Psalm of Asaph; when David saw the angel destroying the people, and wept and said, *let thine hand* be against me, and against my seed, and not against these innocent sheep; and, secondarily, a prediction of the siege of the city of the Jews, forty years after the Ascension, by Vespasian, and Titus his son, who slew myriads of the Jews and destroyed Jerusalem; and the Jews are rejected even to this day.

1. O God, why hast thou forgotten us forever? and *wherefore* hast thou made thine anger so fierce against the sheep of thy pasture?

2. Remember thy congregation, which thou hast purchased of old, and the rod of thine inheritance, *which* thou hast redeemed; this mount Zion, wherein thou hast dwelt.

3. Lift up thy servants above them that rage against us with power; *consider* all that the enemy doeth wickedly to thy sanctuary.

Ps. LXXIV. Ver. 1. *Wherefore hast thou made thine anger so fierce,* ܐܚܡܬܟ ܢܥܫܢ. A. V. *Why doth thine anger smoke,* יֶעְשַׁן אַפְּךָ. The same verb is used here, though not in the same conjugation, but it has a different meaning in the two languages.

Ver. 3. *Lift up thy servants above them that rage against us with power,* ܐܙܥܪ ܟܚܝܠܟ ܥܠ ܐܝܠܝܢ ܕܡܬܚܡܬܝܢ ܥܠܝܢ ܚܣܝܢܐܝܬ. A. V. *Lift up thy feet unto the perpetual desolations,* הָרִימָה פְעָמֶיךָ לְמַשֻּׁאוֹת. The variation here turns partly upon the word לְמַשֻּׁאוֹת, upon which see note to Ps. LXXIII. 18. The LXX. seem to derive it from נָשָׂא, translating it ἐπὶ τὰς ὑπερηφανίας αὐτῶν.

4. Thine enemies boast themselves in the midst of thy festivals; they set up their ensigns *for* signs;

5. And thou knowest, as *he which is* very high exalted, *that* with axes, like the thicket of wood,

6. They have hewn asunder the gates, and broken *them* down together with hatchets and hammers.

7. Yea, they have burned thy sanctuary with fire, and they have defiled *by casting down* the dwelling-place of thy Name to the ground.

8. And they said in their hearts, let us destroy them altogether, and let us bring to an end all the solemnities of God in the earth.

9. They see not their signs; there is no more any prophet, neither is there among us any that is wise.

10. How long, O God? Shall the enemy reproach and provoke thy Name forever?

Ver. 4. *In the midst of thy festivals,* ܒܓܘ ܥܕܥܐܕܝܟ. A. V. *In the midst of thy congregations,* בְּקֶרֶב מוֹעֲדֶיךָ. LXX., ἐν μέσῳ τῆς ἑορτῆς σου.

Ver. 5, 6. *And thou knowest, as he which is very high exalted, that with axes, like the thicket of wood, they have hewn asunder the gates and broken them down together with hatchets and hammers.* Heb., *A man was famous according as he had lifted up axes upon the thick trees. But now they break down the carved work thereof at once with axes and hammers.* It is difficult to reconcile the two texts. The Hebrew is very obscure.

Ver. 8. *And let us bring to an end all the solemnities of God in the earth,* ܢܘܩܕ ܟܠܗܝܢ ܟܢܘܫ̈ܬܗ ܕܐܠܗܐ ܡܢ ܐܪܥܐ. A. V. *They have burnt up all the synagogues of God in the land,* שָׂרְפוּ כָל־מוֹעֲדֵי־אֵל בָּאָרֶץ. LXX., καταπαύσωμεν τὰς ἑορτὰς κυρίου ἀπὸ τῆς γῆς.

Ver. 9. *They see not their signs.* Heb., *We see not our signs.*

11. Wherefore hast thou withdrawn thy hand, even thy right hand, from the midst of thy solemn feasts?

12. Our God is King; for thou hast given commandment of old concerning the deliverance of Jacob.

13. Thou didst divide the seas by thy power, and didst break the heads of the dragons in the waters.

14. Thou brakest the heads of Leviathan in pieces, and gavest him *to be* meat to a strong people.

15. Thou didst cleave the fountains in the valleys; thou driedst up mighty rivers.

16. The day is thine; the night also is thine; thou hast prepared the light and the sun.

17. Thou hast set all the borders of the earth; summer and winter, thou hast created them.

18. Remember, O Lord, the reproach of the enemy; the foolish people have provoked thy Name.

19. Give not over to destruction the soul that con-

Ver. 11. *Wherefore hast thou withdrawn thy hand, even thy right hand, from the midst of thy solemn feasts?* ܠܡܢܐ ܐܗܦܟܬ ܐܝܕܟ ܘܬܟܣܝܗ݁ ܡܢ ܓܘ ܥܘܒܟ. A. V. *Why withdrawest thou thy hand, even thy right hand? pluck it out of thy bosom,* לָמָּה תָשִׁיב יָדְךָ וִימִינְךָ מִקֶּרֶב חוֹקְךָ כַלֵּה. The translator seems to have read מִקֶּרֶב חוֹקְךָ, omitting כַלֵּה, the word which follows.

Ver. 12. *Our God is King; for thou hast given commandment of old concerning the deliverance of Jacob.* Heb., *For God is my King of old, working salvation in the midst of the earth.* In another version the Syriac corresponds more nearly to the Hebrew.

Ver. 14. *To a strong people.* Heb., *to the people inhabiting the wilderness.*

Ver. 15. *In the valleys,* ܒܢܚܠܐ. A. V. *And the flood,* וָנָחַל.

Ver. 18. *Have provoked.* Heb., *have blasphemed.*

Ver. 19. *Give not over to destruction the soul that confesseth thee,*

fesseth thee, and forget not the souls of thy poor forever.

20. Have respect, O Lord, unto thy covenant; for the habitations of the earth are full of darkness and iniquity.

21. Let not the poor man sit ashamed; let the poor and needy praise thy Name.

22. Arise, O God, and judge thine own cause, and remember how the foolish reproach thee daily;

23. And forget not the voice of thine enemies, and the tumult of them that rise up against thee, that increaseth continually.

ܠܐ ܬܬܠ ܢܦܫܐ ܕܡܘܕܝܐ ܠܟ ܠܚܝܘܬܐ A. V. *O deliver not the soul of thy turtledove unto the multitude of the wicked,* אַל־תִּתֵּן לְחַיַּת נֶפֶשׁ תּוֹרֶךָ. The translator read לְחַיַּת נֶפֶשׁ תּוֹדֶךָ. The LXX. partially adopted the same reading; μὴ παραδῷς τοῖς θηρίοις ψυχὴν ἐξομολογουμένην σοι.

Ver. 20. *For the habitations of the earth are full of darkness and iniquity.* Heb., *for the dark places of the earth are full of the habitations of cruelty.*

Ver. 21. *Let not the poor man sit ashamed,* ܠܐ ܢܐܙܠ ܡܣܟܢܐ ܟܕ ܟܐܒ. A. V. *O let not the oppressed return ashamed,* אַל־יָשֹׁב דַּךְ נִכְלָם. For יָשֹׁב, *return,* the translator read יֵשֵׁב.

158 THE BOOK OF PSALMS. [Ps. LXXV.

(LAUD, AND THE BEGINNING OF THE GRADE.)

PSALM LXXV.

A Psalm of Asaph.—Theological truth respecting the Messiah, and warning of the Judgment.

1. Unto thee, O God, do we give thanks; unto thee do we give thanks, and call upon thy Name; we have also told of all thy wondrous works.
2. When I shall receive a *convenient* time, I will also judge uprightly.
3. The earth shall be humbled, and all its inhabitants; thou hast fixed the inhabitants thereof.
4. Thou saidst unto the fools, deal not foolishly; and to the wicked, lift not up the horn;

Ps. LXXV. Ver. 1. *And call upon thy Name; we have also told of all thy wondrous works,* ܩܪܝܢܢ ܠܫܡܟ: ܘܐܫܬܥܝܢ ܟܠܗܘܢ ܬܕܡܪܬܟ. A. V. *For that thy Name is near thy wondrous works declare,* וְקָרוֹב שְׁמֶךָ סִפְּרוּ נִפְלְאוֹתֶיךָ. The Hebrew, to correspond with the Syriac, would be קָרָאנוּ שְׁמֶךָ סִפַּרְנוּ נִפְלְאוֹתֶיךָ. Something similar the LXX. may have read, who have καὶ ἐπικαλεσόμεθα τὸ ὄνομά σου· διηγήσομαι πάντα τὰ θαυμάσιά σου.

Ver. 2. *When I shall receive a convenient time,* ܐܡܬܝ ܕܐܚܒ ܙܒܢܐ. A. V. *When I shall receive the congregation,* כִּי אֶקַּח מוֹעֵד. מוֹעֵד, however, may be rendered *time*, and so the LXX. translate it ὅταν λάβω καιρόν.

Ver. 3. *Thou hast fixed the inhabitants thereof,* ܐܢܬ ܐܩܝܡܬ ܥܡܘܪܝܗ̈. A. V. *I bear up the pillars of it,* אָנֹכִי תִכַּנְתִּי עַמּוּדֶיהָ. The translator wrote ܥܡܘܪܝܗ̈ for ܥܡܘܕܝܗ̈ which would correspond to the Hebrew.

Ver. 4. *Thou saidst.* Heb., *I said.*

5. And lift not up your horn on high, and speak *not* with a proud neck.

6. For there *is* no going forth from the west, nor yet from the desert of the mountains.

7. For God is the judge; he putteth down one and setteth up another.

8. For in the hand of the Lord *there is* a cup, and *it is* full of a mixture of feculent wine; he inclineth *it* from one to another, *and* the dregs thereof, all the wicked of the earth shall wring *them* out and drink *them.*

9. But I shall live forever, and I will sing praises unto the God of Jacob;

10. And all the horns of the wicked will I cut off, but the horns of the righteous shall be exalted.

Ver. 6. *For there is no going forth from the west, nor yet from the desert of the mountains,* ܗܢܐ ܕܢܠ ܡܥܠܐ ܡܢ ܡܕܢܚܐ. ܐܦܠܐ ܡܢ ܡܥܪܒܐ ܘܓܪܒܝܐ. A. V. *For promotion cometh neither from the east, nor from the west, nor from the south,* כִּי־לֹא מִמּוֹצָא וּמִמַּעֲרָב וְלֹא מִמִּדְבַּר הָרִים. In the common versions הָרִים is taken to be Hiphil infinitive of רוּם, *to be exalted,* used here as the nominative in the sentence. By the Syriac translator it was regarded as plural of הַר, *mountain,* after מִדְבַּר in the construct state. So the LXX. translated it ὀρέων.

Ver. 8. *And it is full of a mixture of feculent wine.* Heb., *and the wine is red: it is full of mixture.*

He inclineth it from one to another. Heb., *and he poureth out of the same.*

Ver. 9. *I shall live.* Heb., *But I will declare.*

PSALM LXXVI.

A Psalm of Asaph; — when Rabbah of the children of Ammon was destroyed; and, secondarily, setting forth the vengeance of the Messiah's judgment upon the wicked.

1. In Judah *is* God known; his Name is great in Israel.
2. At Salem shall be his tabernacle, and his dwelling-place in Zion.
3. There brake he the arms of the bows, the shield and the sword in the battle.
4. Illustrious art thou, and anointed, out of thy strong mountain.
5. All the foolish-hearted are troubled, and the mighty men have slept their sleep, and their hands are powerless,

Ps. LXXVI. Ver. 3. *The arms of the bows.* Heb., *the arrows of the bow.*
In the battle. Heb., *and the battle.*
Ver. 4. *Illustrious art thou, and anointed, out of thy strong mountain,* ܢܗܝܪ ܐܢܬ ܡܫܝܚܐ ܡܢ ܛܘܪܐ ܚܣܝܢܐ. For ܚܣܝܢܐ, *anointed,* one version has ܡܝܬܪ, *excellent.* A. V. *Thou art more glorious and excellent than the mountains of prey,* בָּאוֹר אַתָּה אַדִּיר מֵהַרְרֵי־טָרֶף.
Ver. 5. *The foolish-hearted,* ܣܟ̈ܠܝ ܠܒܐ. A. V. *The stout-hearted,* אַבִּירֵי לֵב. The translator either read אֹבְדֵי לֵב or בַּעֲרֵי לֵב. LXX, οἱ ἀσύνετοι τῇ καρδίᾳ.
Are troubled, ܐܬܕܠܚܘ. A. V. *Are spoiled,* אֶשְׁתּוֹלְלוּ. LXX., ἐταράχθησαν. Both translators read אִתְחוֹלְלוּ.
And the mighty men have slept their sleep, and their hands are powerless. Heb., *they have slept their sleep; and none of the men of might have found their hands.*

6. At thy rebuke, O God of Jacob; the riders upon horses have slumbered,

7. And thou art to be feared; *and* who shall stand before thee in this indignation?

8. Thou didst cause judgment to be heard from heaven; the earth seeth and feareth,

9. When God ariseth to judge, and to save all the poor of the earth.

10. For the thoughts of man shall confess thee, and the remainder of his wrath shall take away indignation.

11. Vow and pray unto the Lord your God; let all that are round about him bring presents unto him that ought to be feared.

12. Which humbleth the spirit of princes, and *is* terrible above the kings of the earth.

Ver. 6. *The riders upon horses.* Heb., *both the chariot and horse.* LXX., οἱ ἐπιβεβηκότες τοὺς ἵππους.

Ver. 7. *In this indignation.* Heb., *when once thou art angry.*

Ver. 8. *Seeth and feareth.* Heb., *feared and was still.*

Ver. 10. *For the thoughts of man shall confess thee, and the remainder of his wrath shall take away indignation,* ܩܶܢܛܳܐ ܘܰܐܘܟܶܡܗܘܢ ܘܟܳܢܶܦܳܐ ܐܰܘܺܝܢ ܓܶܝܪ ܀ ܥܰܡܛܳܐ ܕܬܶܫܒܘܚܬܳܐ ܢܶܐܚܽܘܕ ܠܳܟ. A. V. *Surely the wrath of man shall praise thee; the remainder of wrath shalt thou restrain,* פִּי־חֲמַת אָדָם תּוֹדֶךָּ שְׁאֵרִית חֵמֹת תַּחְגֹּר. In the first hemistich, the LXX. agree with the Syriac translator; ὅτι ἐνθύμιον ἀνθρώπου ἐξομολογήσεταί σοι.

Ver. 12. *Which humbleth.* Heb., *He shall cut off.*

Above the kings. Heb., *to the kings.*

PSALM LXXVII.

A Psalm of Asaph ;— concerning the long suffering of God, and his wondrous works; and how David overcame the enemies of the Lord.

1. I cried unto the Lord with my voice, and he heard me; I lifted up my voice unto him, and he answered me.
2. In the day of my trouble I sought the Lord, and his hand smote me in the night-season, and I rested not; and my soul had no comforter.
3. I remembered God, and was troubled, and I thought *upon him* and my spirit fainted;
4. And dimness seized mine eyes; I was dumb and spake not.
5. I considered the days of old, and I called to remembrance the years of ancient times.
6. I meditated in the night, and communed with mine own heart, and made diligent search of my spirit, and said:

Ps. LXXVII. Ver. 2. *And his hand smote me in the night-season,* ܘܐܝܕܗ ܡܚܬܢܝ ܒܠܠܝܐ. A. v. *My sore ran in the night,* יָדִי לַיְלָה נִגְּרָה. The translator evidently read יָדוֹ לַיְלָה נִגְּדַנִי.

And I rested not. Heb., *and ceased not.*

Ver. 4. *And dimness seized mine eyes; I was dumb and spake not.* Heb., *Thou holdest mine eyes waking; I am so troubled that I cannot speak.*

Ver. 5. *And I called to remembrance the years of ancient times.* Heb., *the years of ancient times.* The translator took the verb from the commencement of the next verse.

Ver. 6. *I meditated in the night.* Heb., *I call to remembrance my song in the night.*

7. Hath the Lord forgotten me forever? and will he be favourable unto me no more?

8. Will he withdraw his mercy from me forever? and will he *not* perform his word throughout all generations!

9. Hath God forgotten to be gracious? Hath he shut up his tender mercies in his displeasure?

10. I said, It is mine infirmity; and they are the repeated strokes of the right hand of the most High.

11. For I have remembered thy wonders of old;

12. And I have meditated upon all thy works, and thought of thy doings.

13. O God, thy way is holy, and there is no one so great as our God.

14. Thou art the God that hast done wonders, and shewn thy power among the heathen.

15. Thou hast with thine arm redeemed thy people, the sons of Jacob and Joseph. Diapsalma.

Ver. 10. *And they are the repeated strokes of the right hand of the most High,* ܘܟܓܢܐ ܘܢܟܣܬܗ ܐܢܬܝ ܐܝܢܐ. ܐܝܢܐ, means *repetition;* ܠܐܝܢܐ ܕܐܝܕܐ, *the repetition of the hand, or a repeated stroke.* A. V. *But I will remember the years of the right hand of the most High,* שְׁנוֹת יְמִין עֶלְיוֹן. שְׁנוֹת, may be the plural of the noun שָׁנָה, *year,* in the construct state, or it may be the infinitive of the verb שָׁנָה, *to change,* or *repeat,* which is its more ordinary meaning in the Syriac. It is not difficult therefore to explain the peculiar reading of the Syriac version. The LXX. somewhat similarly render the phrase; αὕτη ἡ ἀλλοίωσις τῆς δεξιᾶς τοῦ ὑψίστου.

Ver. 11. *For I have remembered thy wonders of old.* The same idea is more copiously expressed in the original.

Ver. 13. *Is holy.* Heb., *is in the sanctuary.*

16. The waters saw thee, O God, the waters saw thee and were afraid; the depths also were troubled,

17. And the clouds poured out waters; the heaven of heavens uttered a voice; thine arrows also flew abroad;

18. And the voice of thy thunders *is* in the heavens; thy lightnings lightened the world; the earth was troubled and shook.

19. Thy way *is* in the sea, and thy paths in the great waters, and thy footsteps are not known.

20. Thou leddest thy people like a flock, by the hand of Moses and Aaron.

PSALM LXXVIII.

A Psalm of Asaph, — in which he intimates *to the Jews* that they should keep the commandments of the Lord, and not be like their fathers.

1. Hear my law, O my people, and be obedient; and incline your ears unto the words of my mouth.

2. For lo! I will open my mouth in parables, and I will utter dark sayings of old;

3. Which we have heard and known, and which also our fathers have told us;

Ver. 18. Literally, *in the wheels*, ܒܓܝܓܠܐ. Erpenius translates *in rota*. A. V. *In the heaven*, בַּגַּלְגַּל. The root בָּלַל signifies *to roll*; hence its derivatives in the Hebrew and Syriac, *a wheel, a whirlwind, the skull,* or *cranium,* and *the circle of the heavens.* LXX., φωνὴ τῆς βροντῆς σου ἐν τῷ τροχῷ.

Ps. LXXVIII. Ver. 1. *And be obedient,* ܘܨܘܬܘ. This is not in the Hebrew.

4. That we should not hide *them* from their children, but narrate to the generation to come the praises of the Lord, and his power, and his wonderful works that he hath done.

5. For he established his testimony in Jacob, and appointed his law in Israel; according as he had commanded our fathers,

6. That they should make *them* known to their children; that in another generation the children should know *them*, who should be born and arise, and declare *them* to their children;

7. That their hope might be in God, and that they might not forget the works of God, but keep his commandments:

8. And not be like their fathers, an evil and provoking generation; a generation that set not their heart aright, and believed not in the God of their spirit;

9. The children of Ephraim, who stretched the string and shot with the bow, and *yet* turned back in the day of battle,

10. Because they kept not the covenant of God, and would not walk in his law;

11. But forgat his works, and his wonders that he had shewed them before their fathers;

Ver. 8. *And believed not in the God of their spirit*, ܠܐ ܗܝܡܢ ܒܐܠܗܐ ܕܪܘܚܗܘܢ. A. V. *And whose spirit was not steadfast with God*, וְלֹא־נֶאֶמְנָה אֶת־אֵל רוּחוֹ.

Ver. 9. *Who stretched the string and shot with the bow.* Heb., *being armed and carrying bows.*

Ver. 10. *Because they kept not.* Heb., *They kept not.*

Ver. 11. *Before their fathers.* This forms part of the 12th verse, but in the Syriac is construed with the 11th. I have arranged the words accordingly.

12. For he had done wonders in the land of Egypt, and in the fields of Zoan.

13. He divided the sea, and caused them to pass through; yea, he made the waters to stand as in bottles.

14. In the day-time, also, he led them with a cloud, and all the night with a light of fire.

15. He clave the rock in the wilderness, and gave them drink as out of the great deep.

16. He brought streams out of the rock, and the waters ran down like rivers.

17. And the people sinned yet more, by provoking the most High in the wilderness.

18. And they tempted God in their hearts, by asking meat for their lust.

19. And they murmured against God and said, Can God furnish a table for us in the wilderness?

20. If he smote the rock, so that the waters gushed out, and the streams flowed withal; can he give us bread also? or can he provide food for his people?

21. Wherefore the Lord heard *this*, and was wroth; and a fire was kindled against Jacob, and anger also came up against Israel;

22. Because they believed not in God, and waited not for his salvation.

23. And he commanded the clouds from above, and the doors of heaven were opened.

24. He sent them down manna to eat, and gave them the bread of heaven.

25. Man did eat angels' food, and he sent them meat to the full.

Ver. 13. *As in bottles.* See note to Ps. xxxiii. 7.

26. He caused the winds to blow in the heaven; and by his power he brought in the south-wind.

27. He sent them down flesh like the dust, and feathered fowls like as the sand of the sea;

28. And they fell among their habitations, and round about their tents.

29. So they did eat, and were well filled, for he gave them their own desires.

30. And they had not given over their lusts, but while their meat *was yet* in their mouths,

31. The wrath of God came upon them, and slew the wealthiest of them, and smote down the chosen men of Israel.

32. For all these things they sinned, and believed not again for his wondrous works.

33. *Therefore* they consumed their days in vanity, and their years in haste.

34. When he slew them, *then* they sought him, and returned and prevented him.

35. They remembered that God was their helper, and the high God their redeemer.

36. *Nevertheless* they did *but* love him with their mouths, and they lied unto him with their tongues.

Ver. 28. *And they fell among their habitations.* Heb., *And he let it fall in the midst of their camp.*

Ver. 32. *Again,* ܠܬܘܒ. A. V. *Still,* עוֹד, construed with the first hemistich of the verse.

Ver. 33. *They consumed.* Heb., *did he consume.*
In haste, ܒܡܣܪܗܒܘܬܐ. A. V. *In trouble,* בֶּבֶּהָלָה. LXX., μετὰ σπουδῆς.

Ver. 34. *And prevented him,* ܘܩܕܡܘܗܝ. A. V. *and inquired early after God,* וְשִׁחֲרוּ־אֵל. The translator doubtless read אֵלָיו.

87. They did not order their hearts with him, and they believed not in his covenant.

38. But he being merciful, and a forgiver of sins, and one that destroyeth not, many a time turned his anger away, and suffered not his whole displeasure to arise.

39. For he remembered that they were *but* flesh; a wind that passeth away, and cometh not again.

40. *But* they provoked him in the wilderness, and angered him in the desert.

41. Yea, they turned and tempted God, and provokĕd the Holy One of Israel.

42. And they remembered not his hand, *nor* the day when he delivered them from the power of the oppressor.

43. How he had wrought his signs in Egypt, and his wonders in the fields of Zoan.

44. For he had turned their rivers into blood, and their streams, that they could drink no water.

45. He sent divers sorts of flies upon them, which devoured them, and frogs which destroyed them.

46. He gave their increase to the locusts, and their labour to the young locusts.

47. He brake their vines with hail, and *destroyed* their fig-trees with the frost.

Ver. 37. *And they believed not.* Heb., *neither were they stedfast.*

Ver. 41. *Provoked,* ܐܰܬܺܝܒ. A. V. *Limited,* יַתְווּ. The Syriac root ܬܳܒ, which is the same with the Hebrew verb used here, means, *to repent,* or *grieve.* LXX, παρώξυναν.

Ver. 42. *From the power of the oppressor.* Heb., *from the enemy.*

Ver. 44. *That they could drink no water.* Heb., *that they could not drink.*

Ver. 47. *Their fig-trees.* Heb., *their sycamore-trees.*

48. He gave up their cattle to the hail, and their possessions to conflagration.

49. He sent upon them the fierceness of his anger; wrath, and indignation, and trouble, he sent by the hand of an evil angel.

50. And he opened ways *that were* evil, and spared not their souls from death, and delivered over their flocks to destruction.

51. He slew all the first-born of Egypt; the chief of all their progeny in the tabernacles of Ham.

Section.

52. He carried away his people like sheep, and led them in the wilderness like a flock.

53. He made them to dwell in hope, so that they feared not; but the sea overwhelmed their enemies.

54. He brought them to the border of his sanctuary, *even* to this mountain which his right hand had purchased.

Ver. 48. *And their possessions to conflagration,* ܘܩܢܝܢܗܘܢ ܠܝܩܕܢܐ. A. V. *And their flocks to hot thunderbolts,* וּמִקְנֵיהֶם לָרְשָׁפִים. The LXX. agree here with the Syriac in an unsubstantial variation; καὶ τὴν ὕπαρξιν αὐτῶν τῷ πυρί.

Ver. 49. *He sent by the hand of an evil angel.* Heb., *by sending evil angels among them.*

Ver. 50. *He opened ways that were evil,* ܦܠܘ ܡܓܢܠ ܚܢܦܐ. A. V. *He made a way to his anger,* יְפַלֵּס נָתִיב לְאַפּוֹ.

Their flocks to destruction, ܢܦܫܬܗܘܢ ܠܡܘܬܐ. A. V. *Their life to the pestilence,* חַיָּתָם לַדֶּבֶר. LXX., τὰ κτήνη αὐτῶν εἰς θάνατον.

Ver. 53. *He made them to dwell in hope.* Heb., *And he led them on safely.*

55. He destroyed the heathen before them, and distributed them by the line of his inheritance; and the tribes of Israel dwelt in their tents.

56. *Yet* they tempted and provoked the most high God, and kept not his testimonies;

57. But turned back, and dealt unfaithfully like their fathers, and were turned aside like a deceitful bow.

58. For they provoked him to anger with their high places, and moved him to jealousy with their idols.

59. And God heard *this*, and was wroth, and was sore displeased against Israel;

60. And he forgat the tabernacle of Shiloh, the tent in which he had dwelt among men.

61. He gave his people into captivity, and his glory into the hand of the oppressor.

62. He delivered his people to the sword, and turned away *his eyes* from his inheritance.

63. The fire consumed their young men, and their maidens were sorely afflicted.

64. Their priests also fell by the sword, and their widows were not lamented.

Ver. 55. *And distributed them by the line of his inheritance.* Heb., *and divided them an inheritance by line.*

Ver. 61. *His people,* ܥܡܗ. A. V. *His strength,* עֻזּוֹ.

Ver. 62. *And turned away his eyes from his inheritance,* ܘܐܗܦܟ ܥܝܢܘܗܝ ܡܢ ܝܪܬܘܬܗ. A. V. *And was wroth with his inheritance,* וּבְנַחֲלָתוֹ הִתְעַבָּר. LXX., καὶ τὴν κληρονομίαν αὐτοῦ ὑπερεῖδε.

Ver. 63. *Were sorely afflicted,* ܐܬܛܪܦܝ. A. V. *Were not given to marriage,* לֹא הוּלָּלוּ.

Ver. 64. *Were not lamented,* ܠܐ ܐܬܐܒܠܝ. A. V. *Made no lamentation,* לֹא תִבְכֶּינָה. LXX., οὐ κλαυσθήσονται.

65. *Then* the Lord awaked as one out of sleep, and like a mighty man whom his wine hath excited.

66. He smote his enemies behind him, and made them the reproach of the world.

67. He refused the tabernacle of Joseph, and favoured not the **tribe of Ephraim.**

68. He chose the **tribe of Judah**; the Mount Zion which he loved.

69. He built his sanctuary upon a high place, and established it in the earth forever.

70. He chose David his servant, and led him away from the flocks of sheep,

71. And from following the ewes giving suck; that he might feed Jacob his people, and Israel his inheritance.

72. So he fed them in the integrity of his heart, and guided them by the prudence of his hands.

Ver. 65. *Whom his wine hath excited,* ܘܐܬܬܥܝܪ ܐܝܟ ܕܡܢ. A. V. *That shouteth by reason of wine,* מִתְרוֹנֵן מִיָּיִן.

Ver. 66. *Behind him,* ܒܣܬܪܗܘܢ. A. V. *In the hinder part,* אָחוֹר. This yields a better meaning than the Syriac.

The reproach of the world, ܚܣܕܐ ܘܚܘܣܕܐ. A. V. *A perpetual reproach,* חֶרְפַּת עוֹלָם. To express this the Syriac should be ܚܣܕܐ ܕܠܥܠܡ or ܚܣܕܐ ܕܠܥܠܡ.

Ver. 69. *Upon a high place.* Heb., *like high palaces.*

In the earth, ܒܐܪܥܐ. A. V. *Like the earth,* כְּאֶרֶץ. LXX., ἐν τῇ γῇ.

Ver. 70. *The flocks of sheep.* Heb., *the sheepfolds.*

Ver. 71. *That he might feed.* Heb., *he brought him to feed.*

PSALM LXXIX.

A Psalm of Asaph;—written concerning the desolation of Jerusalem.

1. O God, the heathen are come into thine inheritance and have defiled thy holy temple, and made Jerusalem a desolation.

2. The dead bodies of thy servants have they given *to be* meat unto the fowls of heaven, and the flesh of thy saints unto the beasts of the field.

3. Their blood have they shed like water round about Jerusalem, and there was none to bury *them;*

4. And we are become a reproach to our neighbours; and a mockery and derision to them that are round about us.

5. How long wilt thou be angry, O Lord? forever? and shall thy wrath burn like fire?

6. Pour out thy wrath upon the heathen that have not known thee, and upon the kingdoms that have not called upon thy Name.

7. For they have devoured Jacob, and laid waste his dwelling-place.

8. O remember not against us our former sins; let thy tender mercies speedily prevent us, for we are brought very low.

9. Help us, O God, our Saviour, for the glory of thy Name; be propitious unto us, and deliver us from our sins for thy Name's sake;

10. That the heathen say not, Where is your God?

Ps. LXXIX. Ver. 10. *That the heathen say not, Where is your God?* Heb., *Wherefore should the heathen say, Where is their God?*

Let the vengeance of the blood of thy servants which is shed, be known among the heathen in our sight.

11. Let the sighing of the prisoner come before thee; by the greatness of thy power, deliver the children from death;

12. And recompense unto our neighbours, sevenfold into their bosom, the reproach wherewith they have reproached thee, O Lord.

13. So we thy people, and sheep of thy pasture, will give thee thanks forever, and tell of thy wondrous works to all generations.

PSALM LXXX.

Written by Asaph.

1. Hear, O thou shepherd of Israel, and lead Joseph like a flock; thou that sittest upon the cherubim, reveal thyself.

Let the vengeance of the blood of thy servants which is shed, be known among the heathen in our sight. Heb., *Let him be known among the heathen in our sight by the revenging of the blood of thy servants which is shed.*

Ver. 11. *The children from death,* ܚܲܝܹ̈ܐ ܡܼܢ ܡܵܘܬܵܐ. A. V. *Those that are appointed to die,* בְּנֵי תְמוּתָה.

Ver. 13. *Tell of thy wondrous works.* Heb., *shew forth thy praise.*

Ps. LXXX. Ver. 1. *And lead,* ܘܕܲܒܲܪ. A. V. *Thou that leadest,* נֹהֵג.

Upon, ܠܥܸܠ. This is not in the Hebrew; it is supplied in the English version by the word *between*.

2. Before Ephraim, and Benjamin, and Manasseh, shew thy strength, and come to our assistance.

3. Turn us again, O God Almighty, and cause thy face to shine, and we shall be saved.

4. O Lord God Almighty, how long wilt thou be angry against the prayers of thy servant?

5. Thou givest them bread to eat with tears, and thou givest them tears to drink.

6. Thou makest us a by-word to our neighbours, and our enemies mock us.

7. Turn us again, O God Almighty, and cause thy face to shine, and we shall be saved. Diapsalma.

8. Thou hast brought a vine out of Egypt; thou hast destroyed the heathen and planted it.

9. Thou didst provide for it, and set its root; and the land was filled with it;

10. And the hills were covered with the shadow of it, and the boughs thereof *were* above the goodly cedars.

Ver. 2. *Shew.* Heb., *stir up.*

Ver. 4. *Almighty,* ܚܰܝܠܬܳܢܳܐ. The corresponding Hebrew צְבָאוֹת is not found here.

Of thy servant, ܥܰܒܕܳܟ؟. A. V. *Of thy people,* עַמֶּךָ. LXX, τοῦ δούλου σου.

Ver. 5. *With tears.* Heb., *of tears.*

And givest them tears to drink. The Hebrew adds שָׁלִישׁ, *in great measure.*

Ver. 6. *A by-word.* Heb., *a strife.*

Mock us. Heb., *laugh among themselves.*

Ver. 9. *Thou didst provide for it.* Heb., *Thou preparedst room before it.*

Ver. 10. *Were above,* ܠܥܶܠ. This is not in the Hebrew, but is supplied in the common version by the words *were like.*

11. She sent out her boughs unto the sea, and her branches above the rivers.

12. Why hast thou *then* cut down her hedge, so that all they which pass by the way do trample upon her?

13. Yea, the boar of the wood hath eaten it, and the wild beasts of the field have devoured it.

14. Return, O God Almighty, and look down from heaven; and behold and visit this vine;

15. And the vigorous stock which thy right hand hath planted, and the son of man whom thou madest strong for thyself.

16. Burn her branches in the fire; let them perish at the rebuke of thy countenance.

17. Let thy right hand be upon the man, even upon the son of man whom thou madest strong for thyself;

Ver. 11. *Above the rivers.* Heb., *unto the river.*

Ver. 12. *Trample upon her.* Heb., *pluck her.*

Ver. 13. *Hath eaten it.* Heb., *doth waste it.*

Ver. 15. *The vigorous stock,* ܐܳܨܳܒ, from ܠܳܨܶܒ, *to strengthen.* Heb., כַּנָּה, translated *vineyard*; more literally, *a plant firmly rooted.*

The son of man, ܟܢܶܫܳܐ. A. V. *Branch,* בֵּן, literally, *Son.* LXX., υἱὸν ἀνθρώπου.

Ver. 16. *Burn her branches in the fire,* ܐܶܩܶܕ ܣܰܘܟܶܝܗ̇ ܡܚܰܦܳܦ. This may also be rendered *he hath burnt her branches in the fire;* but the words in the connection in which they stand convey little meaning. The Hebrew is שְׂרֻפָה בָאֵשׁ כְּסוּחָה, *It is burnt with fire; it is cut down.* שֹׂרַף בָּאֵשׁ כְּסוּחֶיהָ, may have been the reading.

Ver. 17. *Let thy right hand be upon the man.* Heb., *Let thy hand be upon the man of thy right hand.*

18. That we turn not aside from thee; but quicken us, and we will call upon thy Name.

19. Turn us again, O Lord God Almighty, and cause thy face to shine, and we shall be saved.

PSALM LXXXI.

A Psalm of Asaph,—by which David prepared himself for the Festivals *of the Lord.*

1. O praise God, which giveth us strength, and cry aloud unto the God of Jacob.

2. Take the cymbals and the psalteries; pleasant *instruments* with the harps.

3. Blow up the trumpets in the beginning of the months; and at the time of the full moon, upon the solemn feast-days.

4. For *this* was a statute for Israel, and a law of the God of Jacob.

5. This he ordained in Joseph *for* his testimony, when he went out of the land of Egypt, *where* he heard a language that he knew not.

6. I removed the yoke from his shoulder, and freed his hands from the chain.

Ps. LXXXI. Ver. 3. *And at the time of the full moon,* مُحجَّمًا. The Hebrew word is the same, but it is translated, *in the time appointed.*

Ver. 5. *Where he heard a language that he knew not.* The Hebrew expresses this in the first person.

Ver. 6. *The yoke from his shoulder.* Heb., *his shoulder from the burden.*

And freed his hands from the chain. Heb., *his hands were delivered from the pots.*

7. He called upon me in trouble and I delivered him; and covered him with my glorious veil, and proved him at the waters of strife.   Diapsalma.

8. Hear, O my people, and I will speak; and Israel, I will testify unto thee; if thou wilt hear me,

9. There shall be no strange god to thee, neither shalt thou worship any other god.

10. I am the Lord thy God, which brought thee up out of the land of Egypt; open thy mouth, and I will fill it.

11. But my people did not hearken to my voice, and Israel did not obey me;

12. But walked in the desire of their own heart, and after their own counsel.

13. O that my people had hearkened unto me, and Israel had walked in my ways!

14. I had soon destroyed their enemies, and turned my hand against them that hated them.

15. They that hate the Lord deal falsely with him, and their trouble endureth forever.

Ver. 7. *He called upon me in trouble and I delivered him.* Heb., *Thou calledst in trouble, and I delivered thee.*

And covered him with my glorious veil, and proved him, ܘܟܣܝܬܗ ܒܬܫܒܘܚܬܐ ܕܝܠܝ ܘܒܚܢܬܗ. A. V. *I answered thee in the secret place of thunder; I proved thee,* אֶעֶנְךָ בְּסֵתֶר רַעַם אֶבְחָנְךָ.

Ver. 8. *And I will speak.* This is not in the Hebrew.

Ver. 12. *But walked in the desire of their own hearts, and after their own counsel.* Heb., *So I gave them up unto their own hearts' lust: and they walked in their own counsels.*

Ver. 14. The verbs in this verse are future in the Hebrew.

Ver. 15. *They that hate the Lord deal falsely with him, and their*

16. *But* he hath fed him with the finest of the wheat; and with honey out of the rock hath he satisfied him.

PSALM LXXXII.

A Psalm of Asaph. — Reproof of the wicked Jews.

1. God standeth in the congregation of the angels, and in the midst of the angels doth he judge.
2. How long will ye judge unjustly, and accept the persons of the wicked?
3. Judge the fatherless and the needy, and justify the poor and humble.
4. Deliver the poor and needy from the hand of the wicked,
5. Which have not known nor understood, for they

trouble endureth forever, ܀ ܡܶܢܠܳܘܽܡܺܝܢ ܘܟ݂ܕ݂ܢܳܠ ܠܳܒܓ݂ܗ ܟ݁ܰܕ݂. ܡܳܣܶܘܢ ܗܳܣܕ݂ܰܘܣ ܠܓ݂ܕ݂ܰܡ. A. v. *The haters of the Lord should have submitted themselves unto him; but their time should have endured forever,* מְשַׂנְאֵי יְהֹוָה יְכַחֲשׁוּ־לוֹ וִיהִי עִתָּם לְעוֹלָם.

Ver. 16. *But he hath fed him.* A. v. *He should have fed them also,* וַיַּאֲכִילֵהוּ.

Hath he satisfied him. Heb., *should I have satisfied thee.*

Ps. LXXXII. Ver. 1. *In the congregation of the angels,* ܒ݁ܰܟ݂ܢܽܘܫܬ݁ܳܐ. ܘܰܒ݂ܟ݂ܢܽܘܫܬ݁ܳܐ. A. v. *In the congregation of the mighty,* בַּעֲדַת־אֵל.

And in the midst of the angels, ܡܶܨܥܰܬ݂ ܟ݁ܢܽܘܫܬ݁ܳܐ. A. v. *Among the gods,* בְּקֶרֶב אֱלֹהִים.

Ver. 4. *From the hand of the wicked.* Heb., *rid them out of the hand of the wicked.*

were walking in darkness; and all the foundations of the earth are out of course.

6. I have said, Ye *are* gods, and ye *are* all the children of the Highest:

7. *But* now ye shall die like men, and fall like one of the princes.

8. Arise, O God, and judge the earth; for thou shalt inherit all nations.

(LAUD, AND THE BEGINNING OF THE GRADE.)

PSALM LXXXIII.

A Psalm of Asaph;— a supplication to God in behalf of the people that suffered affliction, and a prophecy concerning the dispersion of the enemies of the Lord.

1. O God, who is like unto thee? Hold not thy peace, and be not still, O God.

2. For lo, thine enemies make a tumult; and they that hate thee have lifted up the head above thy people.

3. In their craftiness they imagine a secret thing, and take counsel against thy saints,

4. And say, Come, let us destroy them from *being* a nation, and let the name of Israel be no more remembered.

Ps. LXXXIII. Ver. 1. *Who is like unto thee?* كَــد ڊإڡْڊا جُــب.
A. V. *Keep not thou silence,* אַל־דָּמִי־לָךְ. דָּמִי was derived from דָּמָה, *to be like,* and the clause from a negative was made an interrogative proposition. The LXX. have τίς ὁμοιωθήσεταί σοι;

Ver. 2. *Above thy people.* These words, forming part of verse 3, are connected in the Syriac with verse 2, in which I have included them.

5. For they are agreed in their heart together, and are confederate against thee;

6. The tabernacle of Edom, and of the Arabians; and of Moab and of the Gadarenes;

7. The border of Ammon, and of Amalek, and of Philistia with the inhabitants of Tyre.

8. The Assyrian also hath conspired with them, and they have holpen the children of Lot.

9. Do unto them, as unto the Midianites; and as to Sisera, and as to Jabin at the brook of Kishon;

10. Which were destroyed at En-dor, and became *as* dung upon the earth.

11. Cut them off, and destroy them like Oreb and Zeb, and like Zeba and Zalmunna; *even* all their rulers,

12. Which said, Let us take into our own possession the city of God.

13. Make them, O God, like a wheel, and like stubble before the wind;

14. And as the fire that is left in the wood, and as the flame that consumeth the mountains,

15. So persecute them with thy tempests, and vex them with thy storms.

Ver. 6. *The Arabians.* Heb., *the Ishmaelites.*

The Gadarenes. Heb., *the Hagarenes.*

Ver. 7. *The border,* ܠܬܚܘܡܐ. A. V. *Gebal,* גְּבָל. The translator read גְּבֻל, *border,* and varied the sentence accordingly.

Ver. 11. *Cut them off, and destroy them,* ܣܚܘܦ ܐܢܘܢ ܘܐܘܒܕ ܐܢܘܢ. A. V. *Make their nobles,* שִׁיתֵמוֹ נְדִיבֵמוֹ. The translator may have read שַׂמֵּמוֹ וְאַבְּדֵמוֹ.

Ver. 12. *The city of God.* Heb., *the houses of God.*

Ver. 14. *And as the fire that is left in the wood.* Heb., *As the fire burneth the wood.*

16. Fill their faces with shame, that they may seek thy Name, O Lord.

17. Let them be confounded and troubled forever; let them be put to shame and perish.

18. That they may know that thy Name, O Lord, alone is exalted in all the earth.

PSALM LXXXIV.

A Psalm of the sons of Korah; — the musings of David when he went from Zion to worship in the house of God. Also, said to be a prophecy concerning the Messiah, and concerning his Church.

1. How amiable *are* thy tabernacles, O Lord Almighty!

2. My soul waiteth and longeth for the courts of the Lord; my heart and my flesh give praise unto the living God.

3. Yea, also, the sparrow hath found her an house, and the turtledove a nest; they nourish *their* young by the side of thine altar, O Lord Almighty.

4. My King, and my God, blessed are they that dwell in thine house, for they shall praise thee forever. Diapsalma.

Ver. 18. *That they may know that thy Name, O Lord, alone is exalted in all the earth.* Heb., *That men may know that thou, whose Name alone is Jehovah, art the most High over all the earth.*

Ps. LXXXIV. Ver. 3. *They nourish their young by the side of thine altar.* Heb., *where she may lay her young, even thine altars.*

Ver. 4. *My King and my God.* These words are construed in the Syriac with the 4th verse, in which I have included them.

5. Blessed is the man whose helper thou art, and in whose heart *are* thy ways.

6. *They* go through the valley of weeping, and make it a dwelling-place; and even the law-giver shall be clothed with a blessing.

7. They shall go from strength to strength, and in Zion shall the God of gods be seen.

8. O Lord God Almighty, hear my prayer; and hearken, O God of Jacob;

9. And behold thou, O God our helper, and look upon the face of thine Anointed.

Ver. 5. *Whose helper thou art.* Heb., *whose strength is in thee.*
Thy ways. Heb., *the ways of them.*

Ver. 6. *They go through the valley of weeping.* Heb., *Who passing through the valley of Baca.*

A dwelling-place, ܡܥܡܪܐ. A. V. *A well,* מַעְיָן. The translator probably read מָעוֹן.

And even the law-giver shall be clothed with a blessing, ܕܐܦ ܚܘܣܢܐ ܬܠܒܫ ܒܘܪܟܬܐ. A. V. *The rain also filleth the pools,* גַּם־בְּרָכוֹת יַעְטֶה מוֹרֶה. The sense here will depend upon the meaning of the words מוֹרֶה and בְּרָכוֹת. מוֹרֶה, may be derived from יָרָה *to cast, to throw, to sprinkle;* and hence מוֹרֶה, *rain;* or from יָרָה, *to teach;* and hence מוֹרֶה, *teacher,* or *law-giver.* בְּרָכוֹת may be the plural of בְּרָכָה, *blessing,* or בְּרֵכָה, *pool.* The LXX. render the words like the Syriac translator; καὶ γὰρ εὐλογίας δώσει ὁ νομοθετῶν.

Ver. 7. *Shall the God of gods be seen,* ܢܬܚܙܐ ܐܠܗ ܐܠܗܐ. A. V. *Every one of them appeareth before God,* יֵרָאֶה אֶל־אֱלֹהִים. The translator read אֶל אֱלֹהִים; as did the LXX, who have ὀφθήσεται ὁ θεὸς τῶν θεῶν.

10. For one day in thy dwelling is better than a thousand; I would rather dwell in the house of God, than abide in the tent of the wicked.

11. For the Lord God is our nourisher and helper; the Lord shall give grace and glory, and his good things shall he not withhold from them that walk in integrity.

12. O Lord God Almighty, blessed *is* the man that trusteth in thee.

PSALM LXXXV.

A Psalm of the sons of Korah;— the recompense and the deliverance which they had from God, and a prophecy concerning the Messiah.

1. Lord, thou hast been favourable unto thy land, and thou hast brought back the captivity of Jacob.

2. Thou hast forgiven thy people their iniquity, and hast covered all their sins.

3. Thou hast caused all thy wrath to pass away, and hast turned away the fierceness of thine anger.

4. Turn us, O God our Saviour, and cause thine anger to cease from us;

5. And be not displeased at us forever; neither keep thine anger throughout all generations;

6. But turn us, and quicken us, that thy people may rejoice in thee.

Ver. 10. *I would rather dwell.* Heb., *I had rather be a doorkeeper.*

Ver. 11. *Our nourisher and helper.* Heb., *a sun and shield.*

Ps. LXXXV. Ver. 5, 6, in the original, are in the interrogative form.

Ver. 5. *Keep.* Heb., *draw out.*

7. Shew us thy mercy, O Lord, and grant us thy salvation;

8. That we may hear what the Lord our God will speak; for he speaketh peace with his people, and with his saints that they turn not backward.

9. His salvation is nigh them that fear him; he shall cause his glory to dwell in our land.

10. Mercy and truth have met us, and righteousness and peace shall kiss *us*.

11. Truth shall spring out of the earth, and righteousness hath looked down from heaven.

12. Yea, the Lord also shall give his good things, and the earth shall yield her fruits;

13. And the righteous shall walk before him, and he shall establish his goings in the earth.

Ver. 8. *That we may hear.* Heb., *I will hear.*

That they turn not backward. Heb., *but let them not turn again to folly.*

Ver. 9. *He shall cause his glory to dwell.* Heb., *that glory may dwell.*

Ver. 10. *Have met us,* ازدهٰى. A. V. *Are met together,* נִפְגָּשׁוּ.

Shall kiss us, ادماسل. A. V. *Have kissed each other,* נָשָׁקוּ.

Ver. 13. *And the righteous.* Heb., *Righteousness.*

And he shall establish his goings in the earth. Heb., *and shall set us in the way of his steps.*

PSALM LXXXVI.

A Psalm of David;—when he built a house to the Lord; a prophecy also of the calling of the Gentiles; and, again, the peculiar prayer of the righteous man.

1. Incline thine ear, O Lord, and hear me, for I am poor and needy.
2. Preserve my soul, for thou art good; do thou, O God, save thy servant that trusteth in thee.
3. Be merciful unto me, O Lord, for I cry daily unto thee.
4. Rejoice the soul of thy servant, for unto thee, O Lord, do I lift up my soul.
5. For thou, Lord, art good; and abundant is thy mercy towards all them that call upon thee.
6. Give ear unto my prayer, O Lord, and hearken unto the voice of my cry.
7. In the day of mine affliction have I called upon thee, and thou hast heard me.
8. There is no one like unto thee, O Lord God; neither are there *any works* like unto thy works.
9. All nations whom thou hast made shall come and worship thee, O Lord, and shall praise thy Name.
10. For thou art great; thou, O God, alone doest wondrous things.

Ps. LXXXVI. Ver. 2. *For thou art good,* ܛܳܒ݂ܐ ܐܢ̱ܬ؟ اِنَّ لَيَ.
A. V. *For I am holy,* חָסִיד־אָ֫נִי.

Ver. 5. *And abundant is thy mercy.* Heb., *and ready to forgive; and plenteous in mercy.*

Ver. 8. *O Lord God.* Heb., *among the gods, O Lord.*

11. Shew me thy way, O Lord, and I will walk in the truth; let my heart rejoice in them that fear thy Name.

12. I will give thanks unto thee, O Lord my God, with all my heart; and I will praise thy Name forevermore.

13. For great is thy mercy toward me, and thou hast delivered my soul from the lowest hell.

14. O God, the wicked are risen against me, and the congregation of the mighty have sought after my soul, and have not remembered thee.

15. But thou, O Lord God, *art* merciful and compassionate, long suffering, and plenteous in mercy and truth.

16. O turn unto me, and have mercy upon me; give strength unto thy servant, and save the son of thine handmaid;

17. And shew me a favourable token, that they which hate me may see *it* and be ashamed, because thou, Lord, hast holpen me, and comforted me.

Ver. 11. *Let my heart rejoice in them that fear thy Name,* ܬܣܪܐ ܠܚܒ ܟܠܗܘܢ ܘܐܫܠܡ ܠܫܡܟ. A. v. *Unite my heart to fear thy Name,* יַחֵד לְבָבִי לְיִרְאָה שְׁמֶךָ. The translator read יִחַד, from חָדָה, *to rejoice;* the LXX. also, who have εὐφρανθήτω ἡ καρδία μου.

Ver. 14. *Of the mighty.* Heb., *of violent men.*

And have not remembered thee. Heb., *and have not set thee before them.*

Ver. 15. *But thou, O Lord God, art merciful.* Heb., *But thou, O Lord, art a God full of compassion.*

Ver. 17. *A favourable token.* Heb., *a token for good.*

PSALM LXXXVII.

Concerning the redemption of Jerusalem.

1. His foundations *are* upon his holy hill.
2. The Lord hath loved the gates of Zion more than all the dwellings of Jacob.
3. Glorious things are spoken of thee, O city of our God! Diapsalma.
4. Remember Rahab and Babylon *that* know me; behold, the Philistines, and Tyre, and the Ethiopians; This *man* was born there.
5. And of Zion it is said, that a mighty man was born in her, and he hath established her.
6. The Lord shall number the nations in the Scripture; *for* this *man* was born there.
7. The princes that dwell in thee shall rejoice, and all that are humbled in thee.

Ps. LXXXVII. Ver. 1. *Upon his holy hill.* Heb., *in the holy mountains.*

Ver. 4. *Remember.* Heb., *I will make mention of.*

That know me, ܠܝܕܥܝ. A. V. *To them that know me,* לְיֹדְעָי.

Ver. 5. *That a mighty man,* ܓܒܪܐ ܚܕ. A. V. *This and that man,* אִישׁ וְאִישׁ.

And he hath established her. Heb., *and the Highest himself shall establish her.*

Ver. 6. *The Lord shall number the nations in the Scripture,* ܡܪܝܐ ܢܡܢܐ ܟܬܒܐ ܕܥܡܡܐ. A. V. *The Lord shall count when he writeth up the people,* יְהוָה יִסְפֹּר בִּכְתוֹב עַמִּים.

Ver. 7. *The princes that dwell in thee shall rejoice and all that are humbled in thee,* ܢܐܘܕܘܢ ܘܢܨܛܒܝܢ ܟܠܗܘܢ ܬܡܝܡܐ.

PSALM LXXXVIII.

Concerning the people in Babylon.

1. O Lord God of my salvation, I have cried day and night before thee.
2. Let my prayer come before thee, and incline thine ear unto my supplication.
3. For my soul is full of troubles, and my life draweth nigh unto the grave.
4. I am counted with them that go down into the pit, and I am as a man that hath no assistance.
5. Free among the dead, like the slain that lie in the graves, whom thou rememberest no more, and they are perished from thy hands.
6. Thou hast brought me down into the lowest pit, into darkness and the shadows of death.
7. Thy wrath lieth hard upon me, and thou hast brought all thy waves upon me.
8. Thou hast put away mine acquaintance far from me, and thou hast made me an abomination unto them. I am shut up that I cannot come forth;

ܘܠܐܡܚܕܗ ܚܒ݂ܒ. A. V. *As well the singers as the players on instruments shall be there; all my springs are in thee,* וְשָׁרִים כְּחֹלְלִים כָּל־מַעְיָנַי בָּךְ. *The translator may have read* וְשָׁרִים חֹלְלִים וְכָל־מְעַנַּי בָּךְ *The LXX, with a different rendering, have the words* ἀρχόντων *and* εὐφραινομένων.

Ps. LXXXVIII. Ver. 4. *That hath no assistance,* ܘܓܒܪ ܠܐ. A. V. *That hath no strength,* אֵין־אֱיָל. *The words* ܐܝܠ *and* אֱיָל *are the same, but with different meaning, in the two languages.* LXX., ἀβοήθητος.

Ver. 6. *And the shadows of death.* Heb., *in the deeps.*

9. And mine eye dissolveth by reason of my humiliation. Lord, I have called daily upon thee, and I have stretched out my hands unto thee.

10. Behold thou shewest wonders to the dead, and mighty men shall arise and praise thee. Diapsalma.

11. They also that are in the graves shall declare thy loving-kindness, and thy truth in destruction.

12. Thy wonders shall be known in darkness, and thy righteousness in the land that is forgotten.

13. And unto thee have I cried, O Lord, and in the morning shall my prayer prevent thee.

14. O Lord, do not forget my soul, nor turn away thy face from me.

15. I am poor and weary from my youth up; I am lifted up, and cast down, and distracted;

Ver. 9. *Dissolveth*, ܐܟܝ. A. v. *Mourneth*, דָאֲבָה. The same word, with different signification, in the two languages. Verses 10, 11, and 12 are in the interrogative form in the Hebrew.

Ver. 10. *Mighty men*, ܓܒܐ. A. v. *The dead*, רְפָאִים.

Ver. 12. *In the land that is forgotten*, ܐܪܥܐ ܕܛܘܫܝܐ. A. v. *In the land of forgetfulness*, בְּאֶרֶץ נְשִׁיָּה. LXX., ἐν γῇ ἐπιλελησμένῃ.

Ver. 14. *Do not forget*. Heb., *why castest thou off?*
Nor turn away. Heb., *Why hidest thou?*

Ver. 15. *And weary*, ܘܠܐܐ. A. v. *And ready to die*, וְגֹוֵעַ. The translator doubtless read וְיָגֵעַ. The LXX. have ἐν κόποις.

I am lifted up and cast down and distracted, ܐܬܬܪܝܡܬ ܘܐܬܡܟܟܬ ܘܐܬܒܠܗܝܬ. A. v. *While I suffer thy terrors, I am distracted*, נָשָׂאתִי אֵמֶיךָ אָפוּנָה. The translator may have read נָשָׂאתִי וְאֵמֶיךָ וְאָפוּנָה. LXX., ὑψωθεὶς δὲ ἐταπεινώθην καὶ ἐξηπορήθην.

16. And thy wrath goeth over me, and thy trouble hath reduced me to silence.

17. They came round about me daily like water, and set *themselves* together against me.

18. My lovers and my friends hast thou put away from me, and mine acquaintance hast thou removed from me.

PSALM LXXXIX.

Concerning the people in Babylon.

1. I will sing of the mercy of the Lord forever, and with my mouth will I make known his truth to all generations.

2. For thou hast said, The world shall be builded in mercy, and thy truth shall establish the heavens.

3. I have made a covenant with my chosen; and I have sworn unto David my servant;

Ver. 16. *And thy trouble hath reduced me to silence.* Heb., *thy terrors have cut me off.*

Ver. 17. *And set themselves against me.* Heb., *they compassed me about.*

Ver. 18. *And mine acquaintance hast thou removed from me.* Heb., *and mine acquaintance into darkness.*

Ps. LXXXIX. Ver. 2. *For thou hast said.* Heb., *For I have said. The world shall be builded in mercy,* ܒܚܣܕܐ ܡܬܒܢܐ. A. v. *Mercy shall be built up forever,* עוֹלָם חֶסֶד יִבָּנֶה. The translator read, no doubt, חֶסֶד, translating עוֹלָם, *the world,* a signification which the word has in Syriac and Chaldee.

And thy truth shall establish the heavens. Heb., *thy faithfulness shalt thou establish in the very heavens.*

4. That thy seed I will establish forever, and build up thy throne to all generations. Diapsalma.

5. The heavens shall praise thy wonders, O Lord; thy truth also in the congregation of the saints.

6. Who in the heaven of heavens can be compared unto the Lord? And who among the sons of the angels can be likened unto the Lord?

7. God standeth in the congregation of the saints; *he is* great and terrible above all them that *are* round about him.

8. O Lord God Almighty, who is strong like unto thee? or to thy faithfulness round about thee?

9. Thou rulest the raging of the sea, and stillest the tumult of its waves.

10. Thou bringest down the proud like unto them that are slain; thou hast scattered thine enemies with thy strong arm.

11. The heavens are thine; the earth also is thine; thou hast established the world with the fulness thereof.

Ver. 6. *Among the sons of the angels.* Heb., *among the sons of the mighty.*

Ver. 7. *God standeth in the congregation of the saints; he is great and terrible above all them that are round about him.* Heb., *God is greatly to be feared in the assembly of the saints, and to be had in reverence of all them that are about him.*

Ver. 8. *Who is strong like unto thee?* Heb., *who is a strong Lord like unto thee?*

Ver. 10. *Thou bringest down the proud,* ܐܢܬ ܡܡܟܟ ܠܝܐ ܠܫܒܗܪܢܐ. A. V. *Thou hast broken Rahab in pieces,* דִּכְּאתָ כָרָהַב. רָהַב means *pride*, but as used here is regarded as a poetical name of Egypt. The LXX. translate it ὑπερήφανον.

12. Thou hast created the north and the south; Tabor and Hermon sing praise unto thy Name.

13. Thine is the arm, and thine is the strength; thy hand shall be strong and thy right hand shall be exalted.

14. In righteousness and judgment thy throne is established; in mercy and truth they go before thy face.

15. Blessed is the people that know thy praises; they shall walk, O Lord, in the light of thy countenance;

16. And in thy Name shall they rejoice all the day, and in thy righteousness shall they be exalted.

17. For thou art the glory of our strength, and in thy favour shall our horn be exalted.

18. For the Lord is our confidence, and the Holy One of Israel *is* our King.

19. Then he spake in visions with his saints, and said; I have given help to a man, and I have exalted one chosen out of the people.

Ver. 13. *Thine is the arm, and thine is the strength.* Heb., *Thou hast a mighty arm.*

Ver. 14. *In righteousness and judgment thy throne is established,* ܚܲܘܪ̈ܝܡܶܦ݂ܐ̱ܶܝܠ ܡܚܶܓ݂ܒ݂ܰܠ ܦܳܟ݂ܡܳܦ݂ ܚܳܦ݂ܙܡܢܝ. A. V. *Justice and judgment are the habitation of thy throne,* צֶדֶק וּמִשְׁפָּט מְכוֹן כִּסְאֶךָ. The translator seems to have read בְּצֶדֶק וּבְמִשְׁפָּט נָכוֹן כִּסְאֶךָ.

In mercy and truth they go before thy face. Heb., *mercy and truth shall go before thy face.*

Ver. 15. *Thy praises.* Heb., *the joyful sound.*

Ver. 17. *Of our strength.* Heb., *of their strength.*

Ver. 19. *He spake.* Heb., *thou spakest.*

20. Yea, I have found David my servant, and *with* my holy oil have I anointed him.

21. Mine hand hath holpen him, and mine arm also hath strengthened him;

22. And his enemy hath gained no advantage *of him*, and the son of iniquity hath not cast him down.

23. I will cause his enemies to perish before him, and I will destroy them that hate him.

24. My truth and my mercy *shall be* with him, and in my Name shall his horn be exalted. Diapsalma.

Section.

25. I will set his hand in the sea, and his right hand in the rivers.

26. He shall cry unto me, Thou *art* my Father, my God, and my strong deliverer;

27. And I also will make him *my* first-born, and I will exalt him above the kings of the earth.

28. My mercy will I keep for him forevermore, and my covenant shall stand fast with him.

29. His seed will I make *to endure* forever, and his throne as the days of heaven.

30. If his children forsake my law, and walk not in my commandments;

With his saints. Heb., *to thy Holy One.*

To a man, ܠܓܒܪܐ. A. V. *Upon one that is mighty*, עַל־גִּבּוֹר. The Syriac, to correspond, would be ܠܐ ܠܓܒܪܐ.

Ver. 21. *Mine hand hath holpen him.* Heb., *With whom my hand shall be established.*

Ver. 31 of the Hebrew is wanting in the Syriac version; translated, *If they break my statutes, and keep not my commandments.*

32. I will visit their iniquity with the rod, and their sins with the scourge.

33. *Nevertheless*, my mercy will I not take from him, nor suffer my truth to fail;

34. And my covenant I will not despise: I will not alter anything that hath gone out of my lips.

35. Once have I sworn by my holiness unto David, and I will not lie;

36. That his seed shall endure forever, and his throne as the sun before me;

37. And it shall be established forever as the moon, the faithful witness in the heavens.

38. But thou hast forgotten me, and cast me off, and turned away the face of thine Anointed;

39. And thou hast made void the covenant of thy servant, and hast cast his crown upon the ground.

40. Thou hast destroyed his hedges, and overthrown his strongholds;

41. And all that pass by the way trample upon him, and he is a reproach to his neighbours;

42. And thou hast set up the right hand of his adversaries, and made all them that hate him to rejoice.

43. Thou hast also turned the help of his sword, and hast not given him aid in the battle;

Ver. 34. *I will not despise.* Heb., *will I not break.*

Ver. 35. *Unto David, and I will not lie.* Heb., *that I will not lie unto David.*

Ver. 38. *And turned away the face of thine Anointed.* Heb., *thou hast been wroth with thine anointed.*

Ver. 39. *And hast cast his crown upon the ground.* Heb., *thou hast profaned his crown by casting it to the ground.*

Ver. 43. *The help of his sword,* ܚܽܘܠܳܢܳܐ ܕܣܰܝܦܶܗ. A. V. *The edge of his sword,* צוּר חַרְבּוֹ.

44. And thou hast made his victorious ones to cease, and hast cast his throne down to the ground.

45. Thou hast shortened the days of his youth, and covered him with shame.

46. How long wilt thou be angry, O Lord? forever? and shall thy wrath burn like fire?

47. Remember me *that am crying unto thee* from the pit, for thou hast not made all men in vain.

48. What man is he that shall live, and shall not see death? and shall he deliver his soul from the hand of the grave?

49. Lord, where are thy former loving-kindnesses which thou swearest unto David in truth?

And hast not given him aid, ܘܠܐ ܣܢܕܬܝܗܝ. A. V. *And hast not made him to stand,* וְלֹא הֲקֵימֹתוֹ. The LXX., like the Syriac, Ἀπέστρεψας τὴν βοήθειαν τῆς ῥομφαίας αὐτοῦ, καὶ οὐκ ἀντελάβου αὐτοῦ ἐν τῷ πολέμῳ.

Ver. 44. *His victorious ones,* ܡܙܕܟܝܢܘܗܝ. A. V. *His glory,* מִצְּהָרוֹ, literally, *from his glory*. The root צָהַר means *to be pure*; hence צֹהַר, *lustre, glory*. The Syriac root ܙܟܐ means *to conquer*, and in Pahel, *to purify, to cleanse*. The word which I have translated *his victorious ones*, has been also translated *his purity* or *brightness*, and *his victories*.

Ver. 47. *Remember me that am crying unto thee from the pit,* ܐܬܕܟܪܝܢܝ ܕܓܥܐ ܐܢܐ. A. V. *Remember how short my time is,* זְכָר־אֲנִי מֶה־חָלֶד. The Syriac verb ܚܦܪ means *to dig;* hence the derivative *pit*. The Hebrew word, derived from an Arabic root, means *length of life*. Taking the word in the former sense, the translator seems to have read זָכְרֵנִי מֵחָלֶד.

For thou hast not made all men in vain. Heb., *wherefore hast thou made all men in vain?*

50. Remember, Lord, the reproach of thy servant; for I have borne in my life all the slander of the nations.

51. Thine enemies have reproached me, O Lord, and have slandered the footsteps of thine Anointed.

52. Blessed is the Lord forevermore. Amen. Amen.

Ver. 50. *For I have borne in my life all the slander of the nations,* ܘܐܟܝܠܬ ܒܥܘܒܝ ܚܣܕܐ ܕܥܡܡܐ ܣܓܝܐܐ. A. V. *How I do bear in my bosom the reproach of all the mighty people,* שְׂאֵתִי בְחֵיקִי כָּל־רַבִּים עַמִּים. The translator may have read שְׂאֵתִי בְחַיַּי כָּל־דִּיבֵי עַמִּים.

END OF THE THIRD BOOK.

THE FOURTH BOOK.

PSALM XC.

A Psalm of Moses.

1. Lord, thou hast been our dwelling-place, throughout all generations.
2. Before the mountains were conceived, and before the earth brought forth *her fruits*, and before the foundations of the world were laid, from everlasting and to everlasting, thou art God;
3. Which turnest man to humiliation, and sayest, return, ye children of men.
4. For a thousand years in thy sight *are but* as yesterday that hath passed away, and like a watch of the night.

Ps. xc. Ver. 2. *Were conceived,* ܢܬܟܝܠܘܢ. A. v. *Were brought forth,* יֻלָּדוּ.

And before the earth brought forth her fruits, and before the foundations of the world were laid, ܘܥܕܠܐ ܐܬܝܠܕ ܬܐܒܝܠ ܘܐܪܥܐ. A. v. *Or ever thou hadst formed the earth and the world,* וַתְּחוֹלֵל אֶרֶץ וְתֵבֵל.

Ver. 3. *To humiliation,* ܠܡܘܟܟܐ. A. v. *To destruction,* עַד־דַּכָּא. LXX, εἰς ταπείνωσιν.

5. Their generations shall continue *but* a year; and in the morning *they are* like the grass that groweth up;

6. Which in the morning flourisheth and groweth up, but in the evening drieth up and withereth.

7. For we are consumed in thine anger, and by thy wrath are we troubled.

8. Thou hast set our sins before thee; renew our youth in the light of thy countenance.

9. For all our days are consumed in thy wrath, and our years come to an end like a spider's web.

10. Our days, *even* our years *are* threescore years and ten, and hardly fourscore years; 'and the greatest

Ver. 5. *Their generations shall continue but a year,* ܡܶܫܟܚܳܐ ܫܢܰܝܳܐ ܬܶܗܘܶܐ. A. V. *Thou carriest them away as with a flood; they are as a sleep,* זְרַמְתָּם שֵׁנָה יִהְיוּ. For שֵׁנָה, the translator read שָׁנָה, as did the LXX., who have ἔτη; and for זְרַמְתָּם we may conjecture that the reading was זַרְמֹתָם, or זְרֹעֵיהֶם, either of which would give a meaning not unlike the Syriac.

Ver. 6. *Drieth up.* Heb., *is cut down.*

Ver. 8. *Renew our youth,* ܟܰܕ݂ܺܝܬܰܢ. A. V. *Our secret sins,* עֲלֻמֵנוּ. The word is the same, but its meaning varies in the two languages.

Ver. 9. *Like a spider's web,* ܐܰܝܟ݂ ܓܘܳܓܰܝ. A. V. *As a tale that is told,* כְּמוֹ־הֶגֶה. LXX., ὡς ἀράχνη.

Ver. 10. *Our days, even our years.* Heb., *The days of our years.*
And hardly. Heb., *and if by reason of strength they be.*
And the greatest part of them. Heb., *yet is their strength.*
For humiliation cometh upon us and we are hurried away, ܡܶܛܽܠ ܕܳܐܬܶܐ ܥܠܰܝܢ ܡܘܟܳܟܳܐ ܘܡܶܬܚܰܛܦܺܝܢܰܢ. A. V. *For it is soon cut off and we fly away,* כִּי־גָז חִישׁ וַנָּעֻפָה.

part of them *is* labour and sorrows; for humiliation cometh upon us, and we are hurried away.

11. Who knoweth the power of thy wrath, and the fear of thine anger?

12. Teach us the number of our days, that we may enter into the heart of wisdom.

13. Return, O Lord, how long? Wilt thou not comfort thy servants?

14. O satisfy us early with thy mercy, *that* we may sing and rejoice all our days.

15. Make us glad because our iniquity hath ceased, and *there are* years in which we have seen evils.

16. Let thy works appear unto thy servants, and thy glory unto their children.

17. Let the sweetness of the Lord our God be

Ver. 11. *And the fear of thine anger.* Heb., *Even according to thy fear so is thy wrath.*

Ver. 12. *Teach us the number of our days.* Heb., *So teach us to number our days.*

That we may enter into the heart of wisdom, ܘܢܚܘܐ ܠܠܒܐ ܕܚܟܡܬܐ. A. V. *That we may apply our hearts unto wisdom,* וְנָבִיא לְבַב חָכְמָה. The Hebrew, however, may be more naturally rendered like the Syriac.

Ver. 13. *Wilt thou not comfort thy servants?* Heb., *and let it repent thee concerning thy servants.*

Ver. 15. *Because our iniquity hath ceased,* ܡܛܠ ܕܒܛܠ ܥܘܠܢ. A. V. *According to the days wherein thou hast afflicted us,* כִּימוֹת עִנִּיתָנוּ. This difference is susceptible of a very easy explanation. The translator read, no doubt, כִּי מוֹת עֲוֹנוֹתֵנוּ.

Ver. 17. *The sweetness.* Heb., *the beauty.*

Who hath established the work of his hands upon us, and by the work of his hands hath established us. Heb., *and establish thou* upon us; who hath established the work of his hands upon us, and by the work of his hands hath established us.

PSALM XCI.

A Psalm of David;—concerning Hezekiah, the king, who was to be surnamed the son of David; and, spiritually, the victory of the Messiah is spoken of, and of every one that is perfected in him.

1. He that sitteth in the secret place of the most High, and rejoiceth in the shadow of God,
2. Hath said unto the Lord, *thou art* my confidence; God is my refuge in whom I will trust.
3. For he shall deliver thee from the net of the snare, and from talking of vanity.
4. He shall save thee under his feathers, and under his wings shalt thou be concealed; *like* armour his truth shall surround thee.

---

the work of our hands upon us; yea, the work of our hands establish thou it.

Ps. XCI. Ver. 1. *And rejoiceth in the shadow of God.* Heb., *shall abide under the shadow of the Almighty.*

Ver. 2. *Hath said unto the Lord.* Heb., *I will say of the Lord.*

Ver. 3. *The net of the snare.* Heb., *the snare of the fowler.*

From talking of vanity, ܡܢ ܡܡܠܠܐ ܣܪܝܩܐ. A. V. *From the noisome pestilence,* מִדֶּבֶר הַוּוֹת. The translator read מִדַּבֵּר. LXX., ἀπὸ λόγου ταραχώδους.

Ver. 4. *He shall save thee.* Heb., *He shall cover thee.*

Like armour his truth shall surround thee, ܐܠܐ ܢܣܘܓܟ ܩܘܫܬܗ. A. V. *His truth shall be thy shield and buckler,* צִנָּה וְסֹחֵרָה אֲמִתּוֹ. LXX., ὅπλῳ κυκλώσει σε ἡ ἀλήθεια αὐτοῦ.

5. Thou shalt not be afraid for the terror by night, nor for the arrow that flieth by day;

6. Nor for the word that walketh in darkness, nor for the wind that bloweth in the noonday.

7. Thousands shall fall at thy side, and ten thousands at thy right hand, and they shall not come nigh thee.

8. But with thine eyes only shalt thou behold and see the recompense of the wicked.

9. For thou, O Lord, art my confidence, that hast set thy dwelling in the heights.

10. *Therefore*, there shall no evil approach thee, neither shall any plague come nigh thy dwelling;

11. For he shall give his angels charge over thee, that they may keep thee in all thy ways;

12. And upon their arms they shall bear thee up, that thou stumble not with thy foot.

Ver. 6. *The word*, ܡܠܬܐ. A. V. *The pestilence*, דֶּבֶר. See note to verse 3. The LXX here translate the word πράγματος.

Nor for the wind that bloweth, ܡܢ ܪܘܚܐ ܕܢܫܒܐ. A. V. *Nor for the destruction that wasteth*, מִקֶּטֶב יָשׁוּד.

Ver. 7. *They shall not come nigh thee*. Heb., *it shall not come nigh thee*.

Ver. 9. *For thou, O Lord, art my confidence, that hast set thy dwelling in the heights*, : ܐܢܬ ܗܘ ܡܪܝܐ ܬܘܟܠܢܝ ܘܒܡܪܘܡܐ ܣܡܬ ܡܥܡܪܟ. A. V. *Because thou hast made the Lord, which is my refuge, even the most High, thy habitation*, כִּי־אַתָּה יְהוָה מַחְסִי עֶלְיוֹן שַׂמְתָּ מְעוֹנֶךָ. The Hebrew here might be rendered like the Syriac, and perhaps more naturally.

Ver. 12. *And upon their arms.* Heb., *in their hands*.

That thou stumble not with thy foot. Heb., *lest thou dash thy foot against a stone.*

13. Thou shalt tread upon the asp and the basilisk; and the lion and the dragon shalt thou trample under foot.

14. Because he hath sought me, I will deliver him, and I will strengthen him; because he hath known my Name,

15. He shall call upon me, and I will answer him; yea, I *will be* with him in trouble; I will strengthen him, and honour him.

16. With long life will I satisfy him, and shew him my salvation.

(LAUD, AND THE BEGINNING OF THE GRADE.)

PSALM XCII.

Anonymous; concerning the ministry of the Priests, and their morning oblations; a prophecy, also, concerning rest in God.

1. *It is a* good *thing* to give thanks unto the Lord, and to sing praises unto thy Name, O most High;

2. And to shew forth thy loving-kindness in the morning, and thy truth every night.

3. I will play upon an instrument of ten *strings*, and I will play upon the harp;

4. For thou, Lord, hast made me glad through thy works, and I will glory in the work of thy hands.

Ver. 13. *The asp.* Heb., *the lion.*
Ver. 14. *Because he hath sought me.* Heb., *Because he hath set his love upon me.*
And I will strengthen him. Heb., *I will set him on high.*
Ver. 15. *I will strengthen him.* Heb., *I will deliver him.*
Ps. XCII. Ver. 3. *I will play upon an instrument of ten strings, and I will play upon the harp.* Heb., *Upon an instrument of ten strings, and upon the psaltery; upon the harp with a solemn sound.*

5. O Lord, how great are thy works! and thy thoughts are very deep.

6. But an unwise man knoweth not, and a fool doth not understand this.

7. When the wicked spring as the grass, and when all the workers of iniquity do flourish, *it is* that they may perish forever.

8. But thou, O Lord, *art* most High forevermore.

9. For lo! thine enemies, O Lord, — for lo! thine enemies shall perish, and all the workers of iniquity shall be scattered.

10. *But* thou hast exalted my horns like *the horns* of an unicorn, and thou hast anointed me with fragrant oil.

11. Mine eyes, also, have seen *my desire* on mine enemies, and mine ears shall hear *my desire* of the wicked that rise up against me.

12. The righteous shall flourish like the palm-tree, and shall spread abroad like the cedars of Lebanon.

13. Those that be planted in the house of the Lord, and in the courts of our God,

14. Shall still flourish and increase in old age; they shall be fat and well liking;

15. And they shall shew that the Lord is upright: *he is* strong, and there is no unrighteousness in him.

Ver. 10. *And thou hast anointed me with fragrant oil.* Heb., *I shall be anointed with fresh oil.*

Ver. 14. *Shall still flourish.* These words form part of verse 13, but their construction in the Syriac seems to require the position which I have given them.

And increase, ܘܢܐܣܓܘܢ. A. V. *Shall bring forth fruit,* יְנוּבוּן.

PSALM XCIII.

A Psalm of David;—concerning the ministry of the Lord.

1. The Lord reigneth and is clothed with majesty. The Lord is clothed with strength, and is mighty; and he hath established the world that it cannot be moved.
2. Thy throne is established of old, and thou art from everlasting.
3. The floods are lifted up, O Lord; the floods have lift up their voice; the floods are lifted up in purity.
4. The Lord in the heights *is* more glorious than the noise of many waters, *yea than* the mighty waves of the sea.
5. Thy testimonies, also, *are* very sure, and holiness becometh thy house, O Lord, forever.

Ps. XCIII. Ver. 1. *And is mighty,* ܘܠܒܫ. A. V. *Wherewith he hath girded himself,* הִתְאַזָּר.

And he hath established the world. Heb., *the world also is established.*

Ver. 3. *Are lifted up in purity,* ܐܬܬܪܝܡܘ ܒܕܟܝܐ. A. V. *Lift up their waves,* יִשְׂאוּ דָכְיָם. The Syriac here does not convey any intelligible meaning. The translator derived דָכְיָם, a word not elsewhere occurring, and coming from an Arabic root, from the Hebrew זָכַח, *to be pure,* or its equivalent ذَكَا, *to purify.*

Ver. 4. *More glorious.* Heb., *mightier.*

PSALM XCIV.

A Psalm of David;—concerning the congregation of Korah, Dathan, and Abiram; and, spiritually, concerning the persecution of the Church.

1. O Lord God, the avenger; O God, the avenger, reveal thyself.

2. Lift up thyself, thou judge of the earth, and recompense them that bear themselves proudly.

3. Lord, how long shall the wicked, how long shall the wicked boast themselves?

4. And all the workers of iniquity utter, and speak evil, and say,

5. That they have humbled thy people, O Lord, and reduced thine inheritance to subjection?

6. They have slain the widows and the strangers, and have murdered the fatherless;

7. Yet they say, The Lord seeth not, neither doth the God of Jacob regard *it.*

8. Consider, O ye foolish of the people; ye unwise, how long will ye not understand?

9. He that planted the ears, shall he not hear? He that made the eyes, shall he not perceive?

10. He that chastiseth the heathen, shall he not admonish? He that teacheth man knowledge, *shall not he know?*

Ps. xciv. Ver. 4. *And all the workers of iniquity utter and speak evil, and say.* Heb., *How long shall they utter and speak hard things? and all the workers of iniquity boast themselves?*

Ver. 5. *That they have humbled.* Heb., *They break in pieces.*

And reduced thine inheritance to subjection. Heb., *and afflict thine heritage.*

11. The Lord knoweth the thoughts of men, for they are a vapour.

12. Blessed is the man whom thou chastenest, O Lord, and teachest him out of thy law;

13. And givest him rest from the evil days, until the pit be digged for the wicked.

14. For the Lord will not leave his people; neither will he forsake his inheritance.

15. For judgment returneth after the just one, and all the upright in heart shall follow him.

16. Who will rise up for me against the wicked? and who will prepare himself for me against the workers of iniquity?

17. Unless it had been the Lord, who was my helper, my soul had wellnigh dwelt in misery.

18. I said, my feet have slipped; but thy mercy, O Lord, sustained me.

19. In the multitude of the sorrows of my heart, thy comforts have delivered my soul.

Ver. 11. *For they are a vapour.* Heb., *that they are vanity.*

Ver. 13. *And givest him rest,* ܘܡܢܝܚ ܠܗ. A. V. *That thou mayest give him rest,* לְהַשְׁקִיט לוֹ.

Ver. 15. *For judgment returneth after the just one,* ܨܕܝܩܐ. ܘܕܟܐܐ ܢܐܦܠ ܐܬܦܢܝ ܕܝܢܐ. A. V. *But judgment shall return unto righteousness,* כִּי־עַד־צֶדֶק יָשׁוּב מִשְׁפָּט.

Ver. 16. *Will prepare himself.* Heb., *will stand up.*

Ver. 17. *In misery.* Heb., *in silence.*

Ver. 19. *Of the sorrows of my heart,* ܘܚܫܝ. ܘܒܣܘܓܐܐ ܕܚܫܝ. A. V. *Of my thoughts within me,* שַׂרְעַפַּי בְּקִרְבִּי. LXX, τῶν ὀδυνῶν μου ἐν τῇ καρδίᾳ μου.

Have delivered. Heb., *delight.*

20. The throne of the wicked shall not have fellowship with thee, who have framed iniquity against thy law.

21. Yea, they spread *their net* to catch the soul of the righteous, and they condemn the blood of the innocent.

22. But it is the Lord that giveth me strength; God is strong, and *God is my* helper.

23. He hath brought upon them their own iniquity, and put them to silence in their evils; *yea*, the Lord God hath put them to silence.

Ver. 20, in the Hebrew, is in the form of a question. *Who have framed iniquity against thy law,* ܐܝܢܐ ܕܓܒܠ ܟܐܒܐ ܥܠ ܢܡܘܣܟ. A. V. *Which frameth mischief by a law,* יֹצֵר עָמָל עֲלֵי־חֹק.

Ver. 21. *Yea, they spread their net to catch,* ܢܓܒܘܢ ܟܡܐܢܐ. O. A. V. *They press upon, or, gather themselves together against,* יָגֹדּוּ, or יָבוֹאוּ עַל. LXX., θηρεύσουσιν.

Ver. 22. *But it is the Lord that giveth me strength; God is strong, and God is my helper.* Heb., *But the Lord is my defence; and my God is the rock of my refuge.*

Ver. 23. *Hath put them to silence,* ܡܨܡܬ ܐܢܘܢ. A. V. *Shall cut them off,* יַצְמִיתֵם.

PSALM XCV.

A Psalm of David;—literally, when the people passed over Jordan; in which, also, *the Psalmist* sheweth the cutting off of the hope of the Jews; *I was wearied with this generation, so that I sware in my wrath, etc.*

1. O come, let us praise the Lord; and let us sing unto our God the Saviour.
2. Let us come before his presence with thanksgiving, and praise him with psalms.
3. For God is a great Lord, and a King that is great above all gods;
4. In whose hands are the foundations of the earth, and the height of the mountains.
5. The sea is his, and he made it, and his hands formed the dry *land*.
6. O come, let us kneel down and worship him, and let us bless the Lord that made us.
7. For he is our God, and we *are* his people, and the sheep of his pasture. To-day, if ye will hear his voice,
8. Harden not your hearts to anger him like the

Ps. xcv. Ver. 1. *And let us sing unto our God the Saviour.* Heb., *let us make a joyful noise to the Rock of our salvation.*

Ver. 4. *The foundations.* Heb., *the deep places.*

And *the height of the mountains*, ܪ̈ܘܡܬܐ ܕܛܘܪ̈ܐ. A. V. *The strength of the hills is his also,* וְתוֹעֲפֹת הָרִים לוֹ. LXX., τὰ ὕψη τῶν ὀρέων.

Ver. 7. *We are his people, and the sheep of his pasture.* Heb., *we are the people of his pasture, and the sheep of his hand.*

Ver. 8. *To anger him like the provocators.* Heb., *as in the provocation.*

provocators; and as *in* the day of temptation in the wilderness;

9. When your fathers tempted me, and proved *me and* saw my works forty years.

10. I was wearied with this generation, and said, It is a people whose heart doth err, and they have not known my ways;

11. So that I sware in my wrath that they should not enter into my rest.

PSALM XCVI.

A Psalm of David;—a prophecy concerning the coming of the Messiah, and the calling of the Gentiles that *should* believe in him.

1. O sing unto the Lord a new song; sing unto the Lord all the earth.

2. Sing unto the Lord, and bless his Name; shew forth his salvation from day to day.

3. Declare his glory among the heathen, and his works among all people.

4. For our Lord is great, and greatly to be praised; and *he is* to be feared above all gods.

Ver. 9. *Forty years.* The construction requires that these words be included in verse 9, though forming part of verse 10. They are construed with the words that follow them in the original.

Ver. 11. *So that,* ? اَنْ. A. V. *Unto whom,* אֲשֶׁר. LXX., ὡς.

Ps. XCVI. Ver. 3. *His works.* Heb., *his wonders.*

5. For all the gods of the heathen are vain; but the Lord made the heavens.

6. Majesty and glory are before him; strength and praise *are* in his sanctuary.

7. Give unto the Lord, O ye kindreds of the people; give unto the Lord praise and glory.

8. Give unto the Lord the glory *due* unto his Name; bring presents, and come into his courts.

9. Worship the Lord in the court of his holiness; let all the earth tremble before him.

10. Say among the heathen that the Lord reigneth, and hath established the world that it shall not be moved; he shall judge the people righteously.

11. Let the heavens rejoice, and let the earth be glad; let the sea exult, with the fulness thereof.

12. Let the fields glory, and all that is in them; then shall all the trees of the wood sing praise

13. Before the Lord, who cometh to judge the earth; he shall judge the world in righteousness, and the people with truth.

Ver. 5. *Are vain.* Heb., *are idols.*

Ver. 6. *Praise.* Heb., *beauty.*

Ver. 7. *Praise and glory.* Heb., *glory and strength.*

Ver. 9. *In the court of his holiness.* See note to Ps. XXIX. verse 2.

Ver. 11. *Exult.* Heb., *roar.*

Ver. 12. *Glory.* Heb., *be joyful.* The Syriac word here is ܢܷܫܒ݂ܚܘܼܢ.

Ver. 13. *Who cometh.* Heb., *for he cometh; for he cometh.*

PSALM XCVII.

A Psalm of David,—in which he prophesies concerning the coming of the Messiah, and in which, also, he alludes to his revelation at the last.

1. The Lord reigneth, let the earth rejoice; let the multitude of the isles be glad *thereof*.
2. Clouds and darkness *are* round about him; in righteousness and judgment his throne is established.
3. A fire shall consume before him, and burn up his enemies.
4. His lightnings enlightened the world; the earth saw, and was troubled;
5. And the hills melted like wax at the presence of the Lord, *who is* the Lord of the whole earth.
6. The heavens have shewed his righteousness, and all the people have seen his glory.
7. Confounded be all they that serve idols, and boast themselves in graven images; worship him all *ye* his angels.
8. Zion shall hear and rejoice, and the daughters

Ps. XCVII. Ver. 2. *In righteousness and judgment his throne is established.* See note to Ps. LXXXIX. verse 14.

Ver. 3. *Shall consume before him.* Heb., *goeth before him.*

And burn up his enemies. Heb., *and burneth up his enemies round about.*

Ver. 5. *Who is the Lord of the whole earth.* Heb., *at the presence of the Lord of the whole earth.*

Ver. 7. *All ye his angels,* ܠܟܠܗܘܢ ܡܠܐܟܘܗܝ. A.V. *All ye gods,* כָּל־אֱלֹהִים. LXX., πάντες ἄγγελοι αὐτοῦ.

of Judah shall be glad, because of thy judgments, O Lord.

9. For thou art the Lord most High over all the earth, and thou art exalted far above all gods.

10. They that love the Lord hate that which is evil; and he preserveth the souls of his saints, and shall deliver them from the hand of the wicked.

11. *There is* a light which hath sprung up for the righteous, and gladness for the upright in heart.

12. Rejoice in the Lord, O ye righteous, and give thanks at the remembrance of his holiness.

PSALM XCVIII.

A Psalm of David; — concerning the deliverance of the people from Egypt, when they triumphed and prevailed; and, spiritually, a prophecy concerning the coming of the Messiah, and the calling of the Gentiles to the Faith.

1. O sing unto the Lord a new song, for he hath done a marvellous thing; his right hand, and his holy arm, hath gotten him the victory.

2. The Lord hath made known his salvation, and his righteousness hath he openly shewed in the sight of the heathen.

Ver. 10. *They that love the Lord hate that which is evil,* ܐܣܚܡܘܢ ܘܡܟ݁ܢܝ ܣܢܬܝ ܠܒܝܫܐ. A. V. *Ye that love the Lord, hate evil,* אֹהֲבֵי יְהֹוָה שִׂנְאוּ רָע. The translator read שְׂנָאוּ רָע.

Ver. 11. *Hath sprung up,* ܢܕܢܚ. A. V. *Is sown,* זָרֻעַ. LXX., ἀνέτειλε. Both translators seem to have read זָרַח.

3. He hath remembered his mercy and his truth toward the house of Israel, and all the ends of the earth have seen the salvation of our God.

4. Praise the Lord, all the earth; make a loud noise, and sing and give praise.

5. Sing unto the Lord with the harp, and the voice of a psalm;

6. And with the sound of trumpets make a joyful noise before the King, the Lord.

7. Let the sea be moved, with the fulness thereof; the world, and all that dwell therein.

8. Let the floods clap their hands together, and let the hills rejoice

9. Before the Lord, who cometh to judge the earth; with truth shall he judge the world, and the people with equity.

Ps. xcviii. In verse 5 of the Hebrew, the words *with the harp* are repeated at the beginning of the second hemistich.

Ver. 6. *And with the sound of trumpets.* Heb., *With trumpets and sound of cornet.*

Ver. 7. *Be moved,* ܢܕܘܠ. A. V. *Roar,* יִרְעַם. LXX., σαλευθήτω. Some conjecture that the translators read יִרְעַם, or יְעַשׁ.

In verse 8, according to the accentuation of the Hebrew, the word *together* is construed with the second hemistich.

PSALM XCIX.

A Psalm of David, — concerning the destruction of the Midianites, whom Moses and the people of Israel led away captive; a prophecy, also, of the glory of the Messiah's kingdom.

1. The Lord reigneth, let the people tremble; he sitteth upon the Cherubim, let the earth be moved.
2. The Lord *is* great in Zion, and high above all people.
3. Let them praise thy great and terrible Name, for it is holy.
4. The King's strength loveth judgment; thou hast established equity and judgment, and thou hast executed righteousness in Jacob.
5. Exalt ye the Lord our God, and worship at his footstool.
6. Moses is *his* saint, and Aaron among his priests, and Samuel among them that call upon his Name; who called upon the Lord, and he answered them;

Ps. xcix. Ver. 1. *Upon,* ܒ, not in the Hebrew, but corresponding to the word *between,* supplied in the authorized version.

Ver. 4. *Thou hast established equity and judgment, and thou hast executed righteousness in Jacob.* Heb., *thou dost establish equity; thou executest judgment and righteousness in Jacob.*

Ver. 6. *Moses is his saint, and Aaron among his priests,* ܘܫܡܘܐܝܠ ܒܩܪܝܝ ܫܡܗ ܘܐܗܪܘܢ ܒܝܬ ܟܗܢܘܗܝ. A. V. *For he is holy. Moses and Aaron among his priests,* משֶׁה הוּא : קָדוֹשׁ וְאַהֲרֹן בְּכֹהֲנָיו. The difference here arises entirely from punctuation or accentuation, the words being identical. In the Syriac, the words ܘܩܕܝܫ ܗܘ, *is holy,* or *is his saint,* are connected with the verse following, and I have placed them accordingly.

7. And spake unto them in the cloudy pillar; they kept his testimony, and the covenant that he gave them.

8. Thou answeredst them, O Lord our God; thou wast unto them an avenging God; requite them according to their deeds.

9. Exalt the Lord our God, and worship at his holy hill; for the Lord our God is holy.

PSALM C.

Anonymous. — Concerning Joshua, the son of Nun, when he had brought to an end the war of the Ammonites; and, in the New Gospel, concerning the conversion of the Gentiles to the Faith.

1. O, sing praises unto the Lord, all ye lands.
2. Serve the Lord with gladness; come before his presence with a song.
3. Know ye that he is the Lord our God, and he

The translator doubtless was influenced, in making his version, by the historical difficulty that Moses was not a priest in strictness of language, like his brother Aaron.

Ver. 8. *Thou wast unto them an avenging God; requite them according to their deeds,* ܟܐܢܐ ܐܚܕܬ ܠܗܘܢ ܟܕ ܐܠܗܐ ܗܘܝܬ ܠܗܘܢ. ܐܦܪܥ ܐܢܘܢ ܐܝܟ ܚܛܗܝܗܘܢ. A. V. *Thou wast a God that forgavest them, though thou tookest vengeance of their inventions,* אֵל נֹשֵׂא הָיִיתָ לָהֶם וְנֹקֵם עַל־עֲלִילוֹתָם.

Ps. c. Ver. 3. *That he is the Lord our God.* Heb., *that the Lord he is God.*

it is *that* hath made us, and not we ourselves; we *are* his people, and the sheep of his pasture.

4. Enter into his gates with thanksgiving, and into his courts with praise; be thankful unto him, and bless his Name.

5. For the Lord is good, and his mercy *is* everlasting; and his truth *endureth* to all generations.

PSALM CI.

A Psalm of Asaph. — An exhortation of David with reference to those things that are becoming the ministry of the Lord's house; and a prophecy of the glory of him that is pure and perfect in God.

1. I will sing of mercy and judgment, and unto thee, O Lord, will I sing;

2. And I will walk in thy way without blemish. Until when wilt thou *not* come unto me? I have walked within my house in the integrity of my heart;

3. And I have set no wicked thing before mine eyes: I have hated him that doeth evil, and *such an one* hath not cleaved unto me.

4. An evil heart hath departed from me, and I have not known a wicked thing.

Ps. ci. Ver. 2. *And I will walk in thy way without blemish.* Heb., *I will behave myself wisely in a perfect way.*

Ver. 3. *I have hated him that doeth evil.* Heb., *I hate the work of them that turn aside.*

Ver. 4. *And I have not known a wicked thing.* Heb., *I will not know a wicked person.*

5. Whoso privily slandereth his neighbour, him have I destroyed; with him that hath an high look and a proud heart I have not eaten.

6. Mine eyes *shall be* upon the faithful of the land, that they may dwell with me; whoso walketh in the way without blemish, he shall serve me.

7. He that worked deceit shall not dwell within my house; and the lying word shall not be confirmed before mine eyes.

8. I will early put to silence all the wicked of the land, and I will destroy all the workers of iniquity from the city of the Lord.

PSALM CII.

Anonymous. — The lamentation of the Jews, and a prophecy concerning a new people, *even* the Gentiles, by faith.

1. Hear my prayer, O Lord, and let my cry come unto thee.

2. Turn not away thy face from me in the day of mine affliction; but incline thine ear unto me in the day that I call upon thee, and speedily answer me.

Ver. 5. *With him I have not eaten,* ܟܠܝܗ̄ ܠܐ ܐܟܠܬ. A. V. *Him will not I suffer,* אוֹתוֹ לֹא אוּכָל. The translator read אִתּוֹ לֹא אוֹכֵל. So the LXX. have τούτῳ οὐ συνήσθιον.

Ver. 7. *And the lying word shall not be confirmed before mine eyes,* ܘܡܡܠܠ ܕܓܠܐ ܠܐ ܢܬܩܝܡ ܩܕܡ ܥܝܢܝ̈. A. V. *He that telleth lies shall not tarry in my sight,* דֹּבֵר שְׁקָרִים לֹא־יִכּוֹן לְנֶגֶד עֵינָי. The translator read דָּבָר instead of דֹּבֵר.

3. For my days are consumed in smoke, and my bones are whitened like an hearth.

4. My heart is dried like grass, and withered, for I have forgotten the eating of my bread;

5. And by reason of the voice of my groanings, my skin cleaveth to my bones.

6. Yea, I am become like a pelican that is in the wilderness; and I am like an owl in the desert.

7. I have gone apart, and am alone like a sparrow that flieth upon the house-top.

8. Mine enemies reproach me all the day, and they that praise me are sworn against me.

9. For I have eaten ashes like bread, and mingled my drink with weeping;

Ps. CII. Ver. 3. *Are whitened*, ܢܚܪܘ. A. V. *Are burned*, נִחָֽרוּ.

Ver. 4. *My heart is dried like grass, and withered.* Heb., *My heart is smitten, and withered like grass.*

The eating of my bread, ܡܐܟܘܠܬܐ ܕܠܚܡܝ. A. V. *To eat my bread*, מֵאֲכֹל לַחְמִי. The translator probably read מַאֲכַל.

Ver. 5. *My skin cleaveth to my bones.* Heb., *my bones cleave to my skin.*

Ver. 7. *I have gone apart*, ܣܗܕܬ. A. V. *I watch*, שָׁקַדְתִּי.

And am alone like a sparrow that flieth upon the house-top, ܘܗܘܝܬ ܐܝܟ ܨܦܪܐ ܕܦܪܚܐ ܒܠܚܘܕܝܗ ܐܓܪܐ. A. V. *And am as a sparrow alone upon the house-top*, וָאֶהְיֶה כְּצִפּוֹר בּוֹדֵד עַל־גָּג. For בּוֹדֵד the translator read נוֹדֵד.

Ver. 8. *And they that praise me*, ܡܫܒܚܢܝ. A. V. *They that are mad against me*, מְהוֹלָלַי. The translator read מְהַלְלַי, as did the LXX., who have οἱ ἐπαινοῦντές με.

10. Because of thine indignation and wrath; for thou hast lifted me up and cast me down;

11. And my days have declined like a shadow, and I am withered like grass.

12. But thou, O Lord, endurest forever, and thy remembrance to all generations.

13. Do thou arise, and have mercy upon Zion, for the time is come to have mercy upon her.

14. For thy servants take pleasure in her stones, and love the dust thereof.

15. *So* the heathen shall fear thy Name, O Lord, and all the kings of the earth thy majesty.

16. For the Lord buildeth up Zion, and appeareth in glory;

17. And turneth him unto the prayer of the poor, and despiseth not their prayer.

18. This shall be written for the generation to come, and the people that shall be created shall praise the Lord.

19. For he hath looked down from the height of his sanctuary; from heaven did the Lord behold the earth;

20. To hear the groaning of the prisoner, and to deliver the children from death;

21. That they might declare the Name of the Lord in Zion, and his praises in Jerusalem;

Ver. 11. *Have declined,* الْقَذِلَ. A. V. *That declineth,* נָטוּי; spoken of the shadow; for which the translator may have read נָטָיָה.

Ver. 13. *For the time is come to have mercy upon her.* Heb., *for the time to favour her, yea, the set time is come.*

Ver. 20. *The children from death.* Heb., *those that are appointed to death.*

22. When the people are gathered together, and the kingdoms to serve the Lord.

23. They brought down my strength in the earth; but do thou declare unto me the shortness of my days.

24. Take me not away in the midst of my days; and thy years *are* throughout all generations.

25. Of old hast thou established the earth, and the heavens *are* the work of thy hands.

26. They pass away, but thou endurest; yea, all of them wax old like a garment, and like a vesture shall they be changed;

27. But thou art as thou art, and thy years shall not fail.

28. The children, also, of thy servants shall dwell in the earth, and their seed shall be established before thee.

Ver. 23. *They brought down my strength in the earth.* Heb., *He weakened my strength in the way.*

But do thou declare unto me the shortness of my days, ܡܚܰܘܳܐ ܠܺܝ. ܘܰܢܣܰܩܳܟ݂ ܐܶܡܰܪ. The words ܚܰܘܳܐ ܠܺܝ, ܐܶܡܰܪ, forming part of verse 24, in the Hebrew, I have placed in the connection which their construction in the Syriac requires. The Hebrew is קִצַּר יָמָי : אֹמַר אֵלִי, *he shortened my days. I said, O my God.* The translator read הִקְצִיר יָמַי אֱמֹר אֵלַי. The version of the LXX. corresponds with the Syriac: τὴν ὀλιγότητα τῶν ἡμερῶν μου ἀνάγγειλόν μοι.

Ver. 26. *Shall they be changed.* Heb., *shalt thou change them, and they shall be changed.*

Ver. 27. *But thou art as thou art.* Heb., *But thou art the same.*

Ver. 28. *Shall dwell in the earth.* Heb., *shall continue.*

PSALM CIII.

A Psalm of David; — concerning his loss of warmth and vitality in old age; and, again, instruction and thanksgiving from the men of God.

1. Bless the Lord, O my soul, and all my bones, *bless ye* his holy Name.
2. Bless the Lord, O my soul; and forget not all his benefits.
3. Who forgiveth thee all thine iniquity, and healeth all thy diseases;
4. *Who* saveth thee from destruction, *and* supporteth thee with loving-kindness and tender mercies;
5. Satisfying thy body with good things, and renewing thy youth like the eagle's.
6. The Lord executeth righteousness and judgment for all *that are* oppressed.
7. He shewed his ways unto Moses, and his acts unto the children of Israel.
8. The Lord is merciful and gracious, long suffering and plenteous in his mercy.
9. For he is not alway displeased; neither keepeth he his anger forever.
10. For he hath not dealt with us after our sins; neither hath he rewarded us according to our iniquity.

Ps. CIII. Ver. 1. *And all my bones*, ܟܠܗܘܢ ܓܪ̈ܡܝ.
A. v. *And all that is within me*, וְכָל־קְרָבַי.
Ver. 4. *Who saveth thee.* Heb., *Who redeemeth thy life.*
And supporteth thee. Heb., *who crowneth thee.*
Ver. 5. *Thy body.* Heb., *thy mouth.*

11. For as the heavens are high above the earth, so great is his mercy toward them that fear him;

12. And as far as the east is from the west, so far hath he removed our iniquity from us;

13. And like as a father pitieth *his* children, *so* the Lord pitieth them that fear him.

14. For he knoweth our substance; and he remembereth that we *are* dust.

15. *As for* man, his days *are* as grass; and as a flower of the field, so he flourisheth;

16. Upon which when the wind bloweth, it is gone; neither is the place thereof known any more.

17. *But* the mercy of the Lord is from everlasting, even unto everlasting, upon them that fear him; and his righteousness unto children's children;

18. To them that keep his covenant, and remember his commandments, and do them.

19. *As for* the Lord, his throne is established in the heavens, and his kingdom ruleth over all.

20. Bless the Lord, ye angels of his that excel in strength, and keep his commandments.

21. Bless the Lord, all ye his hosts, and *ye* ministers of his that do his pleasure.

22. Bless the Lord, all *ye* works of his, whose dominion is in all the earth; bless the Lord, O my soul.

Ver. 16. *Neither is the place thereof known any more.* Heb., *and the place thereof shall know it no more.*

Ver. 19. *His throne is established.* Heb., *hath prepared his throne.*

Ver. 20. The words לִשְׁמֹעַ בְּקוֹל דְּבָרוֹ, *hearkening unto the voice of his word,* forming part of this verse in the original, are not translated.

Ver. 22. *Whose dominion is in all the earth.* Heb., *in all places of his dominion.*

(LAUD, AND THE BEGINNING OF THE GRADE.)

PSALM CIV.

A Psalm of David;—when he went with the priests to worship before the Ark of the Lord; and in which he teacheth us confession and prayer, and alludeth to the first constitution of created things, and unfoldeth truth concerning the angels.

1. Bless the Lord, O my soul. The Lord my God is exceeding great; he is clothed with majesty and honour;

2. And he is covered *with* light, as *with* a garment; he hath stretched out the heavens like a curtain.

3. He hath built his chambers in the waters, and placed his chariot upon the clouds; and he walketh upon the wings of the wind.

4. He hath made his angels spirit, and his ministers a flaming fire.

5. He hath established the earth upon its foundations, that it should not be removed forever.

Ps. CIV. Ver. 1. *Is exceeding great.* Heb., *thou art very great.*
He is clothed. Heb., *thou art clothed.*
Ver. 2. *And he is covered.* Heb., *Who coverest thyself.*
He hath stretched out. Heb., *who stretchest out.*
Ver. 3. *He hath built*, ܚܫܟ. A. V. *Who layeth the beams*, הַמְקָרֶה.
And placed his chariot upon the clouds, ܘܣܡ ܠܐ ܥܢܢܐ ܟܒܟܒܗ. A. V. *Who maketh the clouds his chariot*, חָשׂם עָבִים רְכוּבוֹ.
Ver. 4. *He hath made.* Heb., *Who maketh.*
Spirit, ܪܘܚܝ. A. V. *Spirits*, רוּחוֹת.

6. Thou coveredst it with the deep, as *with* a garment; and the waters stood above the mountains.

7. At thy rebuke, they flee; and at the voice of thy thunders they are afraid.

8. They went up *as high as* the mountains, and down to the valleys *beneath*, unto the place which thou hast appointed for them.

9. Thou hast set them a bound, that they may not pass over and cover the earth.

10. Thou hast sent the springs into the valleys, and they run among the hills.

11. They give drink to every beast of the field, and the wild asses that thirst are satisfied.

12. By them the fowls of the air have their habitation; *which* sing among the hills.

13. He watereth the hills from his chambers; the earth is satisfied with the fruits of thy works.

14. He causeth the grass to grow for the cattle, and herb for the service of man; that he may bring forth food out of the earth;

15. Wine *that* maketh glad the heart of man, and oil to make him a cheerful countenance, and bread *which* sustaineth man's heart.

Ver. 9. *And cover the earth.* Heb., *that they turn not again to cover the earth.*

Ver. 10. *Thou hast sent.* Heb., *He sendeth.*

Ver. 12. *Which sing among the hills,* ܡܢ ܒܝܢܬ ܣܘܟܐ ܢܬܠܘܢ ܩܠܐ. A. V. *Which sing among the branches,* בֵּין עֳפָאיִם יִתְּנוּ־קוֹל. It is conjectured that the translator, for עֳפָאיִם, read בֵּעֳפָאיִם, or כֵּפִים. The LXX. have ἐκ μέσου τῶν πετρῶν.

Ver. 15. *To make him a cheerful countenance.* Heb., *to make his face to shine.*

16. The trees of the Lord are full *of sap*, and the cedars of Lebanon which he hath planted.

17. There the birds make their nests, and *as for* the stork her nest *is* in the fir-trees.

18. The high hills for the wild goats, and the rocky clefts *are* a covert for the conies.

Section.

19. He appointed the moon for seasons; and the sun knoweth the time of his going down.

20. He maketh darkness, and it is night; and therein all the beasts of the forest do roam;

21. The lions, roaring after their prey, and seeking their meat from God.

22. When the sun ariseth they gather themselves together, and lay them down in their dens.

23. Man goeth forth unto his work, and to his labour, until the evening.

24. O Lord, how manifold are thy works! and in wisdom hast thou made them all, and the earth is full of thy riches.

25. *So is* this great and wide sea, wherein are things creeping innumerable; both great and small beasts.

26. Wherein also go the ships, and *where is* that Leviathan whom thou hast made to play thereupon.

27. These wait all upon thee, that thou mayest give them meat in their season.

Ver. 19. *The time of his going down.* Heb., *his going down.*

Ver. 20. *He maketh.* Heb., *Thou makest.*

Do roam, ܚܕܿܒ݂, literally, *pass through,* or *by.* LXX, διελεύσονται. A. V. *Do creep forth,* תִּרְמֹשׂ.

Ver. 26. *Thereupon,* ܒܓܘܗ. A. V. *Therein,* יִ֗בּ.

28. Thou givest *it* them, and they are nourished; thou openest thine hand, and they are satisfied.

29. Thou turnest away thy face, and they are troubled; thou takest away their breath, and they die, and return to their dust.

30. Thou sendest forth thy spirit, and they are created; and thou renewest the face of the earth.

31. The glory of the Lord shall endure forever; the Lord shall rejoice in his works;

32. Who looketh on the earth and it trembleth, and rebuketh the mountains and they smoke.

33. I will praise the Lord as long as I live, and I will sing unto my God while I have my being.

34. My praise shall be pleasant unto him, and I will be glad in the Lord.

35. But sinners shall be consumed out of the earth, and the unrighteous shall not remain in it. Bless thou the Lord, O my soul.

Ver. 28. *They are nourished.* Heb., *they gather.*
They are satisfied. Heb., *they are filled with good.*

Ver. 32. *Rebuketh,* طار. A. V. *He toucheth,* יִגַּע.

Ver. 34. *My praise shall be pleasant unto him,* ܐܪܚܩܡ ܟܗ ܠܡܚܒܫܘ. A. V. *My meditation of him shall be sweet,* יֶעֱרַב עָלָיו שִׂיחִי.

Ver. 35. *And the unrighteous shall not remain in it.* Heb., *and let the wicked be no more.*

The Psalm in Hebrew concludes with הַלְלוּ־יָהּ, *Praise ye the Lord.*

PSALM CV.

Anonymous;—in which allusion is made to the narrative, *Fear not, Jacob, to go down into Egypt;* and, spiritually, teaching us that we should not fear when any one of us goeth forth to contend with evil spirits; for God is our helper and fighteth for us.

1. O give thanks unto the Lord, and call upon his Name; and shew his deeds among the people.

2. Praise him, and sing unto him, and talk ye of all his wondrous works.

3. Praise his holy Name; let the heart of them rejoice that seek the Lord.

4. Seek the Lord, and be strong; and seek his face evermore.

5. Remember his marvellous works that he hath done; his wonders, and the judgments of his mouth;

6. O ye seed of Abraham his servant, and ye children of Jacob his chosen.

7. He is the Lord our God, whose judgments *are* in all the earth.

8. He hath remembered his covenant forever; the word which he commanded to a thousand generations.

9. For he confirmed his covenant with Abraham, and his oaths unto Isaac;

Ps. cv. Ver. 4. *And be strong,* وكُلِّبُوا. A. V. *And his strength,* וְעֻזּוֹ. The translator read וְעֻזּוּ. LXX, καὶ κραταιώθητε.

Ver. 9. *For he confirmed his covenant with Abraham, and his oaths unto Isaac.* Heb., *Which covenant he made with Abraham, and his oath unto Isaac.*

10. And his testimony unto Jacob; *that it might be for* an everlasting covenant unto Israel;

11. And said, Unto thee will I give the land of Canaan, the lines of your inheritance;

12. When ye were few in number; *when* ye were very few, and *when* ye were strangers in it.

13. They went from one nation to another, and from *one* kingdom to another people;

14. And he suffered no man to do them wrong; he reproved *even* kings for their sakes;

15. *Saying*, Touch not mine Anointed, and do my prophets no harm.

16. Moreover, he called for a famine upon the land, and brake all the staff of their corn.

17. He sent a man before them, *even* Joseph, *who* was sold into bondage.

18. They bound his feet with fetters, and he was laid in iron:

19. Until his word was confirmed; the word of the Lord tried him.

20. The king sent and loosed him, and made him ruler over his people,

Ver. 10. *And his testimony unto Jacob; that it might be for an everlasting covenant unto Israel.* Heb., *And confirmed the same unto Jacob for a law, and to Israel for an everlasting covenant.*

Ver. 12. *When ye were few in number; when ye were very few, and when ye were strangers in it.* Heb., *When they were but a few men in number; yea, very few, and strangers in it.*

Ver. 18. *They bound.* Heb., *they hurt.*

Ver. 19. *Until his word was confirmed.* Heb., *Until the time that his word came.*

Ver. 20. *And made him ruler over his people.* Heb., *even the ruler of the people, and let him go free.*

21. Lord over his house, and ruler of all his substance;

22. That he might chastise *his* princes according to his will, and teach *his* senators wisdom.

Section.

23. Israel also came into Egypt, and Jacob sojourned in the tent of Ham.

24. He increased his people greatly, and made them stronger than their enemies.

25. And he turned their heart to hate his people, and to deal craftily against his servants.

26. He sent Moses his servant, and Aaron whom he had chosen.

27. He shewed his signs by them, and his wonders in the land of Ham.

28. He sent darkness, and made it dark, and they provoked *him by disobedience to* his word.

Ver. 21, in the Hebrew, commences with שָׂמוֹ, '*He made him;* not in the Syriac.

Ver. 22. *That he might chastise,* לֶאְסֹר. A. V. *To bind,* לֶאְסֹר. LXX., τοῦ παιδεῦσαι. Both translators derived the Hebrew word from יָסַר.

Ver. 23. *In the tent.* Heb., *in the land.*

Ver. 27. *He shewed his signs by them.* Heb., *They shewed his signs among them.*

Ver. 28. *And they provoked him by disobedience to his word,* ܘܠܐ ܡܪܕܘ ܥܠ ܡܠܬܗ. A. V. *And they rebelled not against his word,* וְלֹא מָרוּ אֶת־דְּבָרוֹ. LXX., καὶ παρεπίκραναν τοὺς λόγους αὐτοῦ. In both translations the negative was dropped, and the Hebrew verb was derived from מָרַר, *to be bitter,* and not from מָרָה, *to rebel.*

29. He turned their waters into blood, and slew their fish.

30. He made the frogs to abound in their land, even in the chambers of their kings.

31. He spake, and there came all manner of flies, and gnats in all their coasts.

32. He made their rain *to be* hail, and a fire was kindled in their land.

33. He smote their vines and their fig-trees, and brake the trees of their coasts.

34. He spake, and the locusts came, and caterpillars without number, throughout their land.

35. They did eat up all the herbs, and *devoured* the fruits of their ground.

36. He slew all the first-born of Egypt; the chief of all their progeny.

37. He brought them forth with silver and gold, and there was not one among their tribes that was feeble.

38. Egypt was glad at their departing, for the fear of them fell upon them.

39. He spread a cloud around them, and covered them; and fire to give light in the night.

Ver. 32. *And a fire was kindled in their land.* Heb., *and flaming fire in their land.*

Ver. 34. *Throughout their land.* This, in the Hebrew, forms part of the first hemistich of verse 35.

Ver. 35. *And devoured.* I have supplied here what is expressed in the Hebrew by ויאכל.

Ver. 36. *Of Egypt.* Heb., *in their land.*

Their progeny. Heb., *their strength.*

Ver. 39. *He spread a cloud around them, and covered them.* Heb., *He spread a cloud for a covering.*

40. They asked, and he brought them food, and satisfied them with the bread of heaven.

41. He opened the rock, and the waters gushed out; yea, the waters ran in a dry place.

42. For he remembered his holy promise, that Abraham *should be* his servant.

43. He brought forth his people with joy, and his young men with a song;

44. And gave them the lands of the heathen, and they inherited the labour of the people;

45. That they might observe his statutes, and keep his law.

Ver. 40. *Food.* Heb., *quails.*

Ver. 41. *The waters ran in a dry place.* Heb., *they ran in the dry places like a river.*

Ver. 42. *That Abraham should be his servant,* ܘܐܒܪܗܡ ܠܥܒܕܗ. A. V. *And Abraham his servant,* אֶת־אַבְרָהָם עַבְדּוֹ.

Ver. 43. *And his young men with a song,* ܠܥܠܝܡܘܗܝ ܒܬܫܒܘܚܬܐ. A. V. *And his chosen with gladness,* בְּרִנָּה אֶת־בְּחִירָיו. The translator seems to have read אֶת־בַּחוּרָיו, though the words are kindred in signification.

This Psalm ends in Hebrew with Hallelujah.

PSALM CVI.

Anonymous.—*The Psalmist* admonishes them concerning the commandments of the Lord, and teaches us, that, as the Jews sinned, so we should be greatly afraid; that we should not speak in church, nor contend with our brethren for any cause whatever, and especially when we stand, in the time of the Mysteries and of Prayer; and that when we sin, we should repent.

1. O give thanks unto the Lord, for he is good, and his mercy *endureth* forever.

2. Who can narrate the wondrous works of the Lord, and shew forth all his praises?

3. Blessed are they that keep his judgments, and execute his righteousness at all times.

4. Remember us, O Lord, with the favour *that thou bearest unto* thy people; visit us with thy salvation;

5. That we may see the good things of thy chosen; *that* we may rejoice in thy joy, and glory with thine inheritance.

6. We have sinned with our fathers; and we have committed iniquity, and done wickedly.

7. Our fathers understood not thy wonders in Egypt, and they remembered not the multitude of thy mercies, but contended by the waters, *even* at the Red Sea.

Ps. CVI. This Psalm begins in Hebrew with the Hallelujah.

Ver. 4. In the Hebrew the pronominal suffixes are first person singular instead of plural.

Ver. 5. In this verse, also, in the Hebrew, the subject is first person singular instead of plural. One version, however, agrees with the Hebrew.

In thy joy. Heb., *in the gladness of thy nation.*

Ver. 7. *But contended by the waters.* Heb., *but provoked him at the sea.*

8. Nevertheless he saved them for his Name's sake, that he might make his mighty power to be known.

9. He rebuked the Red Sea, also, and it was dried up; so he led them through the deep as through a wilderness;

10. And he saved them from the hand of the enemy, and delivered them from the hand of the oppressor;

11. And the waters covered their oppressors, and there was not one of them left.

12. *Then* believed they his words, and sang his praises.

13. *But* they soon forgat God, and waited not for his counsel.

14. They lusted exceedingly in the wilderness, and tempted God in the desert.

15. He gave them their requests, and sent satiety into their souls.

16. And they envied Moses *in* the camp, and Aaron the saint of the Lord.

17. The earth was opened, and swallowed up Dathan, and covered the congregation of Abiram.

18. A fire was kindled in their companies, and a flame burnt up the unrighteous.

19. They made a calf in Horeb, and worshipped the molten image.

20. Thus they changed their glory into the similitude of an ox that eateth grass;

21. And they forgat God who had delivered them; who had done great things in Egypt;

Ver. 13. *But they soon forgat God.* Heb., *They soon forgat his works.*

Ver. 15. *Satiety,* ܣܒܥܐ. A. V. *Leanness,* רָזוֹן. LXX., πλησμονὴν.

22. And wondrous works in the land of Ham, and fearful things at the Red Sea.

23. Therefore he said that he would destroy them;

Section.

had *it* not *been for* Moses his chosen, who stood before him in the breach, and turned away his anger, that he should not destroy them.

24. Yea, they despised the pleasant land, and believed not his word;

25. But they murmured in their tents, and hearkened not unto the voice of the Lord.

26. Therefore he lifted up his hand against them, that he might destroy them in the wilderness;

27. And that he might scatter their seed among the nations, and destroy them in the lands.

28. Because they were joined unto the idols of Peor, and ate the sacrifices of the dead.

29. Thus they angered him by their works, and provoked him to jealousy with their idols; and suddenly the plague prevailed among them.

30. *Then* stood up Phinehas and prayed, and *so* the plague was stayed;

Ver. 28. *Because they were joined unto the idols of Peor*, ܟܠ ܘܐܬܢܩܦܘ ܠܟܡܘܫ̈ܐ ܕܦܥܘܪ. A. V. *They joined themselves, also, unto Baal-peor*, וַיִּצָּמְדוּ לְבַעַל פְּעוֹר.

Ver. 29. *And provoked him to jealousy with their idols.* This is not in the Hebrew.

And suddenly the plague prevailed among them. Heb., *and the plague brake in upon them.*

Ver. 30. *And prayed*, ܘܨܠܝ. A. V. *And executed judgment*, וַיְפַלֵּל. The Hebrew verb in another conjugation means *to pray.* LXX., καὶ ἐξιλάσατο.

31. And righteousness was counted unto him, unto all generations and for evermore.

32. They angered him, also, at the waters of strife, so that he did evil unto Moses for their sakes;

33. Because they provoked his spirit, so that he spake with his lips;

34. And they did not destroy the nations concerning whom the Lord commanded them;

35. But were mingled among the heathen, and learned their works;

36. And worshipped their idols, which were a snare unto them.

37. They sacrificed their sons and their daughters unto devils;

38. And shed innocent blood, *even* the blood of their sons and of their daughters; *whom* they sacrificed unto the idols of Canaan, and the land was polluted with blood.

39. Thus were they defiled with their own works, and went a-whoring with their own inventions.

40. Therefore the wrath of the Lord waxed hot against his people, insomuch that he abhorred his own inheritance;

41. And he delivered them into the hand of the heathen, and they that hated them ruled over them.

42. Their enemies also oppressed them, and they were brought into subjection under their hands.

43. Many times did he deliver them, *but* they pro-

Ver. 31. *And righteousness was counted unto him.* Heb., *And that was counted unto him for righteousness.*

Ver. 33. *So that he spake,* ܘܡܠܠ. A. V. *So that he spake unadvisedly,* וַיְבַטֵּא.

voked him with their counsels, and were brought low for their iniquity.

44. Nevertheless he regarded their afflictions, and listened to their supplication;

45. And he remembered his covenant, and had mercy upon them; and led them according to the multitude of his mercies.

46. He made them also to be pitied of all those that carried them captives.

47. Save us, O Lord God, and gather us from among the heathen, that we may give thanks unto thy holy Name, and glory with thine inheritance.

48. Blessed is the Lord God of Israel, from everlasting to everlasting; and let all the people say, Amen, Amen.

Ver. 45. *And he remembered his covenant and had mercy upon them.* Heb., *And he remembered for them his covenant.*

And led them, ܘܢܚܡ ܐܢܘܢ. A. V. *And repented,* וַיִּנָּחֶם. The translator doubtless read, וַיְנַחֲמֵם.

Ver. 47. *With thine inheritance.* Heb., *in thy praise.*

Ver. 48. *Amen, Amen.* Heb., *Amen. Hallelujah.* LXX., γένοιτο, γένοιτο.

END OF THE FOURTH BOOK.

THE FIFTH BOOK.

PSALM CVII.

Anonymous. — Written concerning Joel and Abiah, the sons of Samuel, who corrupted the commandments of the Lord. *Intimating, also, that as* God gathered the Jews from the captivity, and brought them up from Babylon, so God, the Only Begotten Son, Jesus the Messiah, gathered the Gentiles from the four corners *of the earth* by preaching unto Baptism.

1. O give thanks unto the Lord, for he is good, and his mercy *endureth* forever.

2. Let the redeemed of the Lord *so* say, whom he hath redeemed from the hand of the oppressor;

3. And gathered them out of all lands, from the east, and from the west, and from the north, and from the south.

4. They wandered in a wilderness of solitude, and found not the way to a city to dwell in.

Ps. CVII. Ver. 4. *They wandered in a wilderness of solitude, and found not the way to a city to dwell in,* ܡܕܝܢܬܐ ܚܕ ܠܡܥܡܪ ܒܗ. ܘܐܫܬܥܝܘ . ܒܐܘܪܚܐ ܐܥܝܗܘܢ ܘܠܐ ܐܕܟܘ ܠܝ ܡܟܣܐ.
A. V. *They wandered in the wilderness in a solitary way; they found no city to dwell in,* תָּעוּ בַמִּדְבָּר בִּישִׁימוֹן דָּרֶךְ עִיר מוֹשָׁב לֹא מָצָאוּ. In the Hebrew, the words דֶּרֶךְ, *a way,* and יְשִׁימוֹן, *solitude, or solitary,* are connected by the accent; in the

5. They hungered and thirsted, and their soul fainted *in them*.

6. They sought the Lord in their afflictions, and he brought them out of their distresses;

7. And caused them to walk in a true way, that they might go to cities of habitation.

8. Let his saints praise the Lord, whose mercies *are shewn* to the children of men.

9. For he hath satisfied the fainting souls, and filled the hungry soul,

10. Of such as sit in darkness, and in the shadows of death, and are bound in poverty and iron;

11. Because they provoked the word of God, and despised the counsel of the most High.

12. He brake their heart with labour; they were weakened, and there was none to help them.

Syriac they are separated by copula. The version of the LXX. is like the Syriac; ἐπλανήθησαν ἐν τῇ ἐρήμῳ ἐν ἀνύδρῳ · ὁδὸν πόλεως κατοικητηρίου οὐχ εὗρον.

Ver. 8. Let his saints praise the Lord, whose mercies are shewn to the children of men. Heb., *Oh that men would praise the Lord for his goodness, and for his wonderful works to the children of men.* The Hebrew of the first hemistich is, יוֹדוּ לַיהוָה חַסְדּוֹ; for which the translator seems to have read יוֹדוּ לַיהוָה חֲסִידָיו.

Ver. 9. And filled the hungry soul. Heb., *and filleth the hungry soul with goodness.*

Ver. 10. Of such as sit. Heb., *Such as sit.*

In poverty, ܒܚܣܟܘܒܐ. A. V. *In affliction,* עֳנִי. LXX., ἐν πτωχείᾳ.

Ver. 11. They provoked. See note to Ps. cv., verse 28.

Ver. 12. He brake. Heb., *Therefore he brought down.*
They were weakened. Heb., *they fell down.*

13. They prayed unto the Lord in their distresses, and he delivered them from their afflictions;

14. And brought them out of darkness and the shadows of death, and brake their bands in sunder.

15. Let his saints praise the Lord, whose mercies *are shewn* to the children of men.

16. For he hath broken the gates of brass, and cut the bars of iron in sunder.

17. He helped them, *and led them* from the way of their sins, for they were brought low through their iniquity;

18. And their soul abhorred all manner of meat, and they drew near unto the gates of death.

19. They sought the Lord in their afflictions, and he brought them out of their distresses.

20. He sent his word, and healed them, and delivered them from destruction.

21. Let his saints praise the Lord, whose mercies *are shewn* to the children of men.

Section.

22. Offer him the sacrifices of praise; praise ye his works with his wonders.

Ver. 17. *He helped them, and led them from the way of their sins,* ܟܒܪ ܐܢܘܢ ܦܨܝ ܐܢܘܢ ܡܢ ܐܘܪܚܐ ܕܚܛܗܝܗܘܢ. A. V. *Fools, because of their transgression,* אֱוִלִים מִדֶּרֶךְ פִּשְׁעָם. The word אֱוִלִים, *fools,* the translator derived from the root אָהַל, or אָיַל, signifying *to be strong;* or he read חוֹעִילָם. So the LXX., who have ἀντελάβετο αὐτῶν ἐξ ὁδοῦ ἀνομίας αὐτῶν.

Ver. 22. *Offer him the sacrifices of praise; praise ye his works with his wonders.* Heb., *And let them sacrifice the sacrifices of thanksgiving, and declare his works with rejoicing.*

23. They that go down to the sea in ships, and do business in great waters;

24. These see the works of the Lord, and his wonders in the depths of the sea.

25. For he raiseth the stormy wind, and the waves of the sea are lifted up.

26. They mount up to the heaven, and they go down again to the deep, and their soul fainteth within them.

27. They reel to and fro, and stagger like drunken men, and are at their wit's end.

28. They cry unto the Lord in their afflictions, and he bringeth them out of their distresses.

29. He maketh the storm to cease, and it is calm; and the waves of the sea are still.

30. Then are they glad, when they be quiet; *so he* bringeth them to the haven which they desire.

31. Let his saints praise the Lord, whose mercies *are shewn* to the children of men.

32. Praise him in the congregation of the people; and exalt him upon the seat of the elders.

33. Who maketh rivers *to be* like a wilderness, and the watersprings a dry ground;

Ver. 25. *For he raiseth.* Heb., *For he commandeth and raiseth.*

Ver. 26. *Fainteth within them.* Heb., *is melted because of trouble.*

Ver. 27. *And are at their wit's end.* This is rather a free translation. The Hebrew literally is, *and all their wisdom is swallowed up;* the Syriac, *and all their wisdom perisheth.*

Ver. 29. *The waves of the sea.* Heb., *the waves thereof.*

Ver. 32. *And exalt him upon the seat of the elders.* Heb., *and praise him in the assembly of the elders.* The words translated *seat* and *assembly* are the same; but their meaning will depend upon the preposition used in connection with them.

34. A fruit-yielding land to be barrenness, for the evil deeds of them that dwell therein.

35. Who maketh the wilderness a standing water, and dry ground, fountains of water.

36. There he maketh the hungry to dwell; and they build cities, and dwell therein.

37. They sow fields, and plant vineyards, and eat of the fruits of their increase.

38. He blesseth them so that they are multiplied greatly, and their cattle are not decreased.

39. Again they are minished and brought low, through greatness of evil and sorrow.

40. He casteth evil upon rulers, and causeth them to wander in a pathless desert, where *is* no way.

41. Yet strengtheneth he the poor, and maketh their families like flocks of sheep;

42. That the righteous may see *it*, and rejoice, and all the unrighteous may stop their mouth.

43. He that *is* wise shall observe these things, and he shall know the loving-kindness of the Lord.

Ver. 36. *And they build cities, and dwell therein.* Heb., *that they may prepare a city for habitation.*

Ver. 37. *And eat of the fruits of their increase.* Heb., *which may yield fruits of increase.*

Ver. 39. *Through greatness of evil and sorrow.* Heb., *through oppression, affliction, and sorrow.*

Ver. 41. *Yet strengtheneth he.* Heb., *Yet setteth he on high from affliction.*

And maketh their families like flocks of sheep. Heb., *and maketh him families like a flock.*

Ver. 42. *The unrighteous.* Heb., *iniquity.*

(LAUD, AND THE BEGINNING OF THE GRADE.)

PSALM CVIII.

A Psalm of David; — when he was prepared with a song for the ministry and psalmody of the House of the Lord; also, *containing an allusion to* the calling of the Gentiles.

1. My heart is prepared, O God, my heart is prepared; I will give praise, and sing with my glory.
2. Awake, my harp; awake, psaltery and harp; I, also, myself am awakened right early.
3. I will praise thee, O God, among the people, and I will sing unto thy Name among the nations.
4. For thy mercy is great, *and reacheth* unto the heavens, and thy truth unto the heaven of heavens.
5. Be thou exalted, O God, above the heavens; and thy glory above all the earth.
6. Wherefore, that thy beloved may be delivered, save me with thy right hand, and answer me.
7. God hath spoken in his holiness; I will rejoice, and I will divide Shechem, and mete out the valley of Succoth.
8. Gilead is mine, and Manasseh is mine; Ephraim *is* the strengthener of mine head; Judah *is* my king;
9. Moab *is* my washpot; upon Edom will I unloose my shoes, and over Philistia will I triumph.
10. Who will bring me into the strong city? and who will lead me into Edom?
11. For lo, thou, O God, hast forgotten us, and thou goest not forth with our host.

Ps. CVIII. Ver. 4. *For thy mercy is great, and reacheth unto the heavens.* Heb., *For thy mercy is great above the heavens.*

12. Give us help against our enemies; for vain is the help of man.

13. God shall make us to get power; for he *it is that* shall tread down our enemies.

PSALM CIX.

A Psalm of David;—when *the people* made Absalom king without his knowledge; for which cause he was slain. And, as respects ourselves, containing an allusion to the sufferings of God the Messiah.

1. Hold not thy peace, O God of my praise;
2. For the mouth of the wicked, and the mouth of the deceitful, are opened against me;
3. They have spoken against me with a lying tongue, and with the voice of hatred; and have fought against me without a cause.
4. Yea, for my love they are my adversaries, even *while* I was praying for them.
5. They have rewarded me evil for good; and hatred for love.

Ver. 13. *God shall make us to get power.* Heb., *Through God we shall do valiantly.*

See also notes to Ps. LVII. and LX.

Ps. CIX. Ver. 3. *And with the voice of hatred.* Heb., *They compassed me about also with words of hatred.* The words, *They have spoken against me with a lying tongue,* form part of the second verse in the Hebrew, but I have placed them with this as being their more natural connection in the Syriac.

Ver. 4. *Even while I was praying for them.* Heb., *but I give myself unto prayer.*

6. Set thou an unrighteous man over them, and let Satan stand at their right hand;

7. And when they are judged, let them go out condemned; and let their prayer become sin.

8. Let their days be few; and whatever is reserved for them, let others take.

9. Let their children be fatherless, and their wives widows.

11. Let the usurer succeed to all that they have; and let strangers search out their power.

12. Let there not be any one to have mercy upon them, and let there not be any to have pity upon their fatherless children.

13. Let their end be destruction, and in the generation following let their name be destroyed.

14. Let the iniquity of their fathers be remembered, and let not the sins of their mothers be blotted out.

15. But let them be before the Lord alway, and let him destroy the memory of them from the earth.

Ver. 6. *Set thou an unrighteous man over them.* The object of the imprecations in this psalm is expressed in the Hebrew in the singular, but in the Syriac in the plural number.

Ver. 8. *And whatever is reserved for them,* ܣܶܟܒܰܡ ܘܶܟ݂ܽܡ ܗܳܘܠ. A. V. *His office,* פְּקֻדָּתוֹ. LXX., καὶ τὴν ἐπισκοπὴν αὐτοῦ.

Ver. 10, of the Hebrew, is wanting in the Syriac version; translated, *Let his children be continually vagabonds, and beg: let them seek their bread also out of their desolate places.*

Ver. 11. *And let strangers search out their power.* Heb., *and let the strangers spoil his labour.*

Ver. 13. *Let their end be destruction,* ܗܳܘܠ ܐܘܒܕܢܐ ܠܚܪܬܗܘܢ. A. V. *Let his posterity be cut off,* יְהִי־אַחֲרִיתוֹ לְהַכְרִית.

Ver. 14. *Be remembered.* Heb., *be remembered with the Lord.*

16. Because they remembered not to do good; but persecuted the poor and needy man, and him whose heart was sorrowful, *even* unto death.

17. They loved cursings, and delighted not in blessings; but they clothed themselves with cursings like as with armour;

18. And they entered into them like waters, and like oil into their bones.

19. *Therefore* let it be unto them like the cloak that they are covered withal, and like a girdle continually.

20. This is the work of them that are adversaries unto the Lord, and of them that speak evil against my soul.

Ver. 16. *And him whose heart was sorrowful, even unto death.* Heb., *that he might even slay the broken in heart.*

Ver. 17. *They loved cursings, and delighted not in blessings,* ܢܬܡܗ ܚܒܢܐ ܡܢ ܪܟܒ ܚܒܬܘܬܟܐ. A. V. *As he loved cursing, so let it come unto him: as he delighted not in blessing, so let it be far from him,* וַיֶּאֱהַב קְלָלָה וַתְּבוֹאֵהוּ וְלֹא־חָפֵץ בִּבְרָכָה וַתִּרְחַק מִמֶּנּוּ.

Ver. 17, 18. *But they clothed themselves with cursings like as with armour; and they entered into them like waters, and like oil into their bones,* ܡܠܒܫܗ ܚܒܢܐ ܐܝܟ ܐܣܠܐ. ܘܬܟܒܣ ܚܣܡ ܐܝܟ ܡܢܐ ܐܝܟ ܡܫܚܐ ܚܝܠܐ ܟܒܥܨܡܬܗ. A. V. *As he clothed himself with cursing like as with his garment, so let it come into his bowels like water, and like oil into his bones,* וַיִּלְבַּשׁ קְלָלָה כְּמַדּוֹ וַתָּבֹא כַמַּיִם בְּקִרְבּוֹ וְכַשֶּׁמֶן בְּעַצְמוֹתָיו.

Ver. 20. *This is the work of them that are adversaries unto the Lord,* ܗܢܐ ܥܒܕܐ ܕܐܠܨܝ ܘܕܡܡܠܠܝ ܠܦܬܢܐ. A. V. *Let this be the reward of mine adversaries from the Lord,* זֹאת פְּעֻלַּת שֹׂטְנַי מֵאֵת יְהוָה. LXX., τοῦτο τὸ ἔργον κ. τ. λ. Gabriel Sio-

21. But do thou for me, O Lord, for thy Name's sake; because thy mercy is good, deliver thou me.

22. For I am poor and needy, and my heart is troubled within me;

23. And my steps have declined like a shadow, and I am tossed up and down as the locust;

24. And my knees are weak through fasting, and my flesh faileth of fatness.

25. I became also a reproach unto them; they looked upon me, and shaked their heads.

26. Help me, O Lord God, and save me according to thy mercy;

27. That they may know that this is thy hand, and *that* thou hast done it.

28. Let them be cursed, but thou shalt be blessed, and thy servant shall rejoice.

29. Let them be clothed with shame that are mine adversaries; and let them be covered with it as with a mantle.

30. I will give thanks unto the Lord with my

nita translates ﺣَﺸْﺮًا, *eventus*, which yields a better sense, though the word will hardly bear the meaning.

Ver. 23. *And my steps have declined like a shadow.* Heb., *I am gone like the shadow when it declineth.*

Ver. 28. *Let them be cursed, but thou shalt be blessed,* ܬܠܐܛܝܢ ܀ ܗܢܘ . ܐܙܠ ܠܟܘ A. V. *Let them curse, but bless thou: when they arise, let them be ashamed,* יְקַלְלוּ־הֵמָּה וְאַתָּה תְבָרֵךְ קָמוּ וַיֵּבֹשׁוּ.

Ver. 29. *And let them be covered with it as with a mantle.* Heb., *and let them cover themselves with their own confusion, as with a mantle.*

mouth; and I will praise him among the multitude.

31. For he standeth on the right hand of the poor, to save his soul from condemnation.

PSALM CX.

A Psalm of David;—concerning the Session of the Lord, and concerning his glorious power. A prophecy, also, of the Messiah, and of his triumph over the adversary.

1. The Lord said unto my Lord, Sit thou at my right hand, until I make thine enemies thy footstool.
2. The Lord shall send thee the rod of strength out of Zion; and he shall rule over thine enemies.
3. Thy people *shall be* glorious in the day of power; in the beauties of holiness from the womb, I have begotten thee, O youth, from the beginning.

Ver. 31. *To save his soul from condemnation*, ܠܡܦܩܗ ܢܦܫܗ ܡܢ ܕܝܢܐ. A. V. *To save him from those that condemn his soul*, לְהוֹשִׁיעַ מִשֹּׁפְטֵי נַפְשׁוֹ. The translator read, probably, מִמִּשְׁפַּט נַפְשׁוֹ.

Ps. CX. Ver. 2. *Shall send thee.* Heb., *shall send.*
The rod of strength. Heb., *the rod of thy strength.*
And he shall rule over thine enemies, ܘܢܫܬܠܛ ܒܥܠܕܒܒܝܟ. A. V. *Rule thou in the midst of thine enemies*, רְדֵה בְּקֶרֶב אֹיְבֶיךָ.

Ver. 3. *Thy people shall be glorious in the day of power*, ܥܡܟ ܡܫܒܚܐ ܒܝܘܡܐ ܕܚܝܠܟ. A. V. *Thy people shall be willing in the day of thy power*, עַמְּךָ נְדָבֹת בְּיוֹם חֵילֶךָ.

4. The Lord hath sworn, and will not lie, that thou art a priest forever in the likeness of Melchizedek.

5. The Lord, at thy right hand, hath broken kings in the day of his wrath.

6. He shall judge the heathen, and shall fill *the places with* the dead bodies; and he shall cut off the head of many in the earth;

7. And he shall drink of the brook in the way; therefore shall his head be exalted.

PSALM CXI.

Anonymous;—concerning the excellency of the works of God, and enjoining upon us to render thanksgiving unto the Messiah. Spoken in the person of the Apostles.

1. I will give thanks unto the Lord with my whole heart, in the council of the upright, *and* in the congregation.

In the beauties of holiness from the womb, I have begotten thee, O youth, from the beginning, : ܚܕܝܘܠ ܡܘܝܡܐ ܩܢ ܟܢܚܓܐ ܩܢ ܡܥܝܡ ܟܘ ܝܟܢܐ ܝܓܝܘܝ. A. V. *In the beauties of holiness from the womb of the morning: thou hast the dew of thy youth,* בְּהַדְרֵי־קֹדֶשׁ מֵרֶחֶם מִשְׁחָר לְךָ טַל יַלְדֻתֶיךָ.

The translator divided differently, and seems to have read מִשַּׁחַר טָלָה יְלִדְתִּיךָ. The LXX. have ἐγέννησά σε.

Ver. 4. *And will not lie.* Heb., *and will not repent.*

In the likeness, ܟ̣ܕܡܘܬܗ. A. V. *After the order,* עַל־דִּבְרָתִי.

Ver. 5. *Hath broken.* Heb., *shall strike through.*

Ver. 6. *And he shall cut off the head of many in the earth.* Heb., *he shall wound the heads over many countries.*

2. The works of the Lord *are* great, and sought out of all them that delight therein.

3. His works *are* glorious and great, and his righteousness endureth forever.

4. He hath given a memorial to his wonderful works; the Lord is full of compassion, and gracious.

5. He hath given food unto them that fear him, and he remembereth his covenant forever.

6. He hath shewed his people the power that *is* in his works, that he may give them the heritage of the heathen.

7. The work of his hands *is* verity and judgment;

8. And they stand fast forever and ever; all his commandments *are* sure, and are done in righteousness and truth.

9. The Lord hath sent redemption unto his people, and he remembereth his covenant forever; holy and reverend is his Name.

10. The fear of the Lord *is* the beginning of wisdom; and a good understanding hath he that doeth thereafter, and his praise endureth forever.

Ps. CXI. Ver. 3. *His works are glorious and great.* Heb., *His work is honourable and glorious.*

Ver. 7, 8. In these verses the construction varies from the Hebrew, but the translation is otherwise literal.

Ver. 9. *The Lord hath sent.* Heb., *He sent.*

And he remembereth, ܘܡܬܕܟܪ. A. V. *He hath commanded,* צִוָּה.

Ver. 10. *Hath he that doeth thereafter,* ܠܟܠ ܕܥܒܕ. Perhaps, however, this might be better translated, *hath he that serveth him.* A. V. *Have all they that do his commandments,* לְכָל־עֹשֵׂיהֶם.

PSALM CXII.

Anonymous;—in which David giveth instruction to Solomon, his son; *Keep the commandments of the Lord, and serve him. Also the calling of the Gentiles, and the judgment of the Messiah.*

1. Blessed is the man that feareth the Lord, and walketh diligently in his commandments.
2. His seed shall be mighty upon earth, and he shall be blessed in the generation of the righteous.
3. Wealth and riches shall increase in his house, and his righteousness shall stand fast forever.
4. Unto the upright there ariseth light in the darkness, and *God* is full of compassion towards the just.
5. The man is good that is merciful and lendeth, and sustaineth his words in judgment.

Ps. CXII. This Psalm commences in Hebrew with the Hallelujah.

Ver. 1. *And walketh diligently,* ܘܣܗܕ. I have translated this freely. The literal meaning is, *and is careful, diligent,* or *exact.* A. V. *That delighteth greatly,* חָפֵץ מְאֹד.

Ver. 2. *And he shall be blessed in the generation of the righteous.* Heb., *the generation of the upright shall be blessed.*

Ver. 3. *Shall increase,* ܢܣܓܐ. This is not expressed in the Hebrew, but is supplied in the authorized version by the words *shall be.*

Ver. 4. *And God is full of compassion towards the just,* ܘܡܪܚܡܢ ܟܠ ܐܢܫ. A. V. *He is gracious, and full of compassion, and righteous,* חַנּוּן וְרַחוּם וְצַדִּיק.

Ver. 5. *The man is good that is merciful and lendeth,* ܓܒܪܐ ܟܗܝܢ ܕܡܪܚܡ ܘܡܘܙܦ. A. V. *A good man sheweth favour, and lendeth,* טוֹב־אִישׁ חוֹנֵן וּמַלְוֶה.

6. He shall not be moved forever; to the righteous there shall be an everlasting remembrance;

7. And he shall not be afraid of evil tidings; for his heart is fixed, trusting in the Lord.

8. Yea, his heart *is* established, and he shall not be afraid, until he see *his desire* upon his enemies.

9. He hath dispersed, and he hath given to the poor; and his righteousness endureth forever, and his horn shall be exalted with honour.

10. The unrighteous, also, shall see *it* and be angry; and he shall gnash with his teeth and vanish away; and the desire of the wicked shall perish.

PSALM CXIII.

Anonymous; — in which reference is made to the diligence to be shewn by the priests, in the ministry of the Lord, in the prime of the morning; and instructing us, who are a new people, regenerated by water and the Spirit, that we should be ready betimes for the service of God, having our hearts sprinkled and washed with the Holy Spirit, and being purified in our minds.

1. Praise, O ye servants of the Lord, praise the Name of the Lord.

And sustaineth his words in judgment, ܡܚܡܣܟ: ܫܓܠܬܗܝ ܒܕܝܢܐ. A. V. *He will guide his affairs with discretion,* יְכַלְכֵּל דְּבָרָיו בְּמִשְׁפָּט. The Hebrew, however, will bear the other meaning. LXX., οἰκονομήσει τοὺς λόγους αὐτοῦ ἐν κρίσει.

Ps. CXIII. This Psalm in the Hebrew begins and ends with the Hallelujah.

2. Blessed be the Name of the Lord from everlasting and to everlasting.

3. From the rising of the sun unto the going down of the same, the Name of the Lord is great;

4. And the Lord is high above all nations, and his glory above the heavens.

5. Who is like unto the Lord our God, who dwelleth on high,

6. And beholdeth the *things that are* humble in heaven and earth?

7. He raiseth up the poor out of the dunghill;

8. That he may set him with the princes of the people.

9. He maketh the barren woman to keep house, and *to be* a joyful mother of children.

Ver. 2. *From everlasting,* ܡܢ ܥܠܡ. A. V. *From this time forth,* מֵעַתָּה.

Ver. 3. *Is great,* ܪܒ ܗܘ. A. V. *Is to be praised,* מְהֻלָּל.

Ver. 6. *And beholdeth the things that are humble,* ܡܢ ܚܘܪ ܡܟܝܟܐ. A. V. *Who humbleth himself to behold the things,* הַמַּשְׁפִּילִי לִרְאוֹת. LXX., καὶ τὰ ταπεινὰ ἐφορῶν.

Ver. 7, 8, are more copiously expressed in the original.

PSALM CXIV.

Anonymous;—from the old Scriptures concerning Moses, who sang praises at the sea; and, as respects ourselves, treating of the call of the Gospel, by which we were made a new people, before barbarous, now spiritual unto God, incarnate in Jesus, the Messiah, who redeemed us by his blood from the curse of scripture, and purified us from sin by his Spirit.

1. When Israel went out of Egypt, and the house of Jacob from a people of strange language;
2. Judah was his holiness, and Israel his praise.
3. The sea saw him and fled, and Jordan turned backward.
4. The mountains skipped like rams, and the little hills like lambs of the flock.
5. What *ailed* thee, O thou sea, that thou fleddest? and thou Jordan that thou didst turn backward?
6. Ye mountains that ye skipped like rams; and ye little hills like lambs of the flock?
7. At the presence of the Lord the earth is moved; at the presence of the God of Jacob;
8. Which turned the rock into standing waters, and the hard rock into fountains of waters.

1. Not unto us, O Lord, not unto us, but unto thy

Ps. cxiv. Ver. 2. *His holiness*, ܩܘܕܫܗ. A. v. *His sanctuary*, לְקָדְשׁוֹ. This, however, might be rendered *his holiness*. LXX., ἁγίασμα αὐτοῦ.

His praise, ܡܫܠܡܢܘܬܗ. A. v. *His dominion*, מַמְשְׁלוֹתָיו.

Ver. 3. *Saw him*, ܚܙܐܘܗܝ. A. v. *Saw it*, רָאָה.

Ver. 7. *The earth is moved*, ܐܬܬܙܝܥܬ ܐܪܥܐ. A. v. *Tremble, thou earth*, חוּלִי אָרֶץ. LXX., ἐσαλεύθη ἡ γῆ.

Ver. 1. *Not unto us*, etc. This is the commencement of Ps.

Name give glory, for thy mercy, and for thy truth's sake;

2. That the heathen say not, Where is their God?

3. Our God is in heaven, and doeth whatsoever he pleaseth.

4. The idols of the heathen *are* silver and gold, the work of men's hands.

5. They have mouths, but they speak not; eyes have they, but they see not;

6. They have ears, but they hear not; noses have they, but they smell not;

7. And they handle not with their hands, and walk not with their feet; neither speak they through their throats.

8. They that make them shall be like unto them, and *so shall* all that put their trust in them.

9. The house of Israel trust in the Lord, and he is their helper and defender.

cxv. according to the division of the Hebrew text and the authorized version.

Ver. 2. *That the heathen say not,* ܠܡܢܐ ܬܐܡܪܘܢ. A. V. *Wherefore should the heathen say,* לָמָּה יֹאמְרוּ הַגּוֹיִם. LXX., μή ποτε εἴπωσι τὰ ἔθνη.

Ver. 4. *The idols of the heathen.* Heb., *Their idols.* LXX., τὰ εἴδωλα τῶν ἐθνῶν.

Ver. 7. *And they handle not with their hands, and walk not with their feet.* Heb., *They have hands, but they handle not: feet have they, but they walk not.*

Ver. 8. *Shall be,* ܢܗܘܘܢ. A. V. *Are,* יִהְיוּ; but this may be rendered *shall be.* LXX., γένοιντο.

Ver. 9. *The house of Israel trust,* ܒܝܬ ܐܝܣܪܐܝܠ ܐܬܬܟܠܘ. A. V. *O Israel, trust thou,* יִשְׂרָאֵל בְּטַח. LXX., οἶκος Ἰσραὴλ ἤλπισεν.

10. The house of Aaron trust in the Lord, and he is their helper and defender.

11. They that fear the Lord, trust in the Lord, and he is their helper and defender.

12. The Lord hath been mindful of us, and hath blessed us; he shall bless the house of Israel; he shall bless the house of Aaron.

13. The Lord shall bless them that fear him, *both* small and great.

14. The Lord shall increase you more and more; you and your children.

15. Ye *are* blessed of the Lord, which made heaven and earth.

16. The heaven of heavens is the Lord's, but the earth hath he given to the children of men.

17. The dead shall not praise the Lord, neither all they that go down into darkness.

18. But we will bless the Lord, from this time forth, and for evermore.

Their helper and defender. Heb., *their help and their shield.* There is a corresponding variation in verses 10, 11.

Ver. 13. *The Lord shall bless them that fear him.* Heb., *He will bless them that fear the Lord.*

Ver. 16. *The heaven of heavens,* ܫܡܝܐ ܕܫܡܝܐ. A. V. *The heaven, even the heavens,* הַשָּׁמַיִם שָׁמַיִם. LXX., ὁ οὐρανὸς τοῦ οὐρανοῦ.

Ver. 17. *Darkness,* ܫܬܩܐ. A. V. *Silence,* דוּמָה. LXX., εἰς ᾅδου.

This Psalm in the Hebrew ends with the Hallelujah.

PSALM CXV.

Anonymous. — The progressive advancement of a new people, turning to Christian worship, like a child to understanding. In its literal sense, containing an allusion to the fact that Saul came and sat at the door of the cave in which David and his men were concealed.

1. I am well pleased that the Lord should hear the voice of my supplication;
2. And *that* he should incline his ear unto me, in the day that I call upon him.
3. For the sorrows of death compassed me, and the pains of hell came upon me; I found affliction and sorrow;
4. And I called upon the Name of the Lord; O Lord, I beseech thee, deliver my soul.
5. Gracious *art* thou, O Lord, and righteous; and thou, O God, *art* full of compassion.
6. The Lord preserveth the little ones; he humbled me, and he hath delivered me.

Ps. cxv. Ver. 1. *I am well pleased that the Lord should hear the voice of my supplication,* ܐܣܬܟܠܬ ܘܬܫܒܚܐ ܕܢܫܡܥ ܡܪܝܐ ܒܩܠܐ ܕܒܥܘܬܝ. A. V. *I love the Lord, because he hath heard my voice and my supplication,* אָהַבְתִּי כִּי־יִשְׁמַע יְהֹוָה אֶת־קוֹלִי תַּחֲנוּנָי. LXX., Ἠγάπησα, ὅτι εἰσακούσεται κύριος τῆς φωνῆς τῆς δεήσεώς μου.

Ver. 2. *And that he should incline his ear unto me, in the day that I call upon him.* Heb., *Because he hath inclined his ear unto me, therefore will I call upon him as long as I live.*

Ver. 6. *The little ones,* ܝܠܘܕܐ. A. V. *The simple,* פְּתָאיִם. LXX., τὰ νήπια.

He humbled me, and he hath delivered me. Heb., *I was brought low, and he helped me.*

7. Return unto thy rest, O my soul, for the Lord hath rewarded thee.

8. For thou hast delivered my soul from death, and my feet from falling;

9. That I might be well pleasing before thee, O God, in the land of the living.

10. I believed and I have spoken; and I was brought very low.

11. I said in my dismay, All men *are* liars.

12. What shall I render unto the Lord for all his benefits toward me?

13. I will take the cup of salvation, and call upon the Name of the Lord;

14. And I will pay my vows unto the Lord in the presence of all the people.

15. Precious in the sight of the Lord is the death of his saints.

16. O Lord, I *am* thy servant; I *am* thy servant, and the son of thine handmaid; thou hast loosed my bonds from off me.

Ver. 8. In this verse in the Hebrew, are the words אֶת־עֵינִי מִן־דִּמְעָה, *mine eyes from tears;* which are not translated.

Ver. 9. *That I might be well pleasing before thee, O God,* ܐܶܫܦܰܪ ܡܶܢ ܩܕܳܡ ܐܰܠܳܗܐ. A. V. *I will walk before the Lord,* אֶתְהַלֵּךְ לִפְנֵי יְהוָֹה. LXX., εὐαρεστήσω ἐνώπιον κυρίου.

Ver. 10. *I believed and I have spoken; and I was brought very low.* Heb., *I believed, therefore have I spoken: I was greatly afflicted.*

Ver. 11. *In my dismay,* ܒ݁ܟ݂ܰܡܺܝܫܽܘܬ݂ܝ̱. A. V. *In my haste,* בְחָפְזִי.

Ver. 14. *The people.* Heb., *his people.*

Ver. 16. *From off me,* ܡܶܢܝ̱, not in the Hebrew.

17. I will offer to thee the sacrifice of praise, and will call upon the Name of the Lord;

18. And I will pay my vows unto the Lord in the presence of all the people;

19. Even in the courts of the Lord's house, and in the midst of thee, O Jerusalem.

PSALM CXVI.

Anonymous;—spoken of the company of Ananias, when they came out of the furnace; and predicting the call of the Gentiles by the preaching of the Gospel.

1. O praise the Lord, all ye nations; praise him, all ye people.

2. For his merciful kindness is great toward us; truly the Lord is everlasting.

Ver. 18. *The people.* Heb., *his people.*

This Psalm ends in the Hebrew with the Hallelujah.

Ps. cxvi. Ver. 2. *Truly the Lord is everlasting,* ܐܺܝܬܰܘܗ̱ܝ ܡܶܛܽܠ ܕܛܳܒ ܗܽܘ ܡܳܪܝܳܐ. A. V. *And the truth of the Lord endureth forever,* וֶאֱמֶת־יְהוָֹה לְעוֹלָם.

This Psalm ends in the Hebrew with the Hallelujah.

PSALM CXVII.

Anonymous;—in its literal sense, referring to Asaph the recorder, and to the priests that ministered unto the Lord; and alluding prophetically to the victorious agonists, and to the Messiah.

1. O give thanks unto the Lord, for he is good, and his mercies *endure* forever.

2. Let Israel say, that his mercies *endure* forever.

3. Let them that are of the house of Aaron say, that his mercies *endure* forever.

4. Let them that fear the Lord say, that his mercies *endure* forever.

5. I called unto the Lord in affliction, and the Lord answered me, *and set me* in a large place.

6. The Lord *is* my helper, I will not fear; what shall man do unto me?

7. The Lord *is* my helper, therefore shall I see *my desire* upon them that hate me.

8. *It is* good to trust in the Lord; better than to put confidence in man.

9. *It is* good to trust in the Lord; better than to put confidence in a prince.

10. All nations compassed me about; but in the Name of the Lord have I destroyed them.

Ps. cxvii. Ver. 6. *My helper,* ܡܥܰܕܪܳܢܝ. A. v. *On my side,* לִי.

Ver. 7. *My helper,* ܡܥܰܕܪܳܢܝ. A. v. *Taketh my part with them that help me,* לִי בְּעֹזְרָי.

Ver. 8. *It is good to trust in the Lord; better than to put confidence in man.* Heb., *It is better to trust in the Lord than to put confidence in man.* There is a corresponding variation in verse 9.

11. They surrounded me, and compassed me about; but in the Name of the Lord have I destroyed them.

12. They compassed me about like bees, and are extinct as the fire of stubble; and in the Name of the Lord have I destroyed them.

13. I was thrust at that I might be overthrown and fall, but the Lord helped me.

14. The Lord is my strength and my glory, and he is become my Saviour.

15. The voice of praise and salvation is in the tabernacle of the righteous; the right hand of the Lord hath done valiantly.

16. The right hand of the Lord hath exalted me; the right hand of the Lord hath done valiantly;

17. That I should not die, but live, and declare the works of the Lord.

18. The Lord hath sorely chastened me, but he hath not delivered me over unto death.

19. Open to me the gates of righteousness, that I may go into them, and give thanks unto the Lord.

20. This is the gate of the Lord, into which the righteous enter.

Ver. 12. *Stubble*, ܩܫܐ. A. v. *Thorns*, קוֹצִים.

Ver. 13. *I was thrust at that I might be overthrown and fall*, ܘܐܬܕܚܝܬ ܘܐܫܬܚܦ ܘܢܦܠ. A. v. *Thou hast thrust sore at me, that I might fall*, דָּחֹה דְחִיתַנִי לִנְפֹּל. LXX., ὠσθεὶς ἀνετράπην τοῦ πεσεῖν.

Ver. 16. *Hath exalted me*, ܐܬܬܪܝܡܬ. A. v. *Is exalted*, רוֹמֵמָה.

Ver. 17. *That I should not die.* Heb., *I shall not die.*

Ver. 19. *That I may go into them.* Heb., *I will go into them.*

21. I will give thanks unto thee, for thou hast heard me, and art become my Saviour.

22. The stone which the builders refused is become the head *stone* of the building.

23. This is the Lord's doing, and it is a wonder in our eyes.

24. This is the day which the Lord hath made; come, let us rejoice and be glad in it.

25. Save me, O Lord; O Lord, deliver me.

26. Blessed is he that cometh in the Name of the Lord; we have blessed you out of the house of the Lord.

27. O Lord, our God, shew us light; and bind our victims with chains, *even* unto the horns of the altar.

28. Thou *art* my God; I will thank thee; thou *art* my God; I will praise thee.

29. O give thanks unto the Lord, for he is good, and his mercy *endureth* forever.

Ver. 22. *Of the building,* ܘܒܢܝܢܠܗ. A. v. *Of the corner,* פִּנָּה.

Ver. 24. *Come,* ܠܐ, not in the Hebrew.

Ver. 25. *Save me, O Lord: O Lord, deliver me.* Heb., *Save now, I beseech thee, O Lord: O Lord, I beseech thee, send now prosperity.*

Ver. 27. *O Lord, our God, shew us light: and bind the victims with chains, even unto the horns of the altar,* ܐܢܬ ܐܠܗܝ ܟܒܢܘ ܠܢ܂ ܘܐܣܪܘ ܟܢܫܐܝܬ ܚܘܒܬܡܗܘܢ ܥܕܡܐ ܠܩܪܢܬܗ ܕܡܕܒܚܐ܂ ܘܚܘܒܐ. A. v. *God is the Lord, which hath shewed us light: bind the sacrifice with cords, even unto the horns of the altar,* אֵל יְהֹוָה וַיָּאֶר לָנוּ אִסְרוּ־חַג בַּעֲבֹתִים עַד־קַרְנוֹת הַמִּזְבֵּחַ.

Ver. 28. *I will praise thee.* Heb., *I will exalt thee.*

(LAUD, AND THE BEGINNING OF THE GRADE.)

PSALM CXVIII.

Anonymous. — A principal meditation upon the excellency that is in God.

Olaph.

1. Blessed are they that are without blemish in the way, and walk in the law of the Lord.
2. Blessed are they that keep his testimony, and seek him with all their heart.
3. They do no iniquity, and they walk in his ways.
4. Thou hast commanded that *men* should keep thy precepts diligently.
5. O that my ways were *so* directed, that I might keep thy precepts!
6. And I shall not be ashamed, when I have kept all thy precepts.
7. I will give thanks unto thee with the uprightness of mine heart, when I have learned thy righteous judgments.
8. I have kept thy precepts; O forsake me not forever.

Beth.

9. Wherewithal shall a young man cleanse his way, that he may keep thy precepts?

Ps. cxviii. Ver. 5. *Thy precepts*, ܦܘܩܕܢܝܟ. A. v. *Thy statutes*, חֻקֶּיךָ. The Syriac ܦܘܩܕܢܐ occurs very frequently in this Psalm, and seems to be used indifferently for the Hebrew פִּקּוּדִים, דָּבָר, מִצְוָה, חֹק, and עֵדָה.

Ver. 8. *Forever.* Heb., *utterly.*

Ver. 9. *That he may keep thy precepts*, ܘܢܛܪ ܦܘܩܕܢܝܟ.

10. With my whole heart have I sought thee; O let me not wander from thy precepts.

11. Thy words have I hid in my heart, that I might not sin against thee.

12. Blessed *art* thou, O Lord; teach me thy precepts.

13. With my lips have I repeated all the judgments of thy righteousness.

14. I have loved the way of thy testimony better than all riches.

15. I have meditated in thy precepts, and I have known thy ways.

16. I have meditated upon thy law, that I might not forget thy words.

Gomal.

17. Hear thy servant, that I may live and keep thy words.

18. Open thou me mine eyes, that I may behold the wondrous things that *are* in thy law.

19. I *am* a stranger with thee; hide not thy precepts from me.

20. My soul hath desired and exceedingly longed for thy judgments at all times.

A. V. *By taking heed thereto according to thy word,* לִשְׁמֹר כִּדְבָרֶךָ.

Ver. 13. *Of thy righteousness.* Heb., *of thy mouth.*

Ver. 15. *And I have known.* Heb., *and have respect unto.*

Ver. 16. *I have meditated upon thy law.* Heb., *I will delight myself in thy statutes.*

Ver. 17. *Hear.* Heb., *Deal bountifully with.*

Ver. 19. *With thee,* عِنْدَك. A. V. *In the earth,* בָאָרֶץ

21. Thou hast rebuked the heathen; and cursed are all they that do err from thy precepts.

22. Remove from me reproach, for I have kept thy testimony.

23. The unrighteous did sit and meditate against me, but I did meditate in thy precepts.

24. I have meditated in thy testimony, and in good counsel.

Dolath.

25. My soul cleaveth unto the dust; quicken thou me, according to thy word.

26. I have declared my ways unto thee, and thou heardest me; teach me thy law.

27. Shew me the way of thy precepts, and I will meditate upon thy wondrous works.

28. My soul fainteth by reason of care; quicken thou me according to thy word.

29. Remove from me the way of the unrighteous, and teach me thy law.

Ver. 21. *Thou hast rebuked the heathen; and cursed are they that do err.* Heb., *Thou hast rebuked the proud that are cursed, which do err.*

Ver. 22. *Reproach.* Heb., *reproach and contempt.*

Ver. 23. *The unrighteous.* Heb., *Princes.*

But I. Heb., *but thy servant.*

Ver. 24. *I have meditated in thy testimony, and in good counsel.* Heb., *Thy testimonies also are my delight and my counsellors.*

Ver. 26. *I have declared unto thee.* Heb., *I have declared.*

Ver. 28. *My soul fainteth by reason of care,* ܢܦܫܐ ܕܠܦܬ ܚܢܢܝܬܐ. A. V. *My soul melteth for heaviness,* דָּלְפָה נַפְשִׁי מִתּוּגָה.

Ver. 29. *Of the unrighteous.* Heb., *of lying.*

Teach me. Heb., *grant me graciously.*

80. I have chosen the way of thy truth, and I have delighted in thy judgments.

81. I have stuck unto thy testimony; O Lord, put me not to shame.

82. I have walked in the way of thy precepts, for thou hast made me glad.

He.

33. Teach me, O Lord, the way of thy precepts, and I shall keep them.

34. Give me understanding, that I may keep thy law, and I will keep it with my whole heart.

35. Make me to go in the path of thy precepts, for therein do I delight.

36. Turn my heart unto thy testimony, and not unto fables.

37. Turn away mine eyes that they may not see falsehood, and quicken thou me in thy ways.

38. Stablish thy word unto thy servant, who feareth thee.

39. Turn away reproach from me, for thy judgments are good.

40. I have delighted in thy precepts, and do thou quicken me in thy righteousness.

Ver. 30. *And I have delighted in thy judgments,* ܐܨܛܒܝܬ ܒܕ̈ܝܢܝܟ. A. V. *Thy judgments have I laid before me,* מִשְׁפָּטֶיךָ שִׁוִּיתִי.

Ver. 32. *For thou hast made me glad.* Heb., *when thou shalt enlarge my heart.*

Ver. 36. *Unto fables,* ܠܡܬܠܐ. A. V. *To covetousness,* אֶל־בָּצַע. ܡܬܠܐ, however, may be derived from ܢܬܠ, and translated *gifts.*

Ver. 39. *Reproach from me.* Heb., *my reproach which I fear.*

Vau.

41. Let thy mercies come unto me, O Lord; even thy salvation, which thou hast promised.

42. So shall I have wherewith to answer them that reproach me, for I trust in thy words.

43. Let not the word of truth be taken out of my mouth, for I have hoped in thy judgments.

44. I will keep thy law forever and ever;

45. And I will walk at liberty, for I delight in thy precepts.

46. I will speak in righteousness before kings, and will not be ashamed.

47. And I will meditate in thy precepts, which I have loved.

48. My hands also will I lift up unto thy precepts which I have loved; and in them will I meditate, *even* in thy precepts, and I will rejoice in thy truth.

Zain.

49. Remember thy word unto thy servant, in which thou hast caused him to trust;

50. And in which I have been comforted in my humiliation; for thy word hath quickened me.

51. The unrighteous have oppressed me, yet have I not declined from thy law.

Ver. 46. *I will speak in righteousness.* Heb., *I will speak of thy testimonies.*

Ver. 48. *And I will rejoice in thy truth.* This is not in the Hebrew.

Ver. 49. *In which thou hast caused him to trust.* Heb., *upon which thou hast caused me to hope.*

Ver. 51. *The unrighteous have oppressed me,* ܟܶܐܦ݂ܠܺܝ ܟܳܠ ܟܳܬܶܒ݂.

52. I remembered thy judgments, O Lord, which were of old, and received comfort; and they have been my correction.

53. Sadness hath taken hold upon me, because of sinners that have forsaken thy law.

54. Thy precepts have been my song, *in* the house of my pilgrimage.

55. I have remembered thy Name, O Lord, in the night, and have kept thy law;

56. And I have received comfort, because I have kept thy precepts.

Cheth.

57. At midnight have I meditated, that I might keep thy precepts.

58. I have longed for thy favour with my whole heart; quicken me, according to thy word.

59. I thought on my ways, and turned my feet unto thy paths.

A. v. *The proud have had me greatly in derision,* הֵלִיצֻנִי זֵדִים עַד־מְאֹד. For הֱלִיצֻנִי, the translator seems to have read חִלְּצֻנִי.

Ver. 52. *And they have been my correction.* This is not in the Hebrew.

Ver. 56. *And I have received comfort,* ܗܳܕܶܐ ܗܘܳܬ݂ ܠܝ̣. A. v. *This I had,* זֹאת הָיְתָה־לִּי.

Ver. 57. *At midnight,* ܒܦܶܠܓܶܗ ܕܠܺܠܝܳܐ. A. v. *Thou art my portion, O Lord,* חֶלְקִי יְהֹוָה. The word חֵלֶק, means *division,* and thence *portion.* The translator evidently understood it here of a division of time; perhaps for יְהֹוָה, reading לַיְלָה.

Ver. 58. *I have longed for.* Heb., *I entreated.*

Quicken me. Heb., *be merciful unto me.*

Ver. 59. *Unto thy paths.* Heb., *unto thy testimonies.*

60. I made ready, and delayed not, that I might keep thy precepts.

61. The cords of the unrighteous have entangled me; yet have I not swerved from thy law.

62. At midnight have I risen, that I might give thanks unto thee; because of thy judgments, O thou most just.

63. I am a lover of all them that fear thee, and of them that keep thy precepts.

64. The earth, O Lord, is full of thy mercies; teach me thy precepts.

Teth.

65. Deal well with thy servant, O Lord, according as thou hast said.

66. Teach me discernment, and grace, and knowledge; for I have believed thy precepts.

67. Before I was humbled, I believed, and kept thy word.

68. Thou *art* good, O Lord, and doest good; teach me thy precepts.

Ver. 61. *The cords of the unrighteous have entangled me*, ܚܒܠܐ ܕܥܘܠܐ ܟܪܟܘܢܝ. A. V. *The bands of the wicked have robbed me*, חֶבְלֵי רְשָׁעִים עִוְּדֻנִי. LXX, σχοινία ἁμαρτωλῶν περιεπλάκησάν μοι.

Yet have I not swerved from. Heb., *but I have not forgotten.*

Ver. 66. *Discernment and grace*, ܛܥܡܐ ܘܛܝܒܘܬܐ. A. V. *Good judgment*, טוּב טַעַם. LXX, χρηστότητα καὶ παιδείαν.

Ver. 67. *I believed, and kept thy word.* Heb., *I went astray: but now have I kept thy word.*

Ver. 68. *O Lord*, ܡܪܝܐ, not in the Hebrew.

69. The iniquity of the proud hath increased; but I have kept thy precepts with my whole heart.

70. Their heart is curdled like milk; but I have kept thy law.

71. It is good for me that I have been humbled; that I might learn thy precepts.

72. The law of thy mouth is better unto me than thousands of gold and silver.

Jud.

73. Thy hands have made me, and fashioned me teach me thy law;

74. That they that fear thee may see and know that I have hoped in thy word.

75. I know, O Lord, that thy judgments are right, and *that* thy truth hath humbled me.

76. Let thy merciful kindnesses be for my comfort, according as thou hast said unto thy servant.

77. Let thy tender mercies come unto me, that I may live; for I have been instructed in thy law.

Ver. 69. *The iniquity of the proud hath increased,* ܣܓܝ ܥܘܠܐ ܕܙܕܘܩܐ. A. V. *The proud have forged a lie against me,* טָפְלוּ עָלַי שֶׁקֶר זֵדִים. LXX., ἐπληθύνθη ἐπ' ἐμὲ ἀδικία ὑπερηφάνων.

Ver. 70. *Their heart is curdled like milk.* Heb., *Their heart is as fat as grease.*

But I have kept. Heb., *but I delight in.*

Ver. 73. *Teach me thy law.* Heb., *give me understanding, that I may learn thy commandments.*

Ver. 74. *That they that fear thee may see and know that I have hoped in thy word.* Heb., *They that fear thee will be glad when they see me; because I have hoped in thy word.*

Ver. 77. *For I have been instructed in thy law.* Heb., *for thy law is my delight.*

78. Let the unrighteous be ashamed, that have brought me low through iniquity; for I have meditated in thy precepts.

79. Let those that fear thee turn unto me, and those that know thy testimony.

80. Let my heart meditate in thy precepts, that I be not ashamed.

Coph.

81. My soul longeth for thy salvation, and I hope in thy word.

82. Mine eyes wait for thy word, *saying*, When wilt thou comfort me?

83. For I am become like a bottle in the cold; yet do I not forget thy precepts.

84. How many are the days of thy servant, and when wilt thou execute judgment for me on them that persecute me?

85. The unrighteous have digged a pit for me, which *is* not after thy law.

86. All thy precepts *are* faithful, and the unrighteous persecute me.

87. They had almost destroyed me upon earth; but I forsook not thy precepts.

88. Quicken me, after thy loving kindness, that I may keep the testimony of thy mouth.

Ver. 78. *That have brought me low through iniquity.* Heb., *for they dealt perversely with me without a cause.*

Ver. 80. *Let my heart meditate.* Heb., *Let my heart be sound.*

Ver. 82. *Wait.* Heb., *fail.*

Ver. 83. *In the cold,* ﺚﻠﺞ. A. V. *In the smoke,* בְּקִיטוֹר.

Ver. 86. *And the unrighteous persecute me.* Heb., *they persecute me wrongfully; help thou me.*

Lomad.

89. O Lord, thou art everlasting, and thy word *is* settled in heaven;

90. And thy truth is unto all generations: thou hast fashioned the earth, and established it.

92. Were it not for thy law, which hath been my meditation, I had perished in my humiliation.

93. I will never forget thy precepts; for in them is my life.

94. I am thine; save me, for I have kept thy precepts.

95. The unrighteous have waited for me, that they might destroy me; but I have considered thy testimony.

96. I have seen an end to every consummation; but thy precept is exceeding broad.

Mem.

97. O how I love thy law! and it is my meditation all the day.

98. Make me wiser than mine enemies; for I have kept thy precepts.

Ver. 89. *O Lord, thou art everlasting.* Heb., *For ever, O Lord.*

Ver. 91 of the Hebrew, translated, *They continue this day according to thine ordinances: for all are thy servants,* is not in the Syriac version.

Ver. 94. *I have kept.* Heb., *I have sought.*

Ver. 96. *To every consummation,* ܠܟܠ ܣܟܐ. A. V. *Of all perfection,* לְכָל־תִּכְלָה. The root כָּלָה, means *to be completed* and *finished*. The derivative, therefore, may mean either *perfection* or *consummation.* LXX., πάσης συντελείας.

Ver. 98. *Make me wiser.* Heb., *Thou hast made me wiser.*

For I have kept thy precepts. Heb., *through thy commandments; for they are ever with me.*

99. Give me more understanding than all my teachers; for thy testimony is my meditation.

100. I understand more than the ancients, because I have kept thy precepts.

101. I have refrained my feet from every evil way; that I might keep thy precepts.

102. I have not swerved from thy judgments; for thou hast taught me.

103. Sweeter *are* thy words unto my palate than honey unto my mouth.

104. I have meditated in thy precepts; therefore do I hate every way of the unrighteous.

Nun.

105. Thy word is a lamp unto my feet, and a light unto my paths.

106. I have sworn, and I have confirmed *it*, that I will keep thy righteous judgments.

107. I am brought very low; quicken me, O Lord, according unto thy word.

108. Accept the words of my mouth, O Lord, and teach me out of thy judgments.

109. My soul is alway in thy hands, and I do not forget thy law.

110. Sinners have laid snares for me; yet I erred not from thy precepts.

Ver. 99. *Give me more understanding.* Heb., *I have more understanding.*

Ver. 104. *I have meditated in thy precepts.* Heb., *Through thy precepts I get understanding.*

Every way of the unrighteous. Heb., *every false way.*

Ver. 108. *The words.* Heb., *the free-will offerings.*

Ver. 109. *In thy hands,* بِكَابِي. A. V. *In my hand,* בְכַפִּי.

111. Thy testimony have I taken as an heritage forever; for it is the delight of my heart.

112. I have inclined my heart; that I may perform thy precepts forever in truth.

Semcath.

113. I hate the unrighteous; but thy law do I love.

114. Thou art my hiding-place, and my refuge, and I hope in thy word.

115. Depart from me, ye unrighteous; that I may keep the precepts of my God.

116. Confirm me in thy word, that I may live; and let me not be ashamed of my hope.

117. Hold thou me up, and I shall be saved; and I will be taught in thy precepts.

118. Alway have I despised all them that do err from thee; for their meditation is evil.

Ver. 112. *Forever in truth.* Heb., *alway, even unto the end.*

Ver. 113. *The unrighteous.* Heb., *vain thoughts.* LXX., παρανόμους.

Ver. 116. *In thy word,* ܒܡܠܬܟ. A. V. *According unto thy word,* כְּאִמְרָתֶךָ. In analogous passages throughout this Psalm, the Hebrew כְּ, *according to,* is translated by the Syriac preposition ܒ, *in,* or *through.*

Ver. 117. *And I will be taught in thy precepts.* Heb., *and I will have respect unto thy statutes continually.*

Ver. 118. *Alway have I despised all them that do err from thee,* ܚܣܕܟ ܐܡܝܢܐܝܬ ܠܟܠ ܕܛܥܝܢ ܡܢܟ. A. V. *Thou hast trodden down all them that err from thy statutes,* סָלִיתָ כָּל־שׁוֹגִים מֵחֻקֶּיךָ. The Syriac ܚܣܕܟ, *alway,* construed with this verse, corresponds to תָּמִיד, *forever,* construed with the preceding verse in the Hebrew. The word סָלִיתָ, the translator

119. Uphold me and I shall be delivered; and I will meditate alway in thy precepts.

120. My flesh trembleth for fear of thee, and I am afraid of thy judgments.

Ee.

121. *Thou that* doest judgment and righteousness, leave me not in the hand of mine oppressors.

122. Delight thy servant with good things, that the proud oppress me not.

123. Mine eyes wait for thy salvation, and for the word of thy righteousness.

124. Deal with thy servant according to thy mercies, and teach me thy law.

125. I *am* thy servant; give me understanding that I may know thy testimony.

derived from סָלָה, though according to the authorized version it is derived from כָּלַל. LXX., ἐξουδένωσας.

For their meditation is evil, ܚܢܘ ܘܟܠܗ ܗܘ ܪܢܝܗܘܢ. A. V. *For their deceit is falsehood,* כִּי־שֶׁקֶר תַּרְמִיתָם. LXX., ὅτι ἄδικον τὸ ἐνθύμημα αὐτῶν. Both translators, for תַּרְמִיתָם, read תַּרְעִיתָם.

Ver. 119. *Uphold me and I shall be delivered; and I will meditate alway in thy precepts.* Heb., *Thou puttest away all the wicked of the earth like dross; therefore I love thy testimonies.* The Syriac here can hardly be called a translation.

Ver. 121. *Thou that doest.* Heb., *I have done.*

Ver. 122. *Delight thy servant,* ܟܣܡܚܝܗܝ ܠܥܒܕܟ. A. V. *Be surety for thy servant,* עֲרֹב עַבְדְּךָ. The translator derived the Hebrew verb from עָרֵב, in the sense *to be sweet, to be pleasant,* etc.

Ver. 123. *Wait.* Heb., *fail.*

126. It is time to serve the Lord; but lo! they have made void thy law.

127. Therefore I love thy precepts better than gold, and better than precious stones.

128. I love all thy precepts, and I hate every way of the unrighteous.

Phe.

129. Thy testimonies are wonderful; therefore my soul keepeth them.

130. Open thy word, and give light; and grant understanding unto the little ones.

131. I opened my mouth, and drew in *my* breath, and waited for thy salvation.

132. Turn unto me, and have mercy upon me; for I have loved thy Name.

Ver. 126. *It is time to serve the Lord,* ܗܢܘ ܙܒܢܐ ܕܬܦܠܘܚ ܠܡܪܝܐ. A. V. *It is time for thee, Lord, to work,* עֵת לַעֲשׂוֹת לַיהוָה.

Ver. 127. *And better than precious stones.* Heb., *yea, above fine gold.*

Ver. 128. *I love all thy precepts.* Heb., *Therefore I esteem all thy precepts concerning all things to be right.*

Every way of the unrighteous. Heb., *every false way.*

Ver. 130. *Open thy word and give light,* ܦܬܚ ܡܠܬܟ ܘܐܢܗܪ. A. V. *The entrance of thy words giveth light,* פֵּתַח דְּבָרֶיךָ יָאִיר.

The little ones. Heb., *the simple.* LXX., νηπίους.

Ver. 131. *And drew in my breath,* ܘܢܓܕܬ ܪܘܚܐ. A. V. *And panted,* וָאֶשְׁאָפָה. LXX., καὶ εἵλκυσα πνεῦμα.

And I waited for thy salvation. Heb., *for I longed for thy commandments.*

Ver. 132. *For I have loved thy Name.* Heb., *as thou usest to do unto those that love thy Name.*

133. Order my going in thy paths, that the unrighteous do not get the dominion over me.

134. Deliver me from the oppression of man, that I may keep thy precepts.

135. Make thy face to shine upon thy servant, and teach me thy law.

136. Streams of waters come from mine eyes, because they keep not thy law.

Tzode.

137. Righteous *art* thou, O Lord; and exceeding upright *are* thy judgments.

138. Thou hast commanded thy testimony in righteousness and truth.

139. Zeal hath tormented me alway, because thine enemies have forgotten thy word.

140. Thy word is very pure; therefore thy servant loveth it.

141. I *am* small and despised; yet do I not forget thy precepts.

142. Thy righteousness endureth forever, and thy law *is* in truth.

143. Affliction and anguish have come upon me; yet have I meditated in thy precepts.

Ver. 133. *In thy paths.* Heb., *in thy word.*
The unrighteous. Heb., *any iniquity.*
Ver. 139. *Zeal hath tormented me alway.* Heb., *My zeal hath consumed me.*
Thine enemies. Heb., *mine enemies.*
Ver. 142. *Is in truth.* Heb., *is the truth.*
Ver. 143. *Yet have I meditated in thy precepts.* Heb., *yet thy commandments are my delights.*

144. Thy testimony is righteous forever; give me understanding, and I shall live.

Koph.

145. I cried unto thee with my whole heart; hear me, O Lord, that I may keep thy precepts.

146. I cried unto thee; save me, that I may keep thy testimony.

147. I rose up early in the morning, and cried, and waited for thy word.

148. Mine eyes prevent the *night* watch, that I may meditate in thy word.

149. Hear my voice, O Lord, according to thy tender mercies, and quicken me in thy judgments.

150. They draw nigh that are my persecutors falsely, and they are far from thy law.

151. Thou *also art* near, O Lord, and all thy precepts *are* in truth; mine eyes prevent the *night* watch, that I may meditate in thy word.

152. Of old, have I known thy testimony; for thou hast established it from everlasting.

Risch.

153. Consider my humiliation, and deliver me; for I have not forgotten thy law.

Ver. 150. *That are my persecutors falsely*, وَكَفَرُوا ةَيَّةً.
A. V. *That follow after mischief*, זֹמָּה רֹדְפֵי. LXX., οἱ καταδιώκοντες με ἀνομίᾳ.

Ver. 151. *Are in truth*. Heb., *are truth*. The last clause of this verse, *Mine eyes prevent the night-watch that I may meditate in thy word*, is not in the Hebrew, and would seem to have been inserted here by mistake.

154. Judge my cause, and deliver me; and quicken me in thy word.

155. Salvation is far from the unrighteous; for they seek not thy precepts.

156. Great are thy tender mercies, O Lord; wherefore quicken me in thy judgments.

157. Many are my persecutors and mine enemies; yet do I not decline from thy testimonies.

158. I have seen the unrighteous, and have known that they keep not thy word.

159. Consider that I love thy precepts, O Lord; and quicken me in thy loving kindness.

160. Thy word *is* true *from* the beginning, and all thy righteous judgments *endure* forevermore.

Schin.

161. Princes have persecuted me without a cause; but my heart standeth in awe of thy word.

162. I have rejoiced in thy word, as he that findeth great spoil.

163. I hate and abhor iniquity; but thy law do I love.

164. Seven times a day do I praise thee, because of thy judgments, O thou most just.

165. Great is the peace of them that love thy law, and in them there is no infirmity.

166. Lord, I have hoped for thy salvation, and done thy precepts.

Ver. 158. *And have known.* Heb., *and was grieved.*

Ver. 163. *Iniquity.* Heb., *lying.*

Ver. 165. *And in them there is no infirmity.* Heb., *and nothing shall offend them.*

167. My soul hath kept thy testimony, and loved it exceedingly.

168. I have kept thy precepts and thy testimonies; and all my ways *are* before thee.

Thau.

169. Let my song come before thee, O Lord; and quicken me in thy word.

170. Let my supplication come before thee; and deliver me in thy word.

171. My tongue shall talk of thy word; for all thy precepts *are* in righteousness.

172. My lips shall speak thy praises, when thou hast taught me thy precepts.

173. Let thine hand help me; for I delight in thy precepts.

174. My soul hath waited for thy salvation; and I have meditated in thy law.

175. Let my soul live, and it shall praise thee; and thy judgment, it shall help me.

176. I have gone astray like a lost sheep; seek thy servant, for I do not forget thy precepts.

Ver. 169. *Let my song come.* Heb., *Let my cry come near.* *Quicken me.* Heb., *give me understanding.*

Ver. 171, 172 are differently arranged in the Hebrew.

Ver. 171. *Are in righteousness.* Heb., *are righteousness.*

Ver. 173. *For I delight in.* Heb., *for I have chosen.*

Ver. 174. *My soul hath waited.* Heb., *I have longed.*

And I have meditated in thy law. Heb., *and thy law is my delight.*

PSALM CXIX.

Anonymous. — The first song of ascension. The people in Babylon pray that they may be delivered; and so we pray that we may be delivered from evil spirits.

1. In mine affliction I cried unto the Lord, and the Lord heard me,
2. And delivered my soul from the lips of the unrighteous, and from deceitful tongues.
3. What shall they give unto thee, or what shall they add unto thee, *these* deceitful tongues?
4. The sharp arrows of a man, like the coals of the oak.
5. Woe is me, that my sojourn is prolonged, and *that* I have my habitation in the tent of Kedar!

Ps. CXIX. Ver. 1. The word *Lord*, when it occurs a second time, is construed in the Hebrew with the second verse.

Ver. 2. *And delivered my soul.* Heb., *Deliver my soul, O Lord. From the lips of the unrighteous.* Heb., *from lying lips.*

Ver. 3. *What shall they give unto thee, or what shall they add unto thee, these deceitful tongues?* ܡܢܐ ܬܬܠ ܠܟ ܘܡܢܐ ܬܘܣܦ ܠܟ ܠܫܢܐ ܢܟܝܠܐ. A. V. *What shall be given unto thee? or what shall be done unto thee, thou false tongue?* מַה־יִּתֵּן לְךָ וּמַה־יֹּסִיף לָךְ לָשׁוֹן רְמִיָּה.

Ver. 4. *The sharp arrows of a man, like the coals of the oak,* ܓܐܪܘܗܝ ܕܓܢܒܪܐ ܫܢܝܢܝܢ ܥܡ ܓܘܡܪܐ ܘܟܕܢܐ. A. V. *Sharp arrows of the mighty, with coals of juniper,* חִצֵּי גִבּוֹר שְׁנוּנִים עִם גַּחֲלֵי רְתָמִים.

Ver. 5. *That my sojourn is prolonged,* ܕܐܘܪܟܬ ܠܝ ܡܥܡܪܝ.

6. My soul hath long dwelt with them that hate peace.

7. For I spake peace *unto them*, but they contended with me.

PSALM CXX.

Anonymous. — *One of the Psalms of ascension from Babylon; also, the promises of good things.*

1. I will lift up mine eyes unto the hill, from whence cometh my helper.
2. My help *cometh* from before the Lord, which made heaven and earth;
3. And he will not suffer thy foot to be moved, and he that keepeth thee will not slumber.
4. For he that keepeth Israel neither slumbereth nor sleepeth.
5. The Lord is thy keeper; the Lord shall cover thee with his right hand.
6. The sun shall not harm thee by day, nor the moon by night.

A. v. *That I sojourn in Mesech,* כִּי־גַרְתִּי מֶשֶׁךְ. The translator seems to have read מְשַׁךְ, giving a substantive meaning to גַרְתִּי. LXX., ἡ παροικία μου ἐμακρύνθη.

Ver. 7. *For I spake peace unto them, but they contended with me.* Heb., *I am for peace: but when I speak, they are for war.*

Ps. cxx. Ver. 1. *My helper.* Heb., *my help.*

Ver. 5. *The Lord shall cover thee with his right hand,* ܛܠܶܠ ܢܶܛܪܳܟ݂ ܒ݁ܝܰܕ݂ ܝܰܡܺܝܢܶܗ ܘܰܢܓ݂ܶܢ. A. v. *The Lord is thy shade upon thy right hand,* יְהוָֹה צִלְּךָ עַל־יַד יְמִינֶךָ.

7. The Lord shall preserve thee from all evils; the Lord shall preserve thy soul.

8. He shall preserve thy going out, and thy coming in, from this time forth, and even forevermore.

PSALM CXXI.

A Psalm of David;— *One of the Psalms* of ascension, when Cyrus commanded the captivity to go up; and, spiritually, the promise of good things.

1. I was glad when they said unto me, we go unto the house of the Lord.

2. My feet were standing in thy gates, O Jerusalem.

3. Jerusalem is builded as a city that a wall surroundeth.

4. Thither the tribes go up, the tribes of the Lord, unto the testimony of Israel, to give thanks unto the Name of the Lord.

5. For there have they fixed thrones of judgment, the thrones of the house of David.

6. Pray for the peace of Jerusalem; they shall be prospered that love thee.

Ver. 7. The word *Lord*, occurring a second time, is construed in the Hebrew with verse 8.

Ps. CXXI. Ver. 2. *My feet were standing.* Heb., according to the authorized version, *our feet shall stand;* but literally, *our feet were standing.*

Ver. 3. *That a wall surroundeth,* ܚܕܪ ܠܗ ܫܘܪܐ. A. V. *That is compact together,* שֶׁחֻבְּרָה־לָּהּ יַחְדָּו.

Ver. 5. *Have they fixed.* Heb., *are set.*

7. Let peace be with thy power, and prosperity within thy palaces.

8. For my brethren and my lovers' sakes, I will speak peace concerning thee.

9. Because of the house of the Lord our God, I will seek thy good.

PSALM CXXII.

A Psalm of David;—*One of the Psalms* of ascension spoken in the person of Zerubbabel, prince of the captivity. — Also a supplicatory prayer.

1. Unto thee do I lift up mine eyes, O dweller in the heavens.

2. As the eyes of servants *look* unto their masters, and as the eyes of a maiden unto her mistress, so our eyes *look* unto thee, O Lord our God, until thou have mercy upon us.

3. Have mercy upon us, O Lord, have mercy upon us; for we have heard many *words* of contempt;

Ver. 7. *With thy power*, ܒܚܝܠܟ. A. V. *Within thy walls*, בְּחֵילָךְ. The word is the same, but in the Syriac its meaning is somewhat more limited than in the Hebrew. LXX., ἐν τῇ δυνάμει σου.

Ver. 8. *I will speak peace concerning thee.* Heb., *I will now say, Peace be within thee.*

Ps. CXXII. Ver. 2. *Look unto their masters.* Heb., *look unto the hand of their masters;* and so in the next clause.

Unto thee, O Lord our God, until thou have mercy upon us. Heb. *upon the Lord our God, until that he have mercy upon us.*

Ver. 3. *For we have heard many words of contempt*, ܣܓܝ ܡܚܣܕܢ ܐܫܬܡܥܢ. A. V. *For we are exceedingly*

4. And our soul is exceedingly filled with the mockery of the scornful, and with the contempt of the proud.

PSALM CXXIII.

Anonymous. — *Thanksgiving.* — *A Psalm of ascension.*

1. Unless the Lord had stood up for us, may Israel say;
2. Unless the Lord had stood up for us, when men rose up against us;
3. They had swallowed us up quick, even when their wrath was kindled against us.
4. They had overwhelmed us in the waters, *and* the stream had gone over our soul.
5. Yea, many waters had gone over our soul.
6. Blessed is the Lord, which hath not given us *as* food to their teeth.
7. Our soul is escaped as a bird out of the snare of the hunter; the snare is broken, and we are delivered.
8. Our help *is* in the Name of the Lord, who made heaven and earth.

filled with contempt, פִּי־רָב שָׂבְעָה בּוּז. For שְׂבַעְנוּ, the translator read שָׂמְעָנוּ.

Ver. 4. *With the mockery of the scornful.* Heb., *with the scorning of those that are at ease.*

Ps. cxxiii. Ver. 4. *They had overwhelmed us in the waters.* Heb., *Then the waters had overwhelmed us.*

Ver. 5. *Yea, many waters.* Heb., *Then the proud waters.*

Ver. 7. *The hunter.* Heb., *the fowlers.*

PSALM CXXIV.

A Psalm of ascension. — Anonymous.

1. They that trust in the Lord in mount Zion shall not be moved, but shall abide forever.

2. As the mountains *are* round about Jerusalem, so the Lord *is* round about his people, from henceforth, and even for ever.

3. For the rod of the unrighteous shall not rest in the lot of the righteous, nor shall the righteous stretch forth their hands unto iniquity.

4. Do good, O Lord, unto *those that be* good, and to them that are upright in their heart.

5. But as for such as pervert their paths, the Lord shall lead them forth with the workers of iniquity; but peace *shall be* unto Israel.

Ps. CXXIV. Ver. 1. *In mount Zion, shall not be moved, but shall abide forever,* ܚܣܝܢ ܙܝܥܣܝܢ : ܠܐ ܣܘܓܐܐ ܐܠܐ ܟܓܒܪܐ ܢܐܚܕܐ. A. V. *Shall be as mount Zion, which cannot be removed, but abideth forever,* כְּהַר־צִיּוֹן לֹא־יִמּוֹט לְעוֹלָם יֵשֵׁב. For כְּהַר, the translator seems to have read בְּהַר.

Ver. 3. *In the lot.* Heb., *upon the lot.*
Nor shall the righteous stretch forth, ܘܠܐ ܢܘܫܛܘܢ ܐܝܕܝܗܘܢ. A. V. *Lest the righteous put forth,* לְמַעַן לֹא־יִשְׁלְחוּ הַצַּדִּיקִים.

Ver. 5. *But as for such as pervert their paths,* ܐܠܝܢ ܕܝܢ ܕܡܣܛܝܢ ܐܘܪܚܬܗܘܢ. A. V. *As for such as turn aside unto their crooked ways,* וְהַמַּטִּים עֲקַלְקַלּוֹתָם.

PSALM CXXV.

One of the Psalms of ascension.—Anonymous.—Spoken concerning Haggai and Zechariah, who went up from Babylon with the captivity; and, spiritually, the expectation of good things to come.

1. When the Lord turneth again the captivity of Zion, we shall be like unto them that rejoice.
2. Then shall our mouth be filled with laughter, and our tongue with praise; then shall they say among the heathen, the Lord hath done great things for them.
3. The Lord hath done great things for us, and *thereof* we are glad.
4. The Lord hath turned our captivity, as the streams in the south.
5. They that sow in tears shall reap in joy.
6. He goeth forth and weepeth, that beareth the seed; he cometh with joy, that bringeth the sheaf.

Ps. CXXV. Ver. 1. *We shall be,* ܗܘܝܢ, literally, *we were,* but the context requires that the word have a future signification.

Like unto them that rejoice, ܐܝܟ ܗܢܘܢ ܕܒܣܝܡܝܢ. A. V. *Like them that dream,* כְּחֹלְמִים. LXX., ὡσεὶ παρακεκλημένοι.

Ver. 4. *The Lord hath turned,* ܘܐܗܦܟ ܡܪܝܐ. A. V. *Turn again, O Lord,* שׁוּבָה יְחֹוָה. The Syriac verb may be imperative.

Ver. 6. *He goeth forth and weepeth, that beareth the seed,* ܡܗܠܟܗܘܐ ܡܗܠܟ ܘܒܟܐ. ܐܢܐ ܕܫܩܝܠ ܙܪܥܐ. A. V. *He that goeth forth and weepeth, bearing precious seed,* הָלוֹךְ יֵלֵךְ וּבָכֹה נֹשֵׂא מֶשֶׁךְ־הַזָּרַע.

He cometh with joy, that bringeth the sheaf, ܐܬܐ ܐܬܐ ܒܚܕܘܬܐ. ܐܢܐ ܕܫܩܝܠ ܟܦܐ. A. V. *Shall doubtless come again with*

PSALM CXXVI.

One of the Psalms of ascension. — Written by David concerning Solomon, and intended also of Haggai and Zechariah, who forwarded the building of the Temple.

1. Except the Lord build the house, they labour in vain that build it; and except the Lord keep the city, its watchmen wake *but* in vain.
2. They are vain that rise up early, and sit up late, *and* eat their bread with sorrows; *for* so he giveth his beloved sleep.
3. Truly children are an heritage of the Lord; the reward of the fruit of the womb.
4. As an arrow in the hand of a mighty man, so are the young children.

rejoicing, bringing his sheaves with him, בָּאִילָא בְרָנָּה נֹשֵׂא אֲלֻמֹּתָיו. I have translated ܟܦܐ, *sheaf;* literally, it means *a handful* of anything.

Ps. CXXVI. Ver. 1. *Its watchmen.* Heb., *the watchman.*

Ver. 2. *They are vain,* ܡܣܬܝܒܗܝܢ ܐܢܝܢ. A. V. *It is vain for you,* שָׁוְא לָכֶם.

And eat their bread with sorrows. Heb., *to eat the bread of sorrows.*

Ver. 3. *The reward of the fruit of the womb,* ܐܓܪܐ ܕܦܐܪ̈ܐ ܕܟܪܣܐ. A. V. *And the fruit of the womb is his reward,* שָׂכָר פְּרִי הַבָּטֶן. The Hebrew, however, without points and accents, might be rendered like the Syriac. LXX., ὁ μισθὸς τοῦ καρποῦ τῆς γαστρός.

Ver. 4. *The young children,* ܒܢܝ̈ܐ ܕܛܠܝܘܬܐ. A. V. *Children of the youth,* בְּנֵי הַנְּעוּרִים.

5. Happy is the man that shall fill his quiver with them; and they shall not be ashamed, when they speak with the enemy in the gate.

PSALM CXXVII.

A Psalm of ascension. — Anonymous. — Intended of Zerubbabel prince of Judah, who forwarded the building *of the Temple;* in which is also indicated the calling of the Gentiles.

1. Blessed is every one that feareth the Lord, and walketh in his paths.
2. When thou shalt eat the labour of thy hands, O man, O well is thee, and happy *shalt* thou *be.*
3. Thy wife *shall be* as an excellent vine upon the sides of thine house; thy children like an olive plant, round about thy table.
4. Thus shall the man be blessed that feareth the Lord.
5. The Lord shall bless thee out of Zion, and thou shalt see the prosperity of Jerusalem all the days of thy life.
6. Yea, thou shalt see thy children's children, and peace upon Israel.

Ps. CXXVII. Ver. 2. *When.* Heb., *for.*

O man, ܟܠܢܫ, not in the Hebrew.

Ver. 3. *Excellent,* ܣܓܘܠܐ. A. v. *Fruitful,* פֹּרִיָּה.

PSALM CXXVIII.

A Psalm of ascension. — Anonymous. — Concerning the oppression of the people; and signifying to us the victory and triumph of the *servants of God.*

1. Mine oppressors have been many from my youth, may Israel say;
2. Mine oppressors have been many from my youth, but they have not prevailed against me.
3. They inflicted scourges upon my back, and prolonged their humiliation.
4. The Lord *is* just, and cutteth asunder the boughs of the unrighteous.
5. Let them turn backward, all they that hate Zion;
6. And let them be as the grass of the house-top, which, when the wind bloweth upon it, withereth and drieth up.

Ps. CXXVIII. Ver. 1. *Mine oppressors have been many.* Heb., *Many a time have they afflicted me.* There is the same variation in the second verse.

Ver. 3. *They inflicted scourges,* ܢ̈ܓܕܘ ܢܓܕ̈ܐ. A. V. *The plowers plowed,* חָרְשׁוּ חֹרְשִׁים.

And prolonged their humiliation, ܘܐܓܪܘ ܡܟܟܗܘܢ. A. V. *They made long their furrows,* הֶאֱרִיכוּ לְמַעֲנוֹתָם. The translator read עֲנוּתָם. LXX, ἐμάκρυναν τὴν ἀνομίαν αὐτῶν, reading עֲווֹנֹתָם.

Ver. 4. *The boughs of the unrighteous.* Heb., *the cords of the wicked.*

Ver. 5. *Let them turn backward.* Heb., *Let them all be confounded and turned back.*

Ver. 6. *Which, when the wind bloweth upon it, withereth and*

7. Neither doth the mower fill his hand therewith, nor he that gathereth *the sheaves*, his bosom.

8. Neither do they which go by, say, The blessing of the Lord *be* upon you; we bless you in the Name of the Lord.

PSALM CXXIX.

A Psalm of ascension.—Intended of Nehemiah the priest; in which allusion is also made to the prayer of the Martyrs.

1. Out of the deep have I cried unto thee, O Lord, and thou heardest my voice.

2. Let thine ears be attentive to the voice of my supplication.

3. If thou, Lord, shouldest mark iniquities, who would be able to stand?

4. For forgiveness is from thee.

drieth up, ܘܐܬܐ ܘܬܡܟܐ ܚܕ ܕܩܡܐ ܡܚܕ ܘܢܓܒ. A. V. *Which withereth afore it groweth up,* שֶׁקַּדְמַת שָׁלַף יָבֵשׁ. The difference here seems to turn upon the variation in meaning, in the two languages, of the word שָׁלַף or ܡܟܕ.

Ver. 7. *He that gathereth the sheaves,* ܡܥܡܪܢܠ. A. V. *He that bindeth sheaves,* מְעַמֵּר.

Ps. CXXIX. Ver. 1. *And thou heardest my voice,* ܘܫܡܥܬ ܩܠܝ. These words form part of the second verse in the Hebrew, but I have included them in the first, with which they are connected in meaning in the Syriac. A. V. *Lord, hear my voice,* אֲדֹנָי שִׁמְעָה בְקוֹלִי.

Ver. 4. *For forgiveness is from thee.* Heb., *But there is forgiveness with thee.* The words לְמַעַן תִּוָּרֵא, *that thou mayest be feared,* forming part of this verse in the Hebrew, are not translated.

5. I hope in the Lord, and my soul waiteth for his word.

6. I have waited for the Lord from the morning watch, even until the morning watch.

7. Let Israel wait for the Lord, for from him *cometh* mercy, and with him *there is* plenteous redemption.

8. And he shall redeem Israel from all his iniquity.

PSALM CXXX.

A Psalm of David. — *One of the Psalms* of ascension. Intended of Joshua, son of Josedek, the high priest; also concerning humility.

1. Lord, mine heart is not lifted up, nor mine eyes lofty; neither do I exercise myself in things too great for me.

Ver. 5. *And my soul waiteth for his word.* Heb., *my soul doth wait, and in his word do I hope.*

Ver. 6. *I have waited for the Lord from the morning watch, even until the morning watch,* ܗܟܝܠ ܚܟܝܬ ܡܢ ܡܛܪܬܐ ܕܨܦܪܐ ܥܕܡܐ ܠܡܛܪܬܐ ܕܨܦܪܐ. A. V. *My soul waiteth for the Lord more than they that watch for the morning: I say, more than they that watch for the morning,* נַפְשִׁי לַאדֹנָי מִשֹּׁמְרִים לַבֹּקֶר שֹׁמְרִים לַבֹּקֶר.

Ver. 7. *From him,* ܥܡܗ ܠܦܘܬ ܡܢ. A. V. *With the Lord,* עִם־יְהֹוָה.

Ps. CXXX. Ver. 1. *Is not lifted up.* Heb., *is not haughty.*

In things too great for me. Heb., *in great matters, or in things too high for me.*

2. But I have humbled my soul, as a child that is weaned of his mother; yea, my soul is even as a weaned child.

3. Let Israel wait for the Lord from this time forth, and forevermore.

(LAUD, AND THE BEGINNING OF THE GRADE.)

PSALM CXXXI.

A Psalm of ascension. — Anonymous. — When *the people* sought to build a house unto the Lord of Sabaoth; — also a prayer of David, and a revelation of the Messiah.

1. Lord, remember David, and all his humiliation,
2. Which sware unto the Lord, and vowed unto the God of Jacob;
3. I will not come into the tabernacle of mine house, nor go up into my bed;
4. And I will not give sleep to mine eyes, nor slumber to mine eyelids;
5. Until I find out a place for the Lord, and an habitation for the God of Jacob.
6. Lo, we heard of it at Ephratah, and found it in the fields.

Ver. 2. *But I have humbled my soul.* Heb., *Surely I have behaved and quieted myself.*

Ps. CXXXI. Ver. 1. *His humiliation,* מַכִּיכוּתֵהּ. A. V. *His afflictions,* עֱנוֹתוֹ. The translator read עֲנָוְתוֹ.

Ver. 4. *To mine eyelids,* ܠܓܒܝܢܝ, literally, *to mine eyebrows.*

Ver. 6. *In the fields.* Heb., *in the fields of the wood.*

7. We will go into his tabernacle, and we will worship at his footstool.

8. Arise, O Lord, into thy rest, thou, and the ark of thy strength.

9. Let thy priests be clothed with righteousness, and thy saints with praise.

10. For thy servant David's sake, turn not away the face of thine Anointed.

11. The Lord hath sworn in truth unto David, and he will not turn from him; of the fruit of thy body will I set upon thy throne.

12. If thy children will keep my covenant, and this testimony that I teach them, of their children *shall there be those that* shall also sit upon thy throne forevermore.

13. For the Lord delighteth in Zion, and hath chosen it for his habitation.

14. This is my rest forever and ever; here will I dwell, for I have desired it;

15. And I will bless her provision, and satisfy her poor with bread.

16. I will clothe her priests with salvation, and her saints with praise.

17. There will I make the horn of David to arise, and I will make a lamp to shine for his Anointed;

Ver. 9. *And thy saints with praise,* ܡܚܣܢܝ ܢܒܩܒܝ. A. V. *And let thy saints shout for joy,* וַחֲסִידֶיךָ יְרַנֵּנוּ.

Ver. 11. *From him,* ܡܢܗ. A. V. *From it,* מִמֶּנָּה.

Ver. 13. *Delighteth.* Heb., *hath chosen.*

And hath chosen it. Heb., *he hath desired it.*

Ver. 16. *With praise.* See note to verse 9.

Ver. 17. *Will I make to arise,* ܐܘܥܐ. A. V. *Will I make to bud,* אַצְמִיחַ. LXX., ἐξανατελῶ.

18. And his enemies will I clothe with shame, but upon himself shall my holiness flourish.

PSALM CXXXII.

A Psalm of David. — *One of the Psalms* of ascension. — Understood of Moses and Aaron, who dwelt in the tabernacle, in the house of the Lord; in which there is also allusion made to a perfect people.

1. How good and how comely *it is* for brethren, when they dwell together in unity!
2. *It is* like the ointment that ran down upon the head, and upon the beard, *even* Aaron's beard; that ran down *also* to the skirts of his garment.
3. As the dew of Hermon, *and as the dew* that descended upon mount Zion; for there the Lord commanded the blessing, even life forevermore.

And I will make to shine, ܘܐܢܗܪ. A. V. *I have ordained*, עָרַכְתִּי.

For his Anointed. Heb., *for mine Anointed.*

Ver. 18. *My holiness*, ܩܘܕܫܝ. A. V. *His crown*, נִזְרוֹ. LXX., τὸ ἁγίασμά μου. Both translators derived the Hebrew word from נֵזֶר, in the sense of *separating*, and *consecrating*; and hence the idea of *holiness.*

Ps. cxxxii. Ver. 1. *For brethren, when they dwell together in unity,* ܠܐܚܐ ܟܕ ܘܚܕܝܢ ܐܟܚܕܐ. A. V. *For brethren to dwell together in unity,* שֶׁבֶת אַחִים גַּם־יָחַד.

Ver. 2. *The ointment.* Heb., *the precious ointment.*

That ran down upon the head and upon the beard. Heb., *upon the head, that ran down upon the beard.*

Ver. 3. *Upon mount Zion.* Heb., *upon the mountains of Zion.*

PSALM CXXXIII.

A Psalm of David; — concerning the priests whom he appointed to attend to the ministry of the Lord by night; and spiritually, the doctrine of life.

1. Bless ye the Lord, all ye servants of the Lord, which by night stand in the house of the Lord.
2. Lift up your hands towards the sanctuary, and bless the Lord.
3. The Lord that made heaven and earth, bless thee out of Zion.

PSALM CXXXIV.

Anonymous. — In its spiritual sense, to be understood of the soul that, conscious, hymns in trance, while watching in union with the Trinity. In which there is also an allusion to the conversion of the people of the Messiah to the Faith.

1. Praise ye the Name of the Lord; praise *him*, O ye servants of the Lord.
2. Ye that stand in the house of the Lord, and in the court of the house of our God.

Ps. cxxxiii. Ver. 2. *Towards the sanctuary*, ܠܩܘܕܫܐ. A. V. *In the sanctuary*, בַּקֹּדֶשׁ. LXX., εἰς τὰ ἅγια.

Ps. cxxxiv. Title. We may suppose an allusion to be made in these somewhat mystical words, to the sacred prophecy of Balaam, of whom it is said, that he "*saw the vision of the Almighty, falling into a trance, but having his eyes open.*"

3. Praise the Lord, for he is good; sing praises unto his Name, for it is pleasant.

4. For the Lord hath chosen Jacob unto himself, and Israel for his congregation.

5. For I know that the Lord our God is greater than all gods;

6. And whatsoever the Lord pleaseth, *that* doeth he in heaven, and in earth; in the seas, and in all deep places.

7. He causeth the clouds to ascend from the ends of the earth, and maketh lightnings for the rain; he bringeth the winds out of his treasuries.

8. Who smote the first-born of Egypt, both of man and beast.

9. *Who* sent his tokens and wonders into the midst of Egypt, upon Pharaoh, and upon all his servants.

10. Who smote great nations, and slew mighty kings.

11. Sihon, king of the Amorites, and Og, king of Bashan, and all the kingdoms of Canaan;

12. And gave their land *for* an heritage unto Israel his people.

13. Thy Name, O Lord, *endureth* forever; thy memorial, O Lord, throughout all generations.

Ver. 4. *For his congregation,* ܠܓܒܝܬܗ. A. V. *For his peculiar treasure,* לִסְגֻלָּתוֹ.

Ver. 5. *For I know that the Lord our God is greater than all gods.* Heb., *For I know that the Lord is great, and that our Lord is above all gods.*

Ver. 9. *Into the midst of Egypt.* Heb., *into the midst of thee, O Egypt.*

Ver. 12. *An heritage.* This word is repeated in the Hebrew.

14. For the Lord judgeth his people, and is comforted in his servants.

15. The idols of the heathen *are* silver and gold, the work of men's hands.

16. They have mouths, but they speak not; eyes have they, but they see not;

17. They have ears, but they hear not, neither is there *any* breath in their mouth.

18. They that make them shall be like unto them, and *so shall* all they that put their trust in them.

19. Bless the Lord, O house of Israel; bless the Lord, O house of Aaron.

20. Bless the Lord, O house of Levi; ye that fear the Lord, bless the Lord.

21. Blessed is the Lord out of Zion; *even* he that dwelleth in Jerusalem.

Ver. 14. *And is comforted in his servants,* ܘܥܠ ܥܒܕܘܗܝ ܢܬܒܝܐ. A. V. *And he will repent himself concerning his servants,* וְעַל־עֲבָדָיו יִתְנֶחָם. LXX., καὶ ἐπὶ τοῖς δούλοις αὐτοῦ παρακληθήσεται.

Ver. 18. *Shall be,* ܢܗܘܘܢ. A. V. *Are,* יִהְיוּ.

This Psalm in the Hebrew begins and ends with the Hallelujah.

PSALM CXXXV.

Anonymous. — Understood of Moses and Israel, singing praises unto the Lord, on account of them that were delivered. Also, concerning the redemption of souls from Gehenna, from the Pharaoh, Satan, by the Messiah, our Saviour, *and their deliverers.*

1. O give thanks unto the Lord, for he is good, and his mercies *endure* forever.
2. O give thanks unto the God of gods; for his mercies *endure* forever.
3. O give thanks unto the Lord of lords; for his mercies *endure* forever.
4. To him who alone doeth great wonders; for his mercies *endure* forever.
5. To him that by his wisdom made the heavens; for his mercies *endure* forever.
6. To him that established the earth above the waters; for his mercies *endure* forever.
7. To him that made great lights; for his mercies *endure* forever:
8. The sun to rule the day; for his mercies *endure* forever:
9. The moon and the stars to rule the night; for his mercies *endure* forever.
10. To him that smote the first-born of Egypt; for his mercies *endure* forever;

Ps. cxxxv. Ver. 6. *To him that established,* ܠܕܐܬܩܢ. A. V. *To him that stretched out,* לְרֹקַע. The same word, with a different meaning, in the two languages.

Ver. 10. *The first-born of Egypt.* Heb., *Egypt in their first-born.*

11. And brought out Israel from among them; for his mercies *endure* forever;

12. With a mighty hand, and an exalted arm; for his mercies *endure* forever.

13. To him that divided the Red Sea; for his mercies *endure* forever.

14. And made Israel to pass through the midst of it; for his mercies *endure* forever.

15. To him that overthrew Pharaoh and his host in the Red Sea; for his mercies *endure* forever.

16. To him which led his people through the wilderness; for his mercies *endure* forever.

17. To him which smote great kings; for his mercies *endure* forever.

18. And slew mighty kings; for his mercies *endure* forever.

19. Sihon, king of the Amorites; for his mercies *endure* forever;

20. And Og, the king of Bashan; for his mercies *endure* forever;

21. And gave their land *for* an heritage; for his mercies *endure* forever;

22. *Even* an heritage unto Israel his servant; for his mercies *endure* forever.

23. To him who remembered us in our humiliation; for his mercies *endure* forever;

24. And hath redeemed us from our enemies; for his mercies *endure* forever.

25. To him that giveth food to all flesh; for his mercies *endure* forever.

Ver. 12. *An exalted.* Heb., *a stretched out.*

Ver. 13. *That divided the Red Sea.* The Hebrew has לִגְזָרִים, *into parts*, which is not translated.

26. O give thanks unto God that *is* in heaven; for his mercies *endure* forever.

PSALM CXXXVI.

A Psalm of David; — The words of the saints that were carried away captive to Babylon.

1. By the rivers of Babylon, there we sat down and wept, when we remembered Zion.
2. We hanged our harps upon the willows that were in the midst thereof.
3. For there they that carried us away captive required of us songs; and they that led us away, said unto us, Sing us some of the songs of Zion.
4. How shall we sing unto you the songs of the Lord in a strange land?
5. If I forget thee, O Jerusalem, let my right hand forget me.
6. Let my tongue cleave to the roof of my mouth, unless I remember thee; unless I prefer Jerusalem above my chief joy.

Ps. cxxxvi. Ver. 3. *And they that led us away,* ܡܘܒܠܢܝ. A. V. *And they that wasted us,* וְתוֹלָלֵינוּ. LXX., οἱ ἀπαγαγόντες ἡμᾶς.

Said unto us, ܐܡܪܘ ܠܢ. A. V. *Required of us mirth,* שִׂמְחָה.

Ver. 4. *Unto you,* ܠܟܘܢ, not in the Hebrew.

Ver. 5. *Forget me,* ܬܛܥܝܢܝ. A. V. *Forget her cunning,* תִּשְׁכַּח.

7. Remember, O Lord, the children of Edom, in the day of Jerusalem; who said, Uncover *it*, uncover *it*, *even* to the foundations thereof.

8. O daughter of Babylon, the spoiler, happy *shall* he *be* that rewardeth thee as thou hast served us.

9. Happy *shall* he *be* that shall take thy children, and dash *them* against the stones.

PSALM CXXXVII.

Written by David. — Thanksgiving with prophecy.

1. I will give thanks unto the Lord with my whole heart; even before kings will I sing praise unto thee.

2. I will worship in thy holy temple, and give thanks unto thy Name, for thy mercy, and for thy truth; for thou hast magnified thy word above every name.

3. In the day when I cried unto thee, thou answeredst me, and increasedst the strength of my soul.

Ver. 7. *Uncover it*, ܩܠܘ. A. V. *Rase it*, עָרוּ.

Ver. 8. *The spoiler*, ܚܪܘܒܐ. A. V. *Who art to be destroyed*, הַשְּׁדוּדָה.

Ps. CXXXVII. Ver. 1. *Kings*, ܡܠܟܐ. A. V. *The gods*, אֱלֹהִים.

Ver. 2. *Above every name*, ܟܠ ܫܡ ܡܢ. A. V. *Above all thy Name*, עַל־כָּל־שִׁמְךָ. The LXX. translate the whole passage ὅτι ἐμεγάλυνας ἐπὶ πᾶν τὸ ὄνομα τὸ ἅγιόν σου.

Ver. 3. *And increasedst the strength of my soul*, ܐܘܣܦܬ ܚܝܠܐ ܘܢܦܫܝ. A. V. *And strengthenedst me with strength in my soul*, תַּרְהִבֵנִי בְנַפְשִׁי עֹז.

4. All the kings of the earth shall praise thee, O Lord, for they have heard the word of thy mouth.

5. Yea, they shall praise the ways of the Lord, for great is the glory of the Lord;

6. And the Lord is high, which hath respect unto *him that is* lowly; but such as be exalted, he knoweth afar off.

7. Though I walk through affliction, thou shalt revive me; in the wrath of mine enemies, thou shalt stretch forth thy hand, and deliver me.

8. Let thy right hand rest upon me, O Lord; thy tender mercies, O Lord, *endure* forever; therefore, forsake not the work of thine hands.

Ver. 5. *They shall praise the ways of the Lord.* Heb., *they shall sing in the ways of the Lord.*

Ver. 6. *And the Lord is high, which hath respect unto him that is lowly.* Heb., *Though the Lord be high, yet hath he respect unto the lowly.*

Ver. 7. *In the wrath.* Heb., *against the wrath.*

And deliver me, ܘܦܨܢܝ. A. V. *And thy right hand shall save me,* וְתוֹשִׁיעֵנִי יְמִינֶךָ.

Ver. 8. *Let thy right hand rest upon me, O Lord,* تكنفني ܐܝܕܟ ܥܠܝ. A. V. *The Lord will perfect that which concerneth me,* יְהֹוָה יִגְמֹר בַּעֲדִי. The words, *thy right hand,* construed in the Syriac with the eighth, are construed in the Hebrew with the seventh verse, as will appear in the translation. I have placed them in their proper connection.

PSALM CXXXVIII.

A Psalm of David;—when one who was called Shimei, the son of Gera, cried out and reproached him, because he had rebelled, saying, O thou shedder of blood! And, in its spiritual sense, theological truth, and prayer with supplication.

1. Lord, thou hast searched me, and known me.
2. Thou knowest my down-setting and mine uprising; thou understandest my thoughts from on high.
3. Thou knowest my way and my paths; thou hast searched out all my ways.
4. If there be variation in my tongue, thou, O Lord, knowest *it; even* all these things from the beginning to the end.
5. Thou hast formed me, and laid thine hand upon me.

Ps. CXXXVIII. Ver. 2. *From on high*, ܡܢ ܪܘܚܩܐ. A. V. *Afar off*, מֵרָחוֹק.

Ver. 3. *Thou knowest my way and my paths*, ܐܘܪܚܝ ܘܫܒܝܠܝ ܝܕܥ ܐܢܬ. A. V. *Thou compassest my path and my lying down*, אָרְחִי וְרִבְעִי זֵרִיתָ, literally, *thou hast sifted*, or, *searched*, and thence, *known*.

Ver. 4. *If there be variation in my tongue*, ܐܢ ܡܣܬܓܦܠ ܠܝ ܒܠܫܢܝ. A. V. *For there is not a word in my tongue*, כִּי אֵין מִלָּה בִּלְשׁוֹנִי. LXX., ὅτι οὐκ ἔστι λόγος ἄδικος ἐν γλώσσῃ μου. Symmachus, οὐκ ἔστιν ἐν ἐμοὶ ἑτερολογία.

Thou, O Lord, knowest it, ܐܢܬ ܡܪܝܐ ܝܕܥ ܐܢܬ ܠܗ. A. V. *But lo, O Lord, thou knowest it altogether*, הֵן יְהוָה יָדַעְתָּ כֻלָּהּ. The word כֻלָּהּ, the translator connected with the succeeding words as will appear.

Even all these things from the beginning to the end. Ver. 5.

6. Beyond me is this knowledge, and *it is* wonderful; I have made a strong effort, but I cannot *attain unto it*.

7. Whither shall I go from thy spirit? and where shall I hide from thy presence?

8. If I ascend up into heaven, thou *art* there; and if I go down into hell, thou art there also.

9. And if I lift up my wings like the eagle, and dwell in the uttermost parts of the sea;

10. Even there shall thy hand hold me, and thy right hand shall lead me.

ܟܠܕܬܢܝ ܘܩܫ ܣܥܪܬ ܡܠܫܢܘܐܠ. *Thou hast formed me,* ܒܟܠܕܘܗܝ. A. V. *Thou hast beset me behind and before,* אָחוֹר וָקֶדֶם צַרְתָּנִי. The LXX. translate the whole passage in accordance with the Syriac, σὺ ἔγνως πάντα τὰ ἔσχατα καὶ τὰ ἀρχαῖα· σὺ ἔπλασάς με. I have altered the arrangement of the verses to bring the words into their natural connection.

Ver. 6. *Beyond me is this knowledge, and it is wonderful,* ܩܠܒ ܡܢܝ ܬܘܕܥܐ ܘܡܬܕܡܪܢܐ. A. V. *Such knowledge is too wonderful for me,* פְּלִאיָה דַעַת מִמֶּנִּי. It will be observed that in the Syriac there is no adjective to authorize a degree of comparison, and the words literally rendered are unintelligible. Perhaps, however, they will bear the meaning which I have given them and which approximates to the Hebrew.

Ver. 7. *Shall I hide,* ܐܛܫܐ. A. V. *Shall I flee,* אֶבְרָח.

Ver. 8. *And if I go down,* ܘܐܢ ܐܚܘܬ. A. V. *If I make my bed,* וְאַצִּיעָה. LXX., ἐὰν καταβῶ.

Ver. 9. *And if I lift up my wings like the eagle,* ܘܐܢ ܐܪܝܡ ܟܢܦܝ ܐܝܟ ܢܫܪܐ. A. V. *If I take the wings of the morning,* אֶשָּׂא כַנְפֵי־שָׁחַר.

11. I said, the darkness shall be light to me, and the night shall be light about me;

12. For the darkness hideth not from thee, but the night shall be as clear as the day; and the darkness *is* as the light *to thee.*

13. For thou hast fashioned my reins, and received me from my mother's belly. Diapsalma.

14. I will praise thee for the wonder that thou hast done; for thy works are very high exalted, and *that* my soul knoweth right well;

15. And my bones were not hid from thee, which

Ver. 11. *I said, the darkness shall be light to me,* ܐܡܪܬ ܕܚܫܘܟܐ ܢܛܫܢܝ. A. V. *If I say, surely the darkness shall cover me,* וָאֹמַר אַךְ־חֹשֶׁךְ יְשׁוּפֵנִי.

Ver. 13. *For thou hast fashioned,* ܐܢܬ ܓܒܠܬ ܟܘܠܝܬܝ. A. V. *For thou hast possessed,* כִּי־אַתָּה קָנִיתָ.

And received me from my mother's belly, ܘܩܒܠܬܢܝ ܡܢ ܟܪܣܐ ܕܐܡܝ. A. V. *Thou hast covered me in my mother's womb,* תְּסֻכֵּנִי בְּבֶטֶן אִמִּי. LXX., ἀντελάβου μου ἐκ γαστρὸς μητρός μου.

Ver. 14. *For the wonder that thou hast done,* ܥܠ ܬܕܡܪܬܐ ܕܐܥܒܕܬ. A. V. *For I am fearfully and wonderfully made,* עַל כִּי נוֹרָאוֹת נִפְלֵיתִי.

For thy works are very high exalted. Heb., *marvellous are thy works.*

Ver. 15. *My bones,* ܓܪܡܝ. A. V. *My substance,* עָצְמִי. LXX., τὸ ὀστοῦν μου. Both translators read עַצְמִי.

Which thou didst form, ܕܥܒܕܬ. A. V. *When I was made,* אֲשֶׁר־עֻשֵּׂיתִי. LXX., ὃ ἐποίησας. The translators doubtless read אֲשֶׁר־עָשִׂיתָ.

thou didst form in secret, *when* I descended into the lower parts of the earth.

16. Mine eyes have seen my recompense; in thy books shall all these things be written. Behold the days are shortened, and there is no man in them.

17. But very dear unto me, O God, are they that love thee, and great is their power;

When I descended into the lower parts of the earth, ܬܣܓܐ ܒܓܘ ܬܚܬܝܬܗ ܕܐܪܥܐ. A. V. *And curiously wrought in the lowest parts of the earth,* רֻקַּ֑מְתִּי בְּֽתַחְתִּיּ֥וֹת אָֽרֶץ׃.

Ver. 16. *Mine eyes have seen my recompense; in thy books shall all these things be written. Behold the days are shortened, and there is no man in them,* ܚܙܝܢ ܥܝܢܝ ܦܘܪܥܢܝ ܘܥܠ ܟܬܒܝܟ ܟܠ ܗܠܝܢ ܢܬܟܬܒܢ: ܗܐ ܝܘܡܬܐ ܐܬܟܪܝܘ ܘܠܝܬ ܒܗܘܢ ܐܢܫ. Being unable to assign any tolerable meaning to these words, I have contented myself with translating them literally. A. V. *Thine eyes did see my substance, yet being unperfect; and in thy book all my members were written, which in continuance were fashioned, when as yet there was none of them,* גָּלְמִ֤י ׀ רָ֘א֤וּ עֵינֶ֗יךָ וְעַֽל־סִפְרְךָ֮ כֻּלָּ֪ם יִכָּ֫תֵ֥בוּ יָמִ֥ים יֻצָּ֑רוּ וְלֹא אֶחָ֣ד בָּהֶֽם. For גָּלְמִי, the translator evidently read גְּמוּלִי, the Hebrew יָצַר, meaning both *to create* and *to shorten*. The Syriac text therefore is susceptible of an easy explanation.

Ver. 17. *But very dear unto me are they that love thee,* ܠܝ ܕܝܢ ܛܒ ܬܩܢܝܢ ܪܚܡܝܟ. A. V. *How precious also are thy thoughts unto me,* וְלִ֤י מַה־יָּקְר֣וּ רֵעֶ֣יךָ. LXX., ἐμοὶ δὲ λίαν ἐτιμήθησαν οἱ φίλοι σου. The Hebrew רֵעֶיךָ, may mean either *thy thoughts* or *thy friends.*

Ver. 17, 18. *And great is their power; and their rulers,* ܘܛܒ ܥܫܢܘ ܘܫܠܝܛܢܝܗܘܢ. A. V. *How great is the sum of them!*

18. And their rulers, should I number them, would be more than the sand: when I awake, I am still with thee.

19. O that thou wouldest slay the wicked, O God, and that bloodthirsty men would depart from me!

20. For they have spoken against thee, and taken thy city deceitfully.

21. I hate them, O Lord, that hate thee; and I am wroth with them that rise up against thee.

22. Yea, I hate them with a perfect hatred, and count them mine enemies.

23. Search me, O God, and know my heart; and try me, and know my goings;

24. And see if there be any way of falsehood in me; lead me in thy way that *is* everlasting.

מֶה עָצְמוּ רָאשֵׁיהֶם. The Hebrew word רֹאשׁ, may mean *head*, or *leader;* or *the sum*, or *whole number*. It is taken in the former sense by the Syriac translator, and construed with succeeding words. I have arranged the verse accordingly.

Ver. 19. *O that thou wouldest slay the wicked, O God!* Heb., *Surely thou wilt slay the wicked, O God.*

And that bloodthirsty men would depart. This, in the Hebrew, is imperative.

Ver. 20. *For they have spoken against thee, and taken thy city deceitfully,* ܡܢܐ ܘܡܠܠܘ ܥܠܝܟ ܟܡܝܢܐܝܬ ܐܟܒܝܫܘ. A. V. *For they speak against thee wickedly, and thine enemies take thy name in vain,* אֲשֶׁר יֹמְרוּךָ לִמְזִמָּה נָשֻׂא לַשָּׁוְא עָרֶיךָ. The Hebrew עָרֶיךָ, may mean *thine enemies*, or *thy cities*. LXX., ὅτι ἐρεῖς εἰς διαλογισμόν · λήψονται εἰς ματαιότητα τὰς πόλεις σου.

Ver. 21. In the Hebrew this verse is in the interrogative form.

Ver. 23. *My goings*. Heb., *my thoughts*.

PSALM CXXXIX.

Written by David,—when Saul cast a javelin at him to slay him, and it entered the wall; and, spiritually, the words of him that cleaveth unto God, and contendeth with them that hate him.

1. Deliver me, O Lord, from the evil man, and preserve me from the unrighteous men;
2. Which imagine mischief in their heart, and stir up strife all the day:
3. Which have sharpened their tongue like a serpent, and adder's poison is under their lips.
4. Keep me, O Lord, from the hand of the unrighteous, and preserve me from the violent men who have purposed to overthrow my goings.
5. The proud, also, have hid snares for me, and spread the cords of their nets about my paths, and cast a net around me. Diapsalma.
6. I said unto the Lord, thou *art* my God; hear the voice of my supplication,
7. O Lord, my strong deliverer, *and* the covering of my head in the day of battle.

Ps. cxxxix. Ver. 2. *And stir up strife all the day*, ܣܛܢ ܢܩܫܐ ܩܪܒܐ. A. V. *Continually are they gathered together for war*, כָּל־יוֹם יָגוּרוּ מִלְחָמוֹת. LXX., παρετάσσοντο πολέμους. The Hebrew verb was either thought to be יָגוּדוּ, or it was derived from נָרָה.

Ver. 5. *The proud, also, have hid snares for me, and spread the cords of their nets about my paths, and cast a net around me.* Heb., *The proud have hid a snare for me, and cords; they have spread a net by the wayside; they have set gins for me.*

Ver. 7. *O Lord, my strong deliverer, and the covering of my head*

8. Grant not, O Lord, his desire to the unrighteous, and let not his imagination ascend into my head.

9. Let the iniquity of their own lips cover them.

10. Let burning coals come down upon them; let them fall into the fire, and let them not be able to rise.

11. Let not an evil speaker be established in the earth; and let his own mischief hunt the unrighteous man to destruction.

12. I know that the Lord maintaineth the cause of the poor, and the cause of the needy.

13. Surely the righteous shall give thanks unto thy Name, and the upright shall dwell in thy presence.

in the day of battle. Heb., *O God the Lord, the strength of my salvation, thou hast covered my head in the day of battle.*

Ver. 8. *And let not his imagination ascend into my head,* ܠܐ ܬܣܩ ܡܚܫܒܬܗ ܠܪܝܫܝ. The word ܠܪܝܫܝ, forms part of the 9th verse, as does the corresponding word in the Hebrew, but in the Syriac it is connected with words going before, and I have accordingly placed it in the 8th verse. A. V. *Further not his wicked device, lest they exalt themselves,* זְמָמוֹ אַל־תָּפֵק יָרוּמוּ. The translator seems to have omitted יָרוּמוּ, reading תָּפֵק, which he connected with the first word of the next verse.

Ver. 9. *Let the iniquity of their own lips cover them,* ܥܘܠܐ ܕܣܦܘܬܗܘܢ ܢܟܣܐ ܐܢܘܢ. A. V. *As for the head of those that compass me about, let the mischief of their own lips cover them,* רֹאשׁ מְסִבָּי עֲמַל שְׂפָתֵימוֹ יְכַסֵּימוֹ.

Ver. 10. *Let them fall into the fire.* Heb., *let them be cast into the fire; into deep pits.*

Ver. 11. *His own mischief.* Heb., *evil.*

PSALM CXL.

A Psalm of David; — as he mused in the ministry of the evening; also the prayers of him that is perfect in God.

1. Lord, I cry unto thee; do thou answer me; hear and receive my words.
2. *Let* my prayers *be set forth* before thee as incense; and the oblation of my hands as the evening oblation.
3. Appoint a guard, O Lord, for my mouth, and a keeper for my lips;
4. That my heart incline not to *any* evil word, and that I may not practice the works of iniquity: as for wicked men, I will not take salt with them.

Ps. CXL. Ver. 1. *Do thou answer me; hear and receive my words.* Heb., *make haste unto me; give ear unto my voice, when I cry unto thee.*

Ver. 2. *Be set forth.* I have supplied here what is expressed in the Hebrew by the word תִּכּוֹן.

The oblation of my hands. Heb., *the lifting up of my hands.*

Ver. 3. *Appoint a guard, O Lord, for my mouth, and a keeper for my lips.* Heb., *Set a watch, O Lord, before my mouth; keep the door of my lips.*

Ver. 4. *That my heart incline not to any evil word.* Heb., *Incline not my heart to any evil thing.*

And that I may not practice the works of iniquity. Heb., *to practice wicked works with men that work iniquity.*

As for wicked men, I will not take salt with them, ܠܡ ܚܠܝ| ܐܘܟܣ ܠܐ ܐܘܟܠ ܟܣܕܗܘܢ. A. V. *And let me not eat of their dainties,* וּבַל־אֶלְחַם בְּמַנְעַמֵּיהֶם. It is conjectured, however, that the true reading of the Syriac is ܐܠܓܢܣܡ, and not ܐܘܟܣܝ, which would correspond with the version of the LXX. who have συνδυάσω.

5. Let the righteous teach me and reprove me; *but* let not the oil of the wicked anoint my head; for my prayer *is* against their wickedness.

6. And their judges were restrained with a hand of stone, and heard my words that they *were* sweet.

Ver. 5. *Let the righteous teach me and reprove me; but let not the oil of the wicked anoint my head*, ܬܚܦܒ ܐܘܣܛܐ ܘܢܚܣܒܢ. A. V. *Let the righteous smite me; it shall be a kindness: and let him reprove me; it shall be an excellent oil, which shall not break my head*, יֶֽהֶלְמֵ֥נִי צַדִּ֨יק חֶ֥סֶד וְֽיוֹכִיחֵ֗נִי שֶׁ֣מֶן רֹ֭אשׁ אַל־יָנִ֣י רֹאשִׁ֑י. LXX., παιδεύσει με δίκαιος ἐν ἐλέει καὶ ἐλέγξει με, ἔλαιον δὲ ἁμαρτωλοῦ μὴ λιπανάτω τὴν κεφαλήν μου. Both translators seem to have read שֶׁ֣מֶן רָשָׁ֑ע for שֶׁ֣מֶן רֹ֭אשׁ, and to have derived יָנִ֣י from an Arabic root, signifying *to anoint*.

For my prayer is against their wickedness, ܒܨܠܘܬܝ ܕܠܩܘܒܠܐ ܕܒܝܫܘܬܗܘܢ. A. V. *For yet my prayer also shall be in their calamities*, כִּי־ע֣וֹד וּ֭תְפִלָּתִי בְּרָעוֹתֵיהֶֽם.

Ver. 6. *And their judges were restrained with a hand of stone, and heard my words that they were sweet*, ܘܐܬܚܒܫܘ ܕܝܢܝܗܘܢ ܒܐܝܕܐ ܕܟܐܦܐ. ܘܫܡܥܘ ܡܠܝ ܕܚܠܝܢ. A. V. *When their judges are overthrown in stony places, they shall hear my words; for they are sweet*, נִשְׁמְט֣וּ בִֽידֵי־סֶ֖לַע שֹׁפְטֵיהֶ֑ם וְשָׁמְע֥וּ אֲמָרַ֗י כִּ֣י נָעֵֽמוּ. The words, however, more literally are, *their judges have been dismissed in the sides of the rock, and have heard my words that they are sweet*, and thus may be supposed to contain an allusion to the incident recorded in 1 Sam. xxiv. when David had Saul at an advantage in the cave, and refused to avail himself of it, simply addressing him in the language of expostulation. The Syriac will harmonize well with this theory of the passage.

7. Like a plough that cutteth the earth, their bones are scattered at the mouth of the pit.

8. But unto thee, O Lord, do I lift up mine eyes, and in thee do I trust; O cast not away my soul.

9. Preserve me from the hand of the proud, who have hid snares for me.

10. Let the unrighteous fall into their own nets together, whilst that I escape.

Ver. 7. *Like a plough that cutteth the earth,* ܐܝܟ ܦܕܢܐ ܘܦܠܚ ܘܐܟܠ. A. V. *As when one cutteth and cleaveth wood upon the earth,* כְּמוֹ פֹלֵחַ וּבֹקֵעַ בָּאָרֶץ. LXX., ὡσεὶ πάχος γῆς διεῤῥάγη ἐπὶ τῆς γῆς.

Their bones. Heb., *our bones.*

Ver. 8. *But unto thee, O Lord, do I lift up mine eyes,* ܐܢܬ ܠܚܦܘܟ ܡܪܢ ܐܪܝܡܬ ܟܬܦܝ A. V. *But mine eyes are unto thee, O God the Lord,* כִּי אֵלֶיךָ יְהֹוִה אֲדֹנָי עֵינָי. For יְהֹוָה אֲדֹנָי, the translator seems to have read יְהֹוָה אָרִים.

O cast not away. Heb., *leave not destitute.*

Ver. 9. *From the hand of the proud, who have hid snares for me.* Heb., *from the snares which they have laid for me, and the gins of the workers of iniquity.*

Ver. 10. *Together.* The Hebrew word, of which this is a translation, is construed in the original with the second hemistich, and rendered *withal* in the common version.

PSALM CXLI.

A Psalm of David;—concerning the famine that continued three years, on account of the iniquity of Saul; and, spiritually, the words of the Agonists, *and* the supplication and prayer that bringeth us near to God.

1. I cried unto the Lord with my voice; with my voice did I make my supplication unto the Lord.
2. Yea, I laid my supplication before him, and shewed before him mine affliction.
3. When my spirit is agitated, thou knowest my paths; in the way of my steps they privily laid snares for me.
4. I looked on *my* right hand, and beheld, but there was no one that knew me; refuge failed me, and there was no avenger for my soul.
5. Then I cried unto thee, O Lord, and said, thou art my hope and my portion, in the land of the living.
6. Hear my supplication, for I am brought very low; deliver me from my persecutors, for they are stronger than I.

Ps. CXLI. Ver. 2. *I laid my supplication.* Heb., *I poured out my complaint.*

Ver. 3. *When my spirit is agitated.* Heb., *When my spirit was overwhelmed within me.*

Ver. 4. *And there was no avenger,* ܘܡܝܐ ܠܐܚܕܐܠܝ. A. V. *No man cared for,* אֵין דּוֹרֵשׁ.

7. Bring my soul out of prison, that I may give thanks unto thy Name; and thy saints will have respect unto me, when thou shalt have rewarded me.

PSALM CXLII.

A Psalm of David;— concerning the Edomites who came against him; and the prayer of him that returneth thanks continually by reason of troubles.

1. Hear my prayer, O Lord, and give ear to my supplication; in thy word answer me, and in thy righteousness.
2. Bring not thy servant into judgment, for in thy sight shall no man living be justified.
3. For the enemy hath persecuted my soul, and humbled my life to the earth; he hath made me to dwell in darkness, like him that hath been long dead.

Ver. 7. *And thy saints will have respect unto me, when thou shalt have rewarded me,* ܘܠܝ ܢܣܟܘܢ ܟܕ ܬܦܪܥܢܝ.
A. V. *The righteous shall compass me about; for thou shalt deal bountifully with me,* כִּי יַכְתִּרוּ צַדִּיקִים כִּי תִגְמֹל עָלָי.

Ps. CXLII. Ver. 1. *In thy word,* ܒܡܠܬܟ. A. V. *In thy faithfulness,* בֶּאֱמֻנָתְךָ. The translator seems to have read בְּאִמְרָתְךָ.

Ver. 2. *Bring not thy servant into judgment.* Heb., *And enter not into judgment with thy servant.*

Ver. 3. *And humbled.* Heb., *he hath smitten.*

4. My spirit is troubled within me, and my heart within me is stirred.

5. I remember thee, O Lord, of old, and meditate on all thy works, and I muse on the works of thy hands;

6. And I stretch forth my hands unto thee; my soul thirsteth after thee like the land.

7. Hear me speedily, O Lord, for my spirit faileth; turn not away thy face from me, that I be not like unto them that go down into the pit.

8. Cause me to hear thy mercy in the morning, for in thee do I trust; shew me thy way, O Lord, that I may walk therein, for I lift up my soul unto thee, O Lord.

9. Deliver me from mine enemies;

10. And teach me to do thy will, for thou art my God; let thy benignant spirit lead me in thy way of life.

11. Comfort me, O Lord, for thy Name's sake; for thy righteousness' sake, bring my soul out of affliction;

Ver. 4. *Is stirred.* Heb., *is desolate.*

Ver. 5. *I remember thee, O Lord,* ܐܬܕܟܪܬܟ ܡܪܝܐ. A. V. *I remember the days,* זָכַ֣רְתִּי יָמִ֑ים.

Ver. 6. *Like the land.* Heb., *as a thirsty land.*

Ver. 8. *Shew me thy way, O Lord, that I may walk therein.* Heb., *cause me to know the way wherein I should walk.* The word *Lord*, at the close of this verse, is construed in the Hebrew with the 9th verse.

Ver. 9. The second clause of this verse in the Hebrew, translated, *I flee unto thee to hide me;* is not in the Syriac version.

Ver. 10. *Let thy benignant spirit lead me in thy way of life.* Heb., *thy spirit is good; lead me into the land of uprightness.*

Ver. 11. *Comfort me,* ܒܝܐܢܝ. A. V. *Quicken me,* תְּחַיֵּ֑נִי; for which the translator may have read תְּנַחֲמֵ֑נִי.

12. And, of thy mercy, put to silence them that hate me, and destroy the enemies of my soul; for I am thy servant.

PSALM CXLIII.

A Psalm of David, — when he slew Asaph, the brother of Goliath. Also the thanksgiving of him that is victorious.

1. Blessed is the Lord who hath taught my hands to war, and my fingers to fight;
2. My refuge and my deliverer, my helper in whom I trust; and *who* subdueth the people under me.
3. Lord, what is man that thou takest knowledge of him? Yea, *what is* man, that thou makest account of him?
4. Man is like a vapour, and his days pass away like a shadow.
5. Bow the heavens, O Lord, and come down; and rebuke the mountains, and they shall smoke.

Ver. 12. *Put to silence,* ܨܡܝ. A. V. *Cut off,* תַּצְמִית.

Ps. CXLIII. Ver. 1. *The Lord.* Heb., *the Lord my strength.*

Ver. 2. *My refuge and my deliverer, my helper in whom I trust.* Heb., *My goodness, and my fortress; my high tower, and my deliverer; my shield, and he in whom I trust.*

Ver. 3. *Yea, what is man,* ܒܪܢܫܐ. A. V. *Or the son of man,* בֶּן־אֱנוֹשׁ. In the Syriac the same word is used in both clauses.

Ver. 4. *Pass away like a shadow.* Heb., *as a shadow that passeth away.*

Ver. 5. *And rebuke.* Heb., *touch.*

6. Cast forth thy lightnings and trouble them; shoot out thine arrows, and scatter them.

7. Stretch forth thine hand from above, and deliver me out of great waters, and from the hand of the unrighteous;

8. Whose mouth speaketh vanity, and their right hand is a right hand of falsehood.

9. I will sing a new song unto thee, O God; and upon a harp of ten strings will I sing praises unto thee.

10. Because thou hast given salvation to the king; and hast delivered David thy servant from the hurtful sword.

11. Deliver me from the hand of the unrighteous, whose mouth speaketh vanity, and their right hand is a right hand of iniquity.

12. Their sons are nourished from their youth like

Ver. 6. *And trouble them.* Heb., *and scatter them.*

And scatter them. Heb., *and destroy them.*

Ver. 7. *And deliver me.* Heb., *rid me, and deliver me.*

Of the unrighteous, ܘܦܨܢܝ. A. V. *Of strange children,* בְּנֵי נֵכָר.

Ver. 9. *And upon a harp of ten strings,* ܒܟܢܪܐ ܕܥܣܪ ܡܢܝܢ. A. V. *Upon a psaltery and an instrument of ten strings,* בְּנֵבֶל עָשׂוֹר. LXX., ἐν ψαλτηρίῳ δεκαχόρδῳ.

Ver. 10. *Because thou hast given salvation to the king.* Heb., *It is he that giveth salvation unto kings.*

And hast delivered. Heb., *who delivereth.*

Ver. 11. See note to verse 7.

Ver. 12. *Their sons are nourished from their youth like a plant,* ܕܒܢܝܗܘܢ ܐܝܟ ܢܨܒܬܐ ܕܡܪܒܝܐ ܡܢ ܛܠܝܘܬܗܘܢ. A. V. *That our sons may be as plants grown up in their youth,* אֲשֶׁר בָּנֵינוּ כִּנְטִעִים מְגֻדָּלִים בִּנְעוּרֵיהֶם.

a plant; and their daughters *are* like brides adorned after the similitude of temples.

13. Their garners are full, and overflowing one into another; their sheep bring forth and nourish in their streets.

14. Their cattle are strong, nor is there a barren one among them; there is neither breaking in, nor complaining in their streets.

And their daughters are like brides adorned after the similitude of temples, ܒܢܬܗܘܢ ܐܝܟ ܟܠܬܐ ܡܨܒܬܢ ܒܕܡܘܬܐ ܕܗܝܟܠܐ. A. V. *That our daughters may be as corner stones, polished after the similitude of a palace*, בְּנוֹתֵינוּ כְזָוִיֹּת מְחֻטָּבוֹת תַּבְנִית הֵיכָל.

Ver. 13. *Their garners are full, and overflowing one into another*, ܐܘܨܪܝܗܘܢ ܡܠܝܢ ܘܡܫܬܦܥܝܢ ܡܢ ܚܕ ܠܚܕ. A. V. *That our garners may be full, affording all manner of store*, מְזָוֵינוּ מְלֵאִים מְפִיקִים מִזַּן אֶל־זַן.

Their sheep bring forth and nourish in their streets, ܥܢܗܘܢ ܝܠܕܢ ܘܡܪܒܝܢ ܒܫܘܩܝܗܘܢ. A. V. *That our sheep may bring forth thousands and ten thousands in our streets*, צֹאונֵנוּ מַאֲלִיפוֹת מְרֻבָּבוֹת בְּחוּצוֹתֵינוּ.

Ver. 14. *Their cattle are strong, nor is there a barren one among them; there is neither breaking in, nor complaining in their streets*, ܬܘܪܝܗܘܢ ܚܣܝܢܝܢ ܘܠܝܬ ܒܗܘܢ ܥܩܪܬܐ: ܠܝܬ ܬܪܥܐ ܘܠܐ ܝܠܠܬܐ ܒܫܘܩܝܗܘܢ. A. V. *That our oxen may be strong to labour; that there be no breaking in, nor going out; that there be no complaining in our streets*, אַלּוּפֵינוּ מְסֻבָּלִים אֵין פֶּרֶץ וְאֵין יוֹצֵאת וְאֵין צְוָחָה בִּרְחֹבֹתֵינוּ.

The whole construction of the Syriac seems to require that the

15. Are the people happy that are in such a case? *Yea rather* blessed are the people, whose God is the Lord.

(LAUD, AND THE BEGINNING OF THE GRADE.)

PSALM CXLIV.

A Psalm of David. — Praise, with theological truth.

1. I will extol thee, my Lord, O King, and I will bless thy Name forever and ever.
2. Everyday will I bless thee, and I will praise thy Name forever.
3. Great is our Lord, and greatly to be praised; and there is no end to his greatness.
4. One generation shall narrate thy works to another, and shall declare thy power;
5. And they shall speak of the might of thy terrour, and proclaim thy wonderful works.

first clause of verse 15 should be in the interrogative form. The version of the LXX. is not unlike the Syriac; ὧν οἱ υἱοὶ ὡς νεόφυτα ἱδρυμένα ἐν τῇ νεότητι αὐτῶν · αἱ θυγατέρες αὐτῶν κεκαλλωπισμέναι περικεκοσμημέναι ὡς ὁμοίωμα ναοῦ · τὰ ταμεῖα αὐτῶν πλήρη ἐξερευγόμενα ἐκ τούτου εἰς τοῦτο · τὰ πρόβατα αὐτῶν πολύτοκα, πληθύνοντα ἐν ταῖς ἐξόδοις αὐτῶν, οἱ βόες αὐτῶν παχεῖς · οὐκ ἔστι κατάπτωμα φραγμοῦ, οὐδὲ διέξοδος, οὐδὲ κραυγὴ ἐν ταῖς ἐπαύλεσιν αὐτῶν · ἐμακάρισαν τὸν λαὸν ᾧ ταῦτά ἐστι, μακάριος ὁ λαὸς οὗ κύριος ὁ θεὸς αὐτοῦ.

Ps. CXLIV. Ver. 4. *Shall narrate.* Heb., *shall praise.*

Thy power. Heb., *thy mighty acts.*

Ver. 5. *And they shall speak of the might of thy terrour, and proclaim thy wonderful works.* Heb., *I will speak of the glorious honour of thy majesty, and of thy wondrous works.*

6. They shall also speak of the fearfulness of thy power, and I will tell of thy greatness;

7. And thy saints shall seek and find the memorial of thy many mercies.

8. The Lord is compassionate and gracious; slow to anger, and of great mercy.

9. The Lord is good, and his tender mercies *are* over all his works.

10. Thy servants shall give thanks unto thee, O Lord; and thy saints shall praise thee.

11. They shall speak of the glory of thy kingdom, and talk of thy power;

12. And they shall shew forth thy might unto men, and the glory of thy kingdom.

13. Thy kingdom *is* an everlasting kingdom, and thy dominion *endureth* throughout all generations: the

Ver. 6. *They shall also speak of the fearfulness of thy power.* Heb., *And men shall speak of the might of thy terrible acts.*

Ver. 7. *And thy saints shall seek and find the memorial of thy many mercies,* ܣܘܥܪ̈ܢܐ ܘܢܬܚܫܒܘܢ ܡܬܢܝܢܐ ܀ ܬܚܒܒ ܐ̈ܢܩܒܝ ܘܬܡܚܣܩ. A. V. *They shall abundantly utter the memory of thy great goodness, and shall sing of thy righteousness,* זֵכֶר רַב־טוּבְךָ יַבִּיעוּ וְצִדְקָתְךָ יְרַנֵּנוּ. For the Syriac ܘܬܡܚܣܩ, we may perhaps read ܢܬܚܫܒܘܢ; and then deriving ܬܚܒܒ from ܚܒܒ, instead of ܚܓܐ, the two texts are substantially coincident.

Ver. 9. *Is good.* Heb., *is good to all.*

Ver. 10. *Thy servants.* Heb., *All thy works.*

Ver. 12. *And they shall shew forth thy might unto men, and the glory of thy kingdom.* Heb., *To make known to the sons of men his mighty acts, and the glorious majesty of his kingdom.*

Ver. 13. *The Lord is faithful in all his words, and righteous in*

Lord is faithful in all his words, and righteous in all his works.

14. The Lord upholdeth all that fall, and raiseth up all them that are bowed down.

15. The eyes of all men *are* directed unto thee; thou givest them food in their season.

16. Thou openest thine hand, and satisfieth the desire of every living thing.

17. The Lord is righteous in all his ways, and merciful in all his works.

18. The Lord is nigh unto them that call upon him in truth;

19. And he fulfilleth the desire of them that fear him; he heareth their supplication, and delivereth them.

20. The Lord preserveth all them that fear him, and destroyeth all the unrighteous.

21. I will speak the praises of the Lord with my mouth; and let all the sons of flesh bless his holy Name forever and ever.

all his works. This is not in the Hebrew, but is found in all the ancient versions, with one exception.

Ver. 15. *Are directed unto thee.* Heb., *wait upon thee.*

Ver. 17. *And merciful.* Heb., *and holy.*

Ver. 18. *Unto them that call upon him in truth.* Heb., *unto all them that call upon him, to all that call upon him in truth.*

Ver. 20. *All them that fear him.* Heb., *all them that love him.*

Ver. 21. *The sons of flesh,* ܟܠ ܒܣܪ. A. V. *Flesh,* בָּשָׂר.

PSALM CXLV.

Spoken by Haggai and Zechariah, the prophets, who went up with the captivity from Babylon, concerning the ministry of the priests to be executed in the morning. Also supplication and praise, with theological truth.

1. Praise the Lord, O my soul.
2. While I live will I praise the Lord, and I will sing praises unto my God, while I have my being.
3. Put not your trust in a prince, nor in the son of man, in whose hand there is no help.
4. For his breath goeth forth, and he returneth to his earth; and in that very day all his thoughts perish.
5. Happy is he that *hath* the God of Jacob for his help; and whose hope *is* in the Lord God;
6. Which made heaven and earth, and the seas, and all that therein is; *which* keepeth truth forever.
7. *Which* executeth judgment for the oppressed; the Lord giveth bread to the hungry; the Lord looseth the prisoners;
8. The Lord openeth *the eyes of* the blind; the Lord raiseth *them that are* bowed down; the Lord loveth the righteous.
9. Yea, he preserveth the poor; he nourisheth the

Ps. CXLV. This Psalm in the Hebrew, begins and ends with the Hallelujah.

Ver. 7, 8. In these verses a slight peculiarity of construction will be noticed.

Ver. 9. *The poor.* Heb., *the strangers.*

fatherless and the widows; but the way of the unrighteous he subverteth.

10. Let the Lord reign forever; thy God, O Zion, unto all generations.

PSALM CXLVI.

A Psalm of Haggai and Zechariah;—concerning Zerubbabel and Joshua the priest, and Ezra, who forwarded the building of Jerusalem; and, as respects ourselves, praise with theological truth.

1. It is good and pleasant to sing praises unto our God, and praise is becoming unto him.
2. The Lord buildeth Jerusalem, and gathereth together the dispersed of Israel.
3. He healeth the broken in heart, and bindeth up their sorrows.
4. He telleth the number of the stars, and hath called them all by *their* names.
5. Great is our Lord, and great *is* his power; and there is no end to his understanding.

He subverteth, ܡܥܩܒ, literally, *he submergeth.* A. V. *He turneth upside down,* יְעַוֵּת.

Ver. 10. *Let the Lord reign.* The verb is imperative; in the Hebrew it is future.

Ps. CXLVI. Ver. 1. *It is good and pleasant to sing praises unto our God, and praise is becoming unto him.* Heb., *Praise ye the Lord: for it is good to sing praises unto our God; for it is pleasant; and praise is comely.*

Ver. 3. *Their sorrows,* ܠܥܨܒܬܗܘܢ. A. V. *Their wounds,* לְעַצְּבוֹתָם.

6. The Lord lifteth up the poor, and casteth the unrighteous down to the ground.

7. Sing unto the Lord with praise; sing praise upon the harp unto the Lord;

8. Who covereth the heaven with clouds, and giveth rain upon the earth; *who* maketh the grass to grow upon the mountains,

9. And giveth food to the cattle, and to the young ravens which cry.

10. The Lord delighteth not in the strength of the horse; neither taketh he pleasure in the legs of a mighty man;

11. But the Lord taketh pleasure in them that fear him; and in them that hope for his mercy.

PSALM CXLVII.

A Psalm of Haggai and Zechariah; when they forwarded the completion of the temple of Jerusalem. — Also praise, with theological truth.

12. Praise the Lord, O Jerusalem; praise thy God, O Zion.

13. For he hath strengthened the bars of thy gates, and hath blessed thy children within thee.

Ver. 6. *The poor.* Heb., *the meek.*

Ver. 8. *And giveth rain upon the earth.* Heb., *who prepareth rain for the earth.*

Ver. 10. *The Lord,* not in the Hebrew.

A mighty man, جَلِيدِ. A. V. *A man,* אִישׁ.

Ps. CXLVII. This Psalm in the Hebrew forms part of Ps. CXLVI., the whole being called Ps. CXLVII.

14. He hath established thy borders in peace, and hath filled thee with the finest of the wheat.

15. He sendeth forth his commandment upon earth, and his word runneth very swiftly.

16. He giveth snow like wool, and scattereth the mists like ashes.

17. He casteth forth the ice like morsels; and who can stand before his cold?

18. He sendeth out his word and melteth them; he causeth the winds to blow, and they make the waters to flow.

19. He sheweth his word in Jacob; his law and his commandments in Israel.

20. He hath not dealt so with all nations, nor hath he shewed them his judgments.

Ver. 14. *He hath established thy borders in peace,* ܡܣ‍ܐܡ ܟܡܓ̈ܐܐ ܒܣ‍ܦܦܣܚܒ. A. V. *He maketh peace in thy borders,* הַשָּׂם־גְּבוּלֵךְ שָׁלוֹם.

Ver. 16. *The mists,* كَهْلِ. A. V. *The hoar frost,* כְּפוֹר.

Ver. 17. *The ice.* Heb., *his ice.*

Ver. 18. *And they make the waters to flow,* ܘܡܐܙܠܝܢ ܡܝܐ. A. V. *And the waters flow,* יִזְּלוּ־מָיִם.

Ver. 19. *In Jacob.* Heb., *unto Jacob.*

In Israel. Heb., *unto Israel.*

Ver. 20. *With all nations.* Heb., *with any nation.*

Nor hath he shewed them his judgments. Heb., *and as for his judgments, they have not known them.*

This Psalm in the Hebrew ends with the Hallelujah.

PSALM CXLVIII.

A Psalm of Haggai and Zechariah. — Theological truth; that as celestial, so terrestrial things should praise the glorious Lord, the Lord of Sabaoth, the God Almighty.

1. Praise ye the Lord from heaven; praise him in the heights.
2. Praise him all ye angels of his; praise him all his hosts.
3. Praise him sun and moon; praise him all ye stars and light.
4. Praise him ye heaven of heavens; and the waters that *be* above the heavens,
5. Let them praise the Name of the Lord; for he spake, and they were; and he commanded, and they were created.
6. He hath established them forever and ever; he hath given a law, and it passeth not away.
7. Praise the Lord from the earth; ye dragons and all deeps.
8. Fire and hail, and snow and frost; winds and storms, the work of his word.

Ps. CXLVIII. This Psalm in the Hebrew begins and ends with the Hallelujah.

Ver. 3. *Stars and light.* Heb., *stars of light.*

Ver. 5. *For he spake and they were,* إِنَّ قَالَ ܗܘܘ ܢܦܫܝ ܘܗܘܘ. This is not in the Hebrew. LXX., ὅτι αὐτὸς εἶπε καὶ ἐγενήθησαν, αὐτὸς ἐνετείλατο καὶ ἐκτίσθησαν.

Ver. 8. *Frost.* Heb., *vapour.*

9. Mountains and all hills; fruitful trees and all cedars.

10. Beasts and all cattle; creeping things, and flying things, and birds.

11. Kings of the earth and all people; princes and all judges of the earth.

12. Young men and maidens; old men and children;

13. Let them praise the Name of the Lord; for his Name only is great, and his glory in the earth and the heavens.

14. He exalteth the horn of his people, and the praise of all his saints; even of the children of Israel, a people near unto him.

Winds and storms, the work of his word, ܘܥܠܥܠܐ ܘܪܘܚܐ ܕܥܒܕ ܡܠܬܗ. A. V. *Stormy wind fulfilling his word,* רוּחַ סְעָרָה עֹשָׂה דְבָרוֹ.

Ver. 10. *And flying things, and birds,* ܘܦܪܚܬܐ ܘܨܦܪܐ. A. V. *And flying fowl,* וְצִפּוֹר כָּנָף.

Ver. 13. *Is great.* Heb., *is excellent.*
In the earth. Heb., *above the earth.*

PSALM CXLIX.

Concerning the new temple. — This psalm anonymous. — Praise, with theological truth.

1. O sing unto the Lord a new song; *and* his praise in the congregation of saints.
2. Let Israel rejoice in him that made him; and let the children of Zion be joyful in their King;
3. And let them praise his Name with cymbals; and let them sing unto him with timbrels and harps.
4. For the Lord taketh pleasure in his people, and giveth salvation to the poor.
5. Let the saints be strengthened in glory, and let them praise him upon their beds;
6. And let them extol God with their throats, *with a twoedged sword in their hands;*

Ps. CXLIX. This Psalm in the Hebrew begins and ends with the Hallelujah.

Ver. 3. *With cymbals,* ܟܦ̈ܐ. A. V. *In the dance,* בְּמָחוֹל.

Ver. 4. *And giveth salvation to the poor,* ܘܢܬܠ ܠܡܣܟܢܐ ܦܘܪܩܢܐ. A. V. *He will beautify the meek with salvation,* יְפָאֵר עֲנָוִים בִּישׁוּעָה.

Ver. 5. *Be strengthened.* Heb., *be joyful.* This variation has been remarked upon before.

And let them praise him. Heb., *let them sing aloud.*

Ver. 6. *Let them extol God with their throats, with a twoedged sword in their hands,* ܢܪܡܪܡܘܢ ܠܐܠܗܐ ܒܓܪܘܢܗܘܢ ܘܣܝܦܐ ܕܬܪܝܢ ܦܘܡܘܗܝ ܒܐܝܕܝܗܘܢ. A. V. *Let the high praises of God be in their mouth, and a twoedged sword in their hand,* רוֹמְמוֹת אֵל בִּגְרוֹנָם וְחֶרֶב פִּיפִיּוֹת בְּיָדָם.

7. To execute vengeance upon the heathen, and punishment upon the people;

8. To bind their kings with fetters, and their nobles with chains of iron;

9. To execute the judgment upon them that is written, and *to give* glory to all his saints.

PSALM CL.

Anonymous. — An exhortation to the general praise of those things that are written and sealed by the Spirit.

1. Praise the Lord in his holiness; praise him in the firmament of his strength.

2. Praise him in his power; praise him in the abundance of his greatness.

3. Praise him with the sound of a trumpet; praise him with psalteries and harps.

4. Praise him with cymbals and timbrels; praise him upon the sweet sounding strings.

Ver. 9. *And to give glory to all his saints,* ܗܘ ܢܬܠ ܫܘܒܚܐ ܠܟܠܗܘܢ ܙܕܝܩܘܗܝ. A. V. *This honour have all his saints,* הָדָר הוּא לְכָל־חֲסִידָיו.

Ps. CL. This Psalm in the Hebrew begins and ends with the Hallelujah.

Ver. 2. *In his power.* Heb., *for his mighty acts.*

In the abundance of his greatness, ܒܣܘܓܐܐ ܕܪܒܘܬܗ. וּבְרֹב גָּדְלוֹ. A. V. *According to his excellent greatness,* כְּרֹב גֻּדְלוֹ.

Ver. 4. *With cymbals and timbrels,* ܒܨܨܠܐ ܘܟܢܪܐ. A. V. *With the timbrel and dance,* בְּתֹף וּמָחוֹל.

5. Praise him upon the loud cymbals; praise him with the voice and a shout.

6. Let everything that hath breath praise the Lord.

The one hundred and fifty Psalms are ended. There are Five Books, Fifteen Grades, Sixty Lauds, and Four thousand eight hundred and thirty-two Verses.* There are those who have added twelve others, but we need them not.

To God be praise forever.

PSALM CLI

This psalm, peculiar to David, is additional; nor is it found in all the copies. — David sang it when he contended alone with Goliath.

1. I was the smallest among my brethren, and a boy in my father's house; I fed my father's flocks.

2. My hands made the organ, and my fingers framed the harp.

3. And who shall shew *it* to my Lord? He is the Lord, and he is my God.

Upon the sweet sounding strings, ܚܩܬܐ ܬܟܢܗܐ. A. V.
With stringed instruments and organs, בְּמִנִּים וְעֻגָב.
Ver. 5. *With the voice and a shout,* ܚܩܠ ܘܟܡܓܐ. A. V.
Upon the high sounding cymbals, בְּצִלְצְלֵי תְרוּעָה.

Ps. CLI. Ver. 3. *And he is my God.* The LXX. have αὐτὸς εἰσακούει.

* This does not indicate the ordinary verse, but a minor division of the text which I have not indicated in the translation.

4. He sent his angel, and took me from my father's sheep; and anointed me with the oil of his anointing.

5. My brethren were fair and tall; but the Lord delighted not in them.

6. I went forth to meet the Philistine, and he cursed me by his idols.

7. But I, when I had drawn his sword, cut off his head, and took away the reproach from the children of Israel.

Ver. 6. *The Philistine.* LXX., τῷ ἀλλοφύλῳ.

THE END.